The Albany Collection:
Treasures and Treasured Recipes

The Women's Council of
The Albany Institute of History & Art

Albany, New York

COMMITTEES

STEERING COMMITTEE
Co-Chairs Marian Potter, Mary Stock

Gretchen Hughs, Ellen Jabbur, Betty Sonneborn

DESIGN AND FORMAT
D. J. Moore Advertising, Inc.

ARTISTIC DIRECTION
Betty Sonneborn

HISTORIC RESEARCH
Allison Bennett

MARKETING COMMITTEE
Denise Maurer, Marion Michaels, Joan Van Patten, Anne Viglione

SUPPORTING COMMITTEE
Marcia Codling, Virginia DeMio, Margo French, Doris Fry
Dinny Goodwin, Billie Kane, Joan Moore
Katherine Prodanovitch, Lois Titus, Anne Viglione

EDITING
Lois Cameron, Margaret Eighmey, Barbara Simpkins, Florence Sutler
Bonnie Taylor, Dorothy Ten Eyck

The invaluable support of all those who assisted with proofreading, testing, and promoting the cookbook is very much appreciated.

ISBN 0-9658063-0-8
Copyright © 1997, The Women's Council of
The Albany Institute of History & Art
1st Printing, 5,000 copies

CONTENTS

Page

Cookbook Committees 2

Foreword 4

Contributors 5

The Menu Collection 7

The Appetizer & Beverage Collection 17

The Bread Collection 41

The Soup, Salad & Sandwich Collection 61

The Eggs, Rice & Pasta Collection 103

The Entrée Collection 113

The Vegetable Collection 173

The Dessert Collection 197

Index 241

Order Forms and Institute Passes 253

FOREWORD

Through this cookbook we hope to give a special insight into one of America's first settlements. *The Albany Collection: Treasures and Treasured Recipes* reflects nearly 400 years of history and entertaining from an historic city, unique in its Dutch/English heritage, that developed from a trading and transportation hub into prominence as New York State's capital.

Recipes have been gathered by members of The Women's Council of The Albany Institute of History & Art from personal travels, friends and families. While some may have been published in other books, periodicals or newspapers, all have proven to be favorites in area homes. Sections with photographs of art and decorative arts from the museum's collections, and menus for special occasions enliven the many pages geared to the pleasure of today's informal entertaining.

The Women's Council was founded in 1961 to assist the Director, Staff and Board of Directors in maintaining a cultural center for the people of the Albany area, giving financial support, offering volunteer services and increasing interest in the Institute within the community. The Institute, founded in 1791, is a museum dedicated to collecting, preserving, interpreting, and promoting interest in the history, art and culture of Albany and the Upper Hudson Valley Region.

From the beginning our financial support has affected every part of the museum, ranging from exhibition assistance, Collections Committee endowment and art scholarships to gallery renovations, security, and annual maintenance. The Women's Council has a proud record of accomplishment through our many volunteer activities including: educational and cultural tours; The Rice Gallery (art sales and rentals); the Luncheon Gallery plus successful special events such as the Elegant Elephant Sale, Heirloom Discovery Day® and our annual Festival of Trees.

The Women's Council gratefully acknowledges those whose enthusiasm and valued assistance made this cookbook possible, as well as those who have given so generously from their own recipe collections. Cookbook Chairs Marian Potter and Mary Stock and their committee members represent the talent and dedication found in our Women's Council. They have tested, tasted, proofread, and edited these recipes to produce an outstanding cookbook. We also extend our thanks to the Institute staff for their assistance.

Our fund-raising projects are a vital component of The Women's Council activities. First-rate programs and amenities for our Institute are possible only with adequate funding. Proceeds from the sale of *The Albany Collection: Treasures and Treasured Recipes* will help support future projects. We hope you will use our cookbook with pleasure for many years to come.

Enjoy!

Anne M. (Polly) Petruska
President
The Women's Council, AIHA

CONTRIBUTORS

Florence Adams
Dolly Albright
Dorothy Allen
Patricia Anklin-Relation
Dorothy T. Ayan
Andrea Hughs-Baird
Donna Baird
Mildred (Midge) Baldwin
Jenny Barbur
Jayne Bassett
Jeanne Bassett
Doris L. Belton
Allison C. Bennett
Susan McCulloch Bennett
Stephanie Biscone
G. May Blackmore
Florence Bogdan
Barbara Bradley
Margo Bradtke
Anne Brewster
Lori Brewster
Elizabeth (Betty) Brown
Janet Brown
Natalie Buchman
Sonya Budka
Olive Byrne
Lois G. Cameron
Pearl Campbell
Frieda Carnell
Joseph Cirabisi
Marcia S. Codling
Sarah Corson
Elizabeth (Beth) Craft
Marjorie Crangle
Cynthia Cromie
Marcia L. Cummings
Mary Lou Cummings
Barbara Cunningham
Lorraine D'Aleo
Joan Davey
Christine Davis
Angrit De Alleaume
Rita V. Delapp
Virginia De Mio
Carroll Devitt
Rae Di Lello
Patricia Dollase
Janis Keane Dorgan
Joan M. Doyle
Ellen Dranichak
Margaret Eighmey
Lia C. Elk
Joy Emery
Ida Fleitz
Mary Grace Fleitz
Diane Fletcher
Joy Ford
Mary Ford
Margo French
Beatrice (Bea) Fricke
Sharon Fricke
Doris H. Fry
Myria Gamber
Teresa Gaus

Donna Gibson
Diana (Dinny) Goodwin
Shirley J. Grady
Tony Guzek
Geraldine (Gerry) Haase
Jeanette (Jan) Hartmuller
Audrey Hawkins
Janet Hengerer
Dorothy Hernandez
Charlene Hickey
Elizabeth (Betty) Huba
Gretchen Hughs
Marijane Ingro
Ellen B. Jabbur
Wilma Jenssen
Elizabeth (Billie) Kane
Jeanne Kane
Nyna Keeton
Gail Kendall
Blanchard Kenney
Pat Kenton
Kaisa Killam
Joanne Glenn Kimmey
Keena Kinsey
Margaret Knouse
Jean B. Lauber
Margaret (Mardie) Leather
Joanne Lenden
Kathryn Liede-Henkins
Judie Linstra
Jean Lyon
Anita Mac Crone
Christie Mahar
Roddy Machanic
Dorothy Malley
Mansion Hill Inn
Carolyn Codling Martel
Bernadette Mayersohn
Mary Alice Maynes
Kate McAllister
Frances (Frankie) McDonald
Kaye McDonald
Mary Jane McGlaflin
Margaret McLaughlin
Hilda McMann
Marion Michaels
Eugenia (Jean) Miele
Ann Moloney
Joan Moore
Sarah (Sally) Moran
Betty Jane (B.J.) Moreen
Mary E. (Mimi) Mounteer
Kathryn Q. Murphy
Thelma Murray
Jean Nickel
Brother James Nilan
Janet Nyquist
Alice O'Brien
Terry O'Brien
Anna O'Connor
Kathleen Odabashian
Diane B. O'Keeffe
Marion Parker
Sarah (Sallie) Pellman
Marcia Perry
Joan Tebbut Persing
Anne M. (Polly) Petruska
Elaine Pidgeon

Ginger Pietrykowski
Marian W. Potter
Katherine Prodanovitch
Lorraine Redden
Camille Ricketts
Jack Riek
Janet Riek
Joan Rittberger
Francis (Doc) Rivett
Lillemor (Lee) Robb
Madeline Rolando
Nancy Reynolds Rooney
Janet Ryan
Isabelle Sanford
Mary D. Shannon
Sheila Davis Sheffield
Fran Sherley
Barbara Simpkins
Deborah Sloan
Manon Smachlow
Hazel P. Smith
Gail Sokol
Elizabeth (Betty) Sonneborn
Lois Spataro
Eunice Spindler
Darcy Phelps Steinke
Mary Stierer
Mary Stock
Connie Strong
Edna (Eddy) Sturges
Robert Sturges
Florence Sutler
Bonnie Taylor
Irene Templeton
Dorothy Ten Eyck
Mary E. Tinney
Leslie Titus
Lois Titus
Dorothea Tobin
Ruth Tobin
Jan Toelke
Theresa N. Traynor
Frances Turmel
Ann Uhl
Midge Van Demark
Joan Van Patten
Polly Van Woert
Anne M. Viglione
Frances Vunck
Betty Wendrem
Ruth Whalen
Kathryn Williams
Cynthia Wilson
Jean Yaguda
Cindy Yonkers

The Cookbook Committee
appreciated the quality and
quantity of the recipes submitted.
Difficult choices were made to
eliminate similar recipes, to
provide variety, and to represent
various ethnic cultures.

THE MARRIAGE FEAST AT CANA
Unidentified Artist
Oil on canvas, c. 1742
AIHA Purchase 1953.24

The Dutch settlers who came to Albany from the
Netherlands in the 17th century brought with them a
love for fine and decorative art. By the 18th century,
their sons and grandsons, prosperous merchants and
landowners, began to commission itinerant artists to
paint family portraits and scripture paintings for their
homes. The source for the scripture paintings has been
traced to family Bibles printed in Holland.

PARTY

Banana-Pineapple Cake
Imperial Pound Cake
Danish Carrot Hazelnut Torte
Angel Whispers
Rum Balls
Chocolate Chip Coconut Bars
Nutmeg Cookie Logs
Ice Cream
Hot Chocolate
Flavored Teas and Coffee

 Founded in 1791, the Institute is one of the oldest museums in the country – older even than the Louvre and the Smithsonian. As a regional museum, the collection focuses on the history, art and culture of the Upper Hudson Valley.

In addition to the changing exhibits throughout the year, Hudson River School paintings, Albany-made silver, early portraits and other decorative arts are featured. A wide range of educational programs, lectures, tours, and art classes are offered. The McKinney Library houses an important collection of diaries, letters, maps, manuscripts, photographs, and ephemera of Albany's past. The collections enrich our entire community, its economy and our families and children.

On the first Sunday in February, the Institute celebrates its birthday as a family festival and Museum Explorers' Day.

DINNER

Cream of Celery Soup
Herb Roasted Orange Salmon
or
Beef Wellington with Mushroom Pâté
Pommes de Terre Dauphinoise
French Style Peas
or
Roasted Vegetables
Spinach - Pear Salad
Lemon Charlotte
Coffee
Tea

In 1940, Albany Mayor John Boyd Thatcher proclaimed a week in May as "Albany Tulip Week." Ninety thousand tulips bloomed in Washington Park that year. The event was not held during World War II and it was not until eight years later that the week honoring tulips was remembered. A local newspaper columnist, Charles Mooney, suggested that there should be an annual Tulip Festival and Mayor Erastus Corning appointed a committee which organized the first event. The tulip was named official flower of the City to commemorate Albany's Dutch heritage. Activities include the crowning of the Tulip Queen, the Tulip Ball, the Pinksterfest (outdoor fair) and the Kinderkermis (children's carnival).

PATIO BUFFET

Chipped Beef Dip
Lobster (or Seafood) Spread
Aram Sandwiches
Celebrity Chili
Deviled Eggs with Mushrooms
Chicken Waldorf Salad
Broccoli Salad with Basil Dressing
Variegated Salad
Beer Bread
Strawberry Angel Delight
Queen Elizabeth's Date Nut Cake
Chocolate Chocolate Chip Cookies
Madison Avenue Punch

The Capital District is known for its many excellent educational institutions. Among them are:

Union College: Founded in 1795 and the first planned college in the United States. Designed by landscape architect Joseph Jacques Ramée, the 100-acre campus includes Jackson's Gardens, eight acres of gardens and woods. The 16-sided Nott Memorial, completed in 1875, is a National Memorial Landmark, named for Eliphalet Nott, Union's President from 1804-1866.

State University of New York at Albany: Oldest State-chartered public institution of higher education in New York. Established in 1844 as a normal school, it has a broad mission of undergraduate and graduate education, research and public service. Today's capacity is 17,000 students.

Rensselaer Polytechnic Institute: A technological university highly respected for its engineering, management, science, architecture, and humanities-social science programs. Founded in 1824, the 260-acre campus is a few blocks from downtown Troy.

The Capital District is also home to The College of Saint Rose, Siena College, Sage Colleges, Emma Willard School, Albany Academy and several other colleges and nationally known high schools.

SUPPER

Potato and Leek Soup
Shaker Braised Flank Steak
Potato Kugel
Shaker Onions
Lemon-Walnut Green Beans
Spicy Cole Slaw
Corn Bread
Double Crust Lemon Pie
or
Black and White Cookies
Shaker Cold Rhubarb Tea

 The Shakers, a celibate religious group led by Mother Ann Lee, first settled in this country in the Albany area in 1776. They established a communal society that was in many ways ahead of its time, emphasizing equality of the sexes, nonviolence, and the care and schooling of children. Their efforts toward perfection and simplicity in daily life are evident in their crafts, architecture and especially in their furniture. The Shakers also recognized that good food, properly cooked and well-digested, is the basis of good health.

A major Shaker burial ground and an 1848 Shaker meeting house, with an interpretive center, comprise today's settlement. There are eight other Shaker buildings on site.

TAILGATE PICNIC

Gouda Cup
Chicken Liver Pâté
Melon Soup
or
Cold Peach Soup
Tailgaters' Loaf
Cottage Cole Slaw
Fresh Seafood Salad
Crunchy Red Potato Salad
Walnut Rolls
Assorted Cheeses
Lemon Squares   Chocolate Macaroons
Iced Tea Soda Beer Wine

 Completed in 1863, the Saratoga Race Track is the oldest thoroughbred track in the country. It was originally built on 125 acres in Saratoga purchased by John Morrissey. In 1864, William Travers was named President of the Racing Association. (The Travers Stakes was named in his honor.)

Today, the Race Track covers 350 acres; the main track is $1^1/8$ miles long; the stabling capacity is 1,830 stalls in a total of 91 barns. The maximum one-day attendance of 53,561 racing fans occurred in 1989; the record one-day handle was $6,529,085 on Travers Day in 1992.

DO-AHEAD LUNCHEON

Autumn Soup
or
Gazpacho Soup

Blend of the Bayou
or
Fresh Asparagus and Ham Pie

Green Bean Salad
or
Parmesan Vegetable Tossed Salad

Zucchini Bread
Coconut Pound Cake
Spicy Tea Punch

 **Quackenbush Square**: A restored area that includes the Quackenbush House built in 1736. The Albany Urban Cultural Park Visitors Center at the Square houses hands-on exhibits and a multi-image audio-visual show tracing the history and architecture of the city.

Schuyler Mansion: Built in 1761 for Philip Schuyler, a noted general of the American Revolution. It was in this elegant Georgian mansion that the Schuylers entertained George Washington, Benjamin Franklin and many other prominent Americans and Europeans. In 1780, Elizabeth Schuyler married Alexander Hamilton in the formal drawing room.

Historic Cherry Hill: Built in 1787 for Philip Van Rensselaer, a commission merchant in Albany, the house was lived in continuously by five generations of the same family until 1963. Possessions were accumulated through the years and included a vast collection of furniture, portraits, textiles, china and documents.

Ten Broeck Mansion: A Federal-style home built for Abraham Ten Broeck and his wife, Elizabeth Van Rensselaer. General Ten Broeck was a locally prominent politician, businessman and patriot who served in the American Revolution. The house was later occupied by four generations of the Olcott family who presented it to the Albany County Historical Association.

RECEPTION

Hot Chili Dip   Shrimp Dip
Great Guacamole Dip
Sausage Biscuit Bites
Crustless Zucchini Quiche
Turkey Ball   Hot Mushroom Turnovers
Asparagus Roll-Ups
Fruited Cheese Log
Sesame Seed Twist Cookies
Caramel Apple Bars   Glazed Walnut Bars
Pfeffernusse   Cherry Flakes
Mulled Cider
Holiday Wassail Punch

 The Festival of Trees has been the primary fund-raiser of the Women's Council of the Albany Institute of History & Art since 1984. It traditionally begins during Thanksgiving week. Scores of trees are sponsored and decorated by community groups and businesses.

The Festival blends innovative and traditional holiday decorations with gingerbread houses, entertainment, electric trains, parties, the Luncheon Gallery, a Festival Café and the Holiday Shop.

MIDNIGHT SUPPER

Champagne
Nut-Filled Brie   Shrimp Mousse
Shrimp and Scallops Gruyère
Sirloin Tip Casserole
Späetzle or Buttered Noodles
Braised Celery and Apple Medley
Honey and Brandy Glazed Carrots
Green Pea/Red Radish Salad
Fresh Fruit Romanoff
Viennese Brownies
Coffee Tea

 Albany's First Night, fashioned after Boston's First Night, was inaugurated in 1986. Following a year of Tricentennial activities and with an interest in promoting the performing arts in the Capital District, Mayor Thomas Whalen initiated this event which attracted 4,000 revelers. Today, this popular family-oriented, non-alcoholic event brings 18,000 to 25,000 revelers each year to Albany. Albany's First Night, with more than 500 performers in more than 60 venues, is thought to offer the greatest number of indoor locations of all First Night cities. Albany was the first city in New York State to host the event.

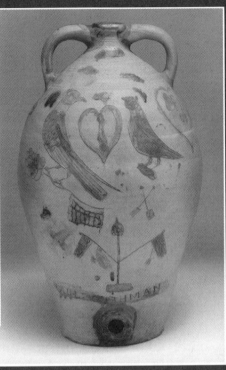

BUTTER CHURN AND WATER KEG
Paul Cushman (1767-1832)
Salt glaze stoneware with incised cobalt decoration
Early 19th century
Butter Churn gift of John P. Remensnyder, 1977.20.7
Water Keg bequest of James Ten Eyck, 1911.5.16

The butter churn is stamped "Paul Cushman, Stoneware Factory
1809/ half a mile west of Albany Goal." An unusual design
element is the fish suckling a cow. The fish is presumably a sturgeon,
so plentiful in the Hudson River at that time that it was known as
"Albany Beef."

The two-handled wine or brandy jug was probably decorated to
commemorate a birthday or other occasion, as evidenced by the
inscription "J.F.M./1818" in the heart shape near the handle.

Baked Carrot Spread

1 cup grated carrots
1 cup mayonnaise
½ teaspoon garlic salt

½ teaspoon lemon pepper
1 cup grated Romano or
mozzarella cheese

Mix all ingredients well and bake uncovered in small casserole at 350° for 25 minutes. Serve hot with crackers.

Note: This makes a delicious spread. No one ever guesses the mystery ingredient—they think it's seafood.

Yield: 2½ cups.

Chipped Beef Dip

1 (8 ounce) package cream
cheese
1 cup sour cream
1 cup mayonnaise

1 (5½ ounce) package chipped
beef, shredded
Worcestershire sauce to taste
1 cup chopped walnuts or
pecans

Mix first 5 ingredients; cook on medium heat stirring constantly until bubbly. Cook and stir a minute or two more. Cool slightly and add chopped nuts. Serve warm with crackers.

Yield: Approximately 3 cups.

Hot Chili Dip

1 (8 ounce) package cream
cheese, softened
1 small grated onion

8 ounces shredded Cheddar
cheese, divided
1 (15 ounce) can chili without
beans

Layer ingredients in order in a 10-inch pie pan, reserving about ¼ of Cheddar cheese for topping. Bake 20 minutes at 350°. Serve with tortilla chips.

Yield: 3 cups.

Chili con Queso

1 clove garlic, chopped
1 large yellow onion, chopped
2 tablespoons butter
¾ pound pasteurized process
   cheese spread
¼ pound pasteurized process
   sharp cheese spread

1 (1 pound) can tomatoes
1½ teaspoons crushed red
   pepper
1 teaspoon chili powder
1 teaspoon paprika
2-3 green chili peppers

Sauté chopped onion and garlic in butter. Add remaining ingredients and cook until thick. Serve in fondue pan to keep hot. Use corn chips to dip.

Yield: 4 cups.

Hot Mushroom Cocktail Spread

8 ounces fresh mushrooms
2 teaspoons butter
2 tablespoons flour
1½ pints (24 ounces) sour cream

1 envelope dry onion soup mix
1 cup grated sharp Cheddar
   cheese

Wash and slice mushrooms. Melt butter in heavy skillet. When hot, add mushrooms. Stir and cook until brown. Remove from heat; sprinkle flour over mushrooms and stir. Mix dry soup and sour cream. Stir into mushrooms. Spread in 9-inch pie pan and top with cheese. Bake uncovered at 350° until bubbly hot, 10-15 minutes. Serve with party rye rounds, chips, or unsalted tortilla chips.

Note: Can be prepared ahead and baked just before serving.

Yield: 3 cups.

Great Guacamole

2 ripe avocados
¼ cup sour cream
2 tablespoons minced onion
Salt to taste
1 teaspoon chili powder

1 clove garlic, crushed
Dash of hot pepper sauce
4 teaspoons lemon juice
2 medium-sized tomatoes,
   peeled and chopped

Cut avocados in half; remove seeds and peel. Mash avocados with fork; put through sieve or whirl in blender until smooth. Stir in the remaining ingredients. Cover. Chill thoroughly.

Yield: 3 cups.

Hummus

1 (15 ounce) can chickpeas,
   reserving liquid
1 clove garlic
1 teaspoon salt

Juice of 2 lemons
3-4 tablespoons tahini
   (sesame seed paste)

Drain chickpeas. Place all ingredients in food processor or blender. Blend until smooth; add ⅔ liquid from chickpeas. Continue blending. Consistency should be like a dip but may be made thicker or thinner depending on personal taste. Serve as a side dish with fish or meat or as an appetizer with pita bread or crackers.

Yield: 2 cups.

Shrimp Dip

1 (4½ ounce) can tiny shrimp
½ cup mayonnaise
½ cup sour cream
¼ teaspoon salt
¼ teaspoon seasoned salt
   flavor enhancer

1 small onion, grated
Dash of cayenne pepper
½ teaspoon paprika
Pinch of sugar

Mix all ingredients except shrimp. Stir in shrimp and chill. Serve with raw vegetables and/or wheat crackers.

Note: Do not use low-fat sour cream (too runny).

Yield: 1½ cups.

Taco Dip

3 ripe avocados
1 tomato, chopped
1½ teaspoons lemon juice
1½ teaspoons garlic powder,
   or several garlic cloves,
   mashed
1 small onion, minced
Hot pepper sauce to taste
1 cup mayonnaise
1 cup sour cream

1 (1½ ounce) package taco
   seasoning
1 (32 ounce) can refried beans
4 ripe tomatoes, chopped, or
   1 (11½ ounce) jar salsa
1 bunch green onions, chopped
8 ounces Cheddar cheese, grated
1 (4½ ounce) can chopped
   ripe olives

Peel and mash avocados. Add 1 tomato, lemon juice, garlic, minced onion and hot pepper sauce; set aside. Mix mayonnaise, sour cream and taco seasoning; set aside. On large platter, spread refried beans as first layer followed by layers of avocado mixture and mayonnaise mixture; sprinkle with 4 remaining tomatoes, green onions and cheese. Top with olives and serve with corn or taco chips.

Yield: 10 servings.

Aram Sandwiches

4 flat flour tortillas
1 (8 ounce) package cream
   cheese
¼ cup mango chutney
¾ teaspoon curry powder
1 head red leaf lettuce,
   cleaned and dried

⅔ pound smoked turkey,
   thinly sliced
1 medium tomato, thinly sliced
1 small cucumber, thinly sliced
½ teaspoon salt
½ teaspoon freshly ground
   pepper

In food processor or blender, combine cream cheese, chutney and curry powder. Blend until smooth. Spread each tortilla flat with a generous coating of cheese mixture. Place 2-3 lettuce leaves on one end of flat tortilla. Top lettuce with turkey, tomato and cucumber. Sprinkle with salt and pepper. Tightly roll (like a jelly roll) starting with covered end. Secure with tooth pick. Refrigerate 6-12 hours. Cut and discard ragged ends. Cut roll diagonally into 1½-inch slices. Serve cut side up. Garnish with parsley.

Yield: 3-4 servings as lunch, 8 servings as appetizers.

Asparagus Roll-Ups

24 slices white sandwich bread
½ cup butter or margarine,
   softened
1 (8 ounce) package cream
   cheese, softened

4 ounces blue cheese, softened
24 spears fresh or frozen
   asparagus, partially
   cooked, well drained
½ cup melted butter

Trim crusts from bread; flatten with rolling pin. Mix softened butter with both cheeses. Spread mixture on each bread slice and top with an asparagus spear. Roll bread around asparagus and dip in melted butter. Cut each roll into thirds and freeze. When ready to serve, bake at 400° for 15 minutes.

Yield: 72 bits.

Banana Rumaki

8-10 slices bacon, cut in half
5 slightly under-ripe bananas

½ cup brown sugar
1 tablespoon curry powder

Blanch bacon in boiling water for 10 minutes. Drain and dry thoroughly. Cut bananas into 1½-inch chunks. Wrap a piece of bacon around each chunk, securing with a toothpick. Combine sugar and curry powder. Sprinkle on bananas. Place on rack in shallow baking pan lined with foil. Bake in 350° oven for about 12 minutes or until bacon is crisp and sugar is slightly caramelized.

Yield: 16-18 servings.

Roasted Garlic Canapés

2 heads garlic
2 tablespoons olive oil
2 (8 ounce) packages cream
   cheese, softened

½ cup butter, softened
¾ teaspoon salt or seasoned salt

Cut off tops of garlic heads; drizzle with oil in either foil or garlic roaster. Cook in 350° oven for 1 hour. Cool. Squeeze pulp out. Pulverize in blender. Add remaining ingredients. Serve on crackers or with vegetables.

Yield: 2½ cups.

Borekas
Israeli Spinach Turnovers

1 (10 ounce) package frozen chopped spinach
1 (8 ounce) container non-fat ricotta cheese
1 1-inch square block of feta cheese, crumbled
2 sheets frozen puff pastry

Cook the spinach according to package directions. Squeeze thoroughly to remove all liquid. Mix the spinach with the ricotta and feta cheeses. Preheat the oven to 350°. Unfold the puff pastry according to package directions. Cut each sheet into nine squares. Divide the spinach and cheese mixture into eighteen even portions and place one portion in the center of each pastry square. Fold the pastry squares into a triangle and press down the center point with your finger. Leave the two side points open. (It's okay if the spinach-cheese mixture seems to ooze out of the side openings.) Place on a greased cookie sheet and bake at 350° for about 15-20 minutes, or until golden brown.

Note: These are best eaten right out of the oven. However, they can be refrigerated or frozen. Reheat in the oven, not in a microwave.

Yield: 18 Borekas.

Chicken Wings

2 pounds chicken wings, tips removed
½ cup plain yogurt
3 tablespoons lemon juice
1 tablespoon Dijon style mustard
3 cloves garlic, minced
1 teaspoon salt
½ teaspoon each of sage, oregano and pepper
½ cup bread crumbs
½ cup freshly grated Parmesan cheese
Salt and pepper
Dash of red pepper (optional)

Combine yogurt, lemon juice, mustard, garlic, salt, sage, oregano and pepper. Cut wings into two pieces and place in yogurt mixture. Marinate chicken for several hours or overnight. Combine crumbs and cheese; add salt, pepper and red pepper. Drain wings; coat with crumbs and chill for 1 hour. Bake at 375° for 30 minutes.

Note: Wings may be refrigerated for several hours before baking.

Yield: 6-8 servings.

Tiny Broccoli Quiches

Pie crust mix for two
  9-inch crusts
2 tablespoons butter or
  margarine, melted
½ (10 ounce) package frozen
  chopped broccoli, thawed

¼ pound Swiss cheese,
  shredded
1 cup half-and-half
3 eggs
1 teaspoon salt

Grease and flour 36 1¾-inch muffin pan cups. Prepare pie crust dough as label directs. On lightly floured surface, with floured rolling pin, roll dough about ⅛-inch thick. Using fluted 3-inch round cookie cutter, cut dough into 36 circles, re-rolling scraps, and line muffin pan cups with circles. Brush pastry lightly with butter. Refrigerate 30 minutes. Preheat oven to 400°. Drain broccoli well on paper towels. Into each cup spoon about 1 teaspoon broccoli and top with some cheese. In small bowl with wire whisk or spoon, mix well the half-and-half, eggs and salt, and spoon about one tablespoon egg mixture into each cup. Bake 25 minutes or until knife comes out clean. Serve hot immediately or cool on wire rack about 15 minutes and freeze.

Note: If frozen, about 35 minutes before serving, preheat oven to 400°. Unwrap and bake frozen quiches 25 minutes or until heated through.

Yield: 36 individual quiches.

Sausage Biscuit Bites

1 pound sharp cheese,
  shredded

1 pound bulk sausage,
  mild or hot
3 cups biscuit baking mix

Crumble sausage and brown in skillet until all red is gone. In large saucepan, heat together the sausage and shredded cheese until melted. Stir in biscuit mix until smooth. Cool. Chill for about 30 minutes. Shape into small balls. Place on ungreased baking sheet. Bake at 400° for 8-10 minutes. Remove; drain on paper towels. Serve warm. May be frozen; reheat in slow oven.

Yield: Approximately 4 dozen.

Hot Mushroom Turnovers

1 (8 ounce) package cream
   cheese, softened
1½ cups all-purpose flour
½ cup butter, softened
3 tablespoons butter
½ pound mushrooms, minced

1 large onion, minced
¼ cup sour cream
1 teaspoon salt
¼ teaspoon thyme
2 tablespoons flour
1 egg, beaten

In a large bowl with mixer at medium speed, beat cream cheese, flour and ½ cup butter until smooth. Shape into ball and wrap with cloth. Refrigerate for 1 hour. In a skillet over medium heat, melt 3 tablespoons butter; cook mushrooms and onions until tender, stirring occasionally. Stir in sour cream, salt, thyme and 2 tablespoons flour. Set aside. On floured surface with floured rolling pin, roll half of dough ⅛-inch thick. With a floured 2¾-inch round cookie cutter, cut as many circles as possible. Re-roll and repeat until all dough has been used. Brush each dough circle with egg. On half of each, place a teaspoon of mushroom mixture and fold. Press edges firmly with a fork to seal. Prick tops. Place turnovers on greased cookie sheet and brush with remaining egg. Bake at 450° for 12-14 minutes until golden brown.

Note: May be frozen after baking and cooling to be reheated later.

Yield: Approximately 42 turnovers.

Spinach Balls

2 (10 ounce) packages frozen
   chopped spinach
2 cups packaged herb stuffing
1 large onion, minced
4 eggs

½ cup Parmesan cheese
¾ cup melted butter
½ tablespoon thyme
1 clove garlic, minced

Cook spinach and drain well. Mix with remaining ingredients. Chill at least 2 hours; roll into 1-inch balls. Place on cookie sheet and bake 30 minutes at 300° until golden brown. Serve hot.

Note: To freeze, place uncovered on cookie sheets and freeze until hard. Once they are hard, put in plastic bags or containers in freezer. Thaw before baking.

Yield: Approximately 50 balls.

Raw Vegetable Pizza

2 (8½ ounce) packages
   crescent roll dough
2 (8 ounce) packages cream
   cheese, softened
¾ cup mayonnaise
1 package Ranch dressing mix

Assorted chopped raw
   vegetables (suggest red and
   green peppers, broccoli,
   cauliflower, grated carrots,
   and/or black olives)

Spread rolls on bottom and up sides of a 15x10x1-inch jelly roll pan. Bake at 350° for 8-10 minutes. Cool. Mix cream cheese, mayonnaise and dressing mix; spread on cooled crust. Add vegetables. Cut into small squares.

Yield: 12-16 servings.

Crustless Zucchini Quiche

5 eggs
½ cup oil
1 cup buttermilk biscuit mix
4 cups thinly sliced zucchini
1 medium onion, chopped
½ cup grated Parmesan cheese
½ cup grated sharp cheese
½ cup grated Swiss cheese

½ cup grated mozzarella cheese
1 tablespoon parsley
½ teaspoon oregano
Dash of garlic powder
Dash of pepper
Thinly sliced smoked sausage
   (optional)

Beat eggs. Add oil and stir in baking mix. Add remaining ingredients. Place in a greased 9-inch square casserole or baking dish. Bake for 40-45 minutes at 350°. Cut into small squares and serve hot or cold.

Note: May use 9-inch pie pan and serve as an entrée.

Yield: 81 1-inch squares.

Nut-Filled Brie

2 pounds Brie
½ cup chopped walnuts
¼ cup sunflower seeds
2 teaspoons dried green
    peppercorns

12 ounces cream cheese,
    softened
Salt and finely ground pepper
    to taste
2-3 tablespoons aquavit

Split Brie into 2 layers. Mix remaining ingredients together, setting aside a few walnuts, sunflower seeds and peppercorns for decoration. Place half of this mixture on cut side of bottom layer of Brie. Cover with remaining half of Brie, cut side down. Spread remaining half of mixture on top and sides of Brie. Decorate. Serve with olives, grapes and French bread.

Yield: 12-16 servings.

Cheese Crisps

4 cups shredded sharp
    Cheddar cheese
2 cups flour
2 teaspoons sugar
½ teaspoon salt
⅛ teaspoon cayenne pepper

⅛ teaspoon dry mustard
1 cup butter or margarine at
    room temperature
Dash Worcestershire sauce
2 cups crispy rice cereal

Mix well all ingredients except cereal. Add cereal. Mix with hands to blend. Form into 1-inch balls. Put on ungreased cookie sheet. Flatten to ¼-inch thickness in crisscross pattern with fork dipped in flour. Bake in 350° oven for 10-12 minutes.

Yield: 8-10 dozen.

Cheese Petit Fours

3 loaves very thinly sliced
   bread (80 slices)
1 pound butter, softened
4 (6 ounce) jars sharp
   pasteurized process cheese
   spread

1 teaspoon hot pepper sauce
1½ teaspoons Worcestershire
   sauce
1 teaspoon garlic powder
Dill weed

Remove crusts from bread. Blend butter and next four ingredients together. Spread on slices of bread. Sprinkle dill weed over each. Stack 4 slices together. Cut into 6 pieces; sprinkle with dill. Freeze. Bake frozen on an ungreased baking sheet at 375° for 15 minutes or until brown.

Yield: 120 pieces.

Rye Cheese Delights

½ cup grated sharp Cheddar
   cheese
½ cup grated mozzarella cheese
¼ cup grated Parmesan cheese

4 scallions, chopped
½ teaspoon garlic powder
½ cup mayonnaise
Party rye bread

Mix all ingredients except bread. Top bread slices with teaspoon of mixture. Broil till brown.

Yield: 72 rounds.

Danish Cheese Mold

1 (9 ounce) package Gouda
   cheese, grated
¾ cup crumbled blue cheese
½ cup sour cream
¼ cup butter or margarine

2 tablespoons cider vinegar
1 tablespoon grated onion
⅛ teaspoon garlic salt
⅛ teaspoon cayenne pepper

Combine all ingredients in medium-size saucepan; cook slowly, stirring constantly 15 minutes or until cheeses are completely melted and mixture is blended. Pour into lightly oiled 3-cup mold and refrigerate. Unmold and serve at room temperature.

Yield: Hors d'oeuvres for 6-8.

Fruited Cheese Log

½ cup dried apricots
1 pound Monterey Jack or mild
   Cheddar cheese, shredded
1 (8 ounce) package cream
   cheese, softened
⅓ cup dry vermouth

1 teaspoon poppy seeds
½ teaspoon seasoned salt
⅓ cup golden raisins
⅓ cup chopped dates
Chopped walnuts

Soak apricots in 1 cup water 2 hours; drain and chop. Blend cheeses. Add next three ingredients and mix well. Add apricots, raisins and dates; mix thoroughly. Turn onto sheet of foil and shape into 9-inch log. Wrap securely in foil and chill until firm. Roll in chopped walnuts. Cover again with foil and store in refrigerator until ready to use.

Yield: Hors d'oeuvres for 8.

Gouda Cup

1 (12 ounce) Gouda cheese
3 tablespoons beer

Dash hot pepper sauce
1 teaspoon bottled steak sauce

Cut wide circle in top of cheese and scoop out to ¼-inch thickness. Refrigerate shell. Soften removed cheese and mash with other ingredients. Let stand one hour to blend. Pile mixture into shell like a cone. Cover with plastic wrap and refrigerate a few days. To serve, bring cheese to room temperature. Surround with crackers.

Yield: Approximately 1 cup spread.

"Hot" Cream Cheese Topping

1 (12 ounce) jar pineapple
   topping for ice cream
1 (10 ounce) jar apple jelly
½ cup horseradish or more
   to taste

1 teaspoon dry mustard
1 (8 ounce) package cream
   cheese

Mix first four ingredients together and pour over the softened cream cheese. Serve with crackers.

Yield: 3 cups.

Rosemary Cheese Wafers

2 cups grated extra-sharp cheese
½ cup butter, softened
1 cup flour
⅛ teaspoon salt
¼ teaspoon dry mustard

½ teaspoon Worcestershire
sauce
2 pinches cayenne pepper
2 tablespoons chopped fresh
rosemary leaves

Blend cheese and butter until smooth. Blend in remaining ingredients until smooth. Form a large ball and refrigerate for ½ hour. Divide into small bits and roll into marble size balls. Place on a foil-lined baking sheet and flatten slightly with fork. Bake in 375° oven for 10-12 minutes until lightly browned around the edges. Watch closely.

Yield: 2 dozen.

Hot Crab Puffs

1 (6 ounce) can lump
crabmeat, drained and
sprinkled with lemon juice
¾ cup finely chopped onion
¾ cup grated fresh Parmesan
cheese

¾ cup mayonnaise (Do not
use the light or no-fat.)
Generous pinch of cayenne
pepper
1 loaf white bread, very thinly
sliced

Use food processor to grate onion and cheese. Blend first 5 ingredients together lightly. Spread on slices of bread and cut bread into quarters. Place on lightly oiled, foil-lined baking sheet. Cover and freeze. When ready to bake, place in a 375° oven for 12-15 minutes; watch closely. Should be slightly puffed and lightly browned.

Yield: 8 dozen puffs.

Devilish Pâté

1 tablespoon unflavored gelatin
1 (10¾ ounce) can beef broth
2 (4 ounce) cans liver pâté

1 (4½ ounce) can deviled ham
1 teaspoon grated onion
1 teaspoon lemon juice

Soften gelatin in broth and then stir over low heat until dissolved. Measure ¾ of this into 3-cup mold. Chill until almost set but still sticky on top. Blend other ingredients into remainder of gelatin mixture and spoon over layer in mold. Chill for several hours or overnight. Unmold and serve with melba toast or crackers.

Yield: 3 cups.

Crabmeat Spread

2 (8 ounce) packages softened
cream cheese
1 (8 ounce) package crabmeat
2 tablespoons finely
chopped onion

1 teaspoon Worcestershire
sauce
1 tablespoon horseradish
4-5 drops hot pepper sauce
½ cup sliced almonds
Paprika

Beat cream cheese 1-2 minutes with electric mixer until creamy. Blend in remaining ingredients, except almonds and paprika. Spread mixture in 9-inch pie plate. Top with almonds and sprinkle with paprika. Bake uncovered at 375° for 20 minutes until golden brown. Serve with crackers or corn chips.

Yield: 3 cups.

Lobster (or Seafood) Spread

2 tablespoons unflavored
gelatin
½ cup water
2 tablespoons lemon juice
1 pint sour cream

1 (12 ounce) bottle chili sauce
2 tablespoons horseradish
1½ cups chopped lobster or
other seafood

In medium saucepan, sprinkle gelatin over water mixed with lemon juice. Let stand 1 minute. Stir over low heat until gelatin is completely dissolved (about 5 minutes). With whisk or rotary beaters, blend in sour cream, chili sauce and horseradish. Fold in seafood. Put into an oiled 5-cup mold; chill until firm. Unmold and serve with crackers.

Yield: 5 cups.

Salmon Ball

1 (8 ounce) package cream
    cheese, softened
1 (16 ounce) can red or
    pink salmon
1 tablespoon prepared
    horseradish
1 tablespoon lemon juice
1 teaspoon liquid smoke

Dash seasoned pepper
Dash garlic salt
2 tablespoons chopped onion
2 tablespoons chopped celery
Dash of dill
Chopped walnuts
Chopped parsley

Drain and clean salmon. Add all ingredients except walnuts and parsley; mix with fork or hands. Roll into a ball and refrigerate until firm. Roll in walnuts and parsley. Serve with crackers.

Note: Should be made the day before serving so flavors will blend.

Yield: 10 servings.

Seafood Cream Cheese Spread

2 (8 ounce) packages cream
    cheese, softened
1 (8 ounce) container sour cream

1 (1.7 ounce) package
    vegetable soup and dip mix
¾ cup cocktail sauce, chilled

TOPPING (choose one of the following):
1 (6 ounce) can white crabmeat,
    rinsed, drained and chilled
1 (4½ ounce) can shrimp,
    rinsed and drained

1 (6½ ounce) can tuna fish,
    drained

In large mixer bowl, beat cheese until fluffy; beat in sour cream and soup mix. Spread cheese mixture over bottom and sides of 10-inch glass pie plate. Chill at least one hour. Just before serving, spread with topping of choice. Top with cocktail sauce. Serve with assorted crackers.

Yield: Hors d'oeuvres for 12.

Shrimp Mousse

1 (8 ounce) package cream
    cheese, softened
1 (10¾ ounce) can tomato soup
2 envelopes unflavored gelatin
½ cup cold water
1 cup mayonnaise

1½ cups mixed chopped celery,
    onions and green peppers
1 pound fresh cooked shrimp,
    cut into pieces
Green olives for garnish

Beat cream cheese and tomato soup together. Dissolve gelatin in cold water. Add to cheese mixture and blend well. Add mayonnaise, chopped vegetables and shrimp. Chill in an oiled 5-cup mold. When set, unmold and garnish with sliced green olives.

Yield: 5 cups.

Chicken Liver Pâté

1 cup chicken livers
1 medium onion, chopped
2 tablespoons Worcestershire
    sauce
1 tablespoon lemon juice

2-4 cloves garlic, crushed
Salt and pepper to taste
Pinch nutmeg
1 cup bread crumbs

Place all ingredients, except bread crumbs, in a small saucepan; add approximately ¼ cup water. Bring to boil; simmer 10 minutes. Cool slightly. Add bread crumbs. Place in blender. Blend until smooth. Chill. Serve with crackers.

Yield: 2 cups.

Turkey Ball

1 (8 ounce) package cream
    cheese, softened
1 cup finely chopped
    cooked turkey
¾ cup finely chopped
    toasted almonds

⅓ cup mayonnaise
2 tablespoons chopped
    chutney
1 tablespoon curry powder
¼ teaspoon salt
Chopped parsley

Mix together the first seven ingredients. Chill several hours. Shape into a ball. Roll in parsley. Serve with crackers.

Yield: One large ball.

Deviled Ham Mousse

1½ envelopes unflavored gelatin
1 (10¾ ounce) can cream of
celery soup
2 (8 ounce) packages cream
cheese

1 cup mayonnaise
1¼ cups finely chopped onion
1½ cups finely chopped celery
1 (6¾ ounce) can deviled ham

Dissolve gelatin in ½ cup hot water. Heat soup, undiluted. Add gelatin mixture. Beat in cream cheese with electric mixer over low heat until smooth. Let mixture cool 15-20 minutes. Add remaining ingredients; beat until smooth and blended thoroughly. Pour into a 6-cup mold that has been oiled. Chill 8 hours or overnight. Unmold and serve with crackers.

Yield: 5-6 cups.

Green Pepper Jelly

6 large green peppers,
cut up small
1½ cups cider vinegar, divided
6 cups sugar

1½ teaspoons crushed
red pepper
2 (6 ounce) bottles liquid
fruit pectin
Green food coloring as desired

Liquefy 3 peppers and ¾ cup of vinegar in food processor. Repeat process with remaining peppers and vinegar. Place in saucepan and bring to boil. Add pectin and boil until candy thermometer reaches 200°; watch closely. Put in 8-ounce jelly jars or frozen food containers. Cover with lids; invert for 1½ hours to disperse minced pepper. Freeze up to 1 year or refrigerate up to 3 weeks.

Note: Delicious poured over a block of cream cheese as an appetizer or hors d'oeuvre . Serve as a condiment with roast lamb or beef.

Yield: Approximately 8 jars.

Better Than Eggnog

3 large eggs
1 quart orange juice
¼ cup lemon juice
2 tablespoons sugar
¼ teaspoon cinnamon
Dash of cloves

⅛ teaspoon ginger
2 quarts vanilla ice cream,
  softened
1 quart ginger ale
Nutmeg

Whisk eggs until frothy. Add the next 6 ingredients and mix. Spoon ice cream into a large punch bowl. Stir in egg mixture until combined. Just before serving, add ginger ale. Sprinkle with nutmeg.

Yield: Approximately 4 quarts.

Popular Party Punch

12 green tea bags
12 black tea bags
½ gallon boiling water
4 cups sugar
4 (12 ounce) cans lemonade
  concentrate, thawed

1 (12 ounce) can limeade
  concentrate, thawed
1 gallon cranberry juice
6 quarts ginger ale

Brew tea bags in boiling water for 2-3 minutes. Dissolve sugar in hot tea. Let cool. Add the next 3 ingredients, reserving ginger ale until just before serving. Add ice or chill. Serve.

Yield: 4 gallons or 85 (12 ounce) servings.

Shaker Cold Rhubarb Tea

4 cups diced unpeeled rhubarb
4 cups water

Grated rind of 1 lemon or orange
¾-1 cup sugar

Simmer rhubarb in water until very tender, about 20-25 minutes. Strain; add rind and sugar. Stir until sugar has dissolved. Cool and serve over ice in tall clear glasses.

Note: The redder the rhubarb skin, the more attractive the drink.

Yield: 4 servings.

Shaker Mocha "Punch"

½ cup instant coffee powder
2 cups hot water
1 cup sugar
1 gallon milk

½ gallon chocolate ice cream, softened
½ gallon vanilla ice cream, softened

In a saucepan combine coffee, water and sugar. Bring to a boil over medium heat, stirring frequently. Remove from heat; cool. Pour into a large serving bowl. Stir in milk; add ice creams. Stir until smooth.

Yield: About 18 servings.

Spicy Tea Punch

2½ cups boiling water
5 tea bags or 5 teaspoons loose tea
¼ teaspoon cinnamon
¼ teaspoon nutmeg

¾ cup sugar
2 cups cranberry juice cocktail
1½ cups water
½ cup orange juice
⅓ cup lemon juice

Pour boiling water over tea and spices. Cover and steep 5 minutes. Remove tea bags or strain. Add sugar and stir until dissolved. Cool. Add cranberry juice, water, orange juice and lemon juice. Chill. Serve over ice cubes.

Yield: 8-12 servings.

Apricot Refresher

1½ cups sugar
8 cups water, divided
1 (12 ounce) can orange juice concentrate, thawed

1 (12 ounce) can lemonade concentrate, thawed
1 (750 ml.) bottle apricot brandy
Ginger ale

Dissolve sugar in 2 cups boiling water. Add remaining water and other ingredients (except ginger ale). Put in freezer ice cube trays. When frozen, serve cubes in glass with ginger ale.

Note: Prepare ahead at least 8-10 hours.

Yield: 18-22 servings.

Sunshine Punch

7 bananas	1 (46 ounce) can unsweetened
8 oranges, peeled and sectioned	pineapple juice
1 (16 ounce) can frozen orange	7 cups unsweetened apple juice
juice concentrate, thawed	Ginger ale to taste and to dilute
	to desired consistency

Mash bananas with fork or in food processor; remove. Process orange sections with slicing blade; add ½ cup orange or pineapple juice, bananas and mix well. Mix with remaining juices in large bowl. Ladle the mixture into bowls and freeze. When mixture is at slushy stage, mix again with a fork to distribute fruit evenly. Return to freezer until 30 minutes before serving in punch bowl. Add ginger ale, serve.

Note: Must prepare ahead.

Yield: 25-35 servings.

Mulled Cider
A Festival of Trees Favorite

1 orange	½ cup sugar
1 lemon	1 gallon apple cider
1½ teaspoons whole cloves	2 cups orange juice
3 (3-inch) sticks cinnamon	1 cup lemon juice

Peel orange and lemon rinds into strips; insert cloves in each strip. Combine rinds, cinnamon, sugar and cider in a large pot; bring to a boil. Cover; reduce heat and simmer 10 minutes. Remove from heat; let cool completely. To serve, add orange and lemon juices to cider mixture; heat thoroughly.

Yield: 5 quarts.

Madison Avenue Punch

2 cups sugar
2½ cups water
1 cup lemon juice
  (about 6 lemons)
1 cup orange juice
  (about 3 oranges)

1 (6 ounce) can pineapple
  juice concentrate, thawed
2 quarts ginger ale
1 quart whiskey (optional)
Fresh mint leaves (optional)

In non-reactive pan, make a simple syrup by boiling sugar and water for 10 minutes. Remove from heat and stir in juices. Leave at room temperature for 1 hour; refrigerate. To serve as a punch, combine chilled juices, ginger ale and whiskey in punch bowl. Garnish with mint.

Note: If smaller portions are desired, mix in glasses by using equal parts fruit base and ginger ale with or without whiskey.

Yield: 16 teetotaler servings.

Champagne Punch

1 (12 ounce) can lemonade
  concentrate, thawed
1¼ lemonade cans of water
1 (750 ml.) bottle champagne,
  chilled

2 quarts ginger ale, chilled
1 pint raspberry sherbet
Strawberries or raspberries
  to decorate

Mix lemonade and water in punch bowl; slowly pour in champagne and ginger ale; stir gently. Carefully set pint of sherbet in center of punch bowl. Decorate.

Yield: 30 4-ounce servings.

Cranberry Holiday Drink

1 (12 ounce) can cranberry
   juice concentrate, thawed
6 ounces white rum
2½ tablespoons sugar

1 ounce Rose's lime juice
1 ounce fresh lime juice
4-5 ice cubes

Put first five ingredients in blender; blend until smooth. Add ice cubes; blend to a slush.

Note: Color lends itself to holiday time.

Yield: 4 servings.

Holiday Wassail

2½ cups sugar
1 cup water
1 lemon, sliced
8 (3- inch) sticks cinnamon
1 quart pineapple juice

1 quart orange juice
5 cups Sauterne
½ cup dry sherry
½ cup lemon juice
Pineapple wedges

Combine sugar, water, lemon slices and cinnamon sticks in a medium saucepan; bring to a boil and cook 5 minutes, stirring constantly. Combine next 5 ingredients in large pot; bring to a boil, cover and simmer 10 minutes. Stir in sugar syrup; heat thoroughly. Remove lemon slices and cinnamon sticks. Garnish each serving with a pineapple wedge.

Yield: 4 quarts.

Kahlua

4 cups sugar
4 cups water
¾ cup dry instant coffee

Fifth of vodka
1 vanilla bean, chopped

Boil sugar and water 10 minutes. Cool; add coffee, vodka and vanilla bean. Pour into one-half gallon jug and shake every day for 3 weeks.

Yield: 2 quarts.

Geppel's Gloggs
Scandinavian Hot Wine

1 bottle red table wine
1 orange, sliced
½ lemon, sliced
1 tablespoon honey
1 whole cinnamon stick
10 whole cloves
1 tablespoon grated fresh
    ginger root

½ cup raisins
½ cup whole blanched
    almonds
2 tablespoons crème de cassis
2 tablespoons dark rum
2 tablespoons aquavit or vodka

Bring wine to a boil in a heavy saucepan; add next 6 ingredients. Boil 2-3 minutes. Remove from heat; add rest of ingredients. Cool and store covered overnight. Heat to serve but do not boil again. Serve in heated mugs or glasses with a few raisins and almonds in each glass.

Yield: 8-10 servings.

Irish Cream Whiskey

1¾ cups whiskey
1 (14 ounce) can sweetened
    condensed milk
1 cup heavy cream
4 eggs

2 tablespoons chocolate syrup
2 tablespoons strong coffee
1 teaspoon vanilla
½ teaspoon almond extract

Blend all ingredients with mixer. Store tightly covered in refrigerator. Can be kept up to one month.

Yield: 5 cups.

CAKEBOARD
John Conger, c. 1820-40
AIHA purchase 1978.146

Unusual mahogany cakeboard used for
baking Nieuwjaarskoeken (New Year's cakes)
and molded cookies. There are two molds
each of leaves and eagles, and a larger figure
of a Dutch man.

Blueberry Coffee Cake

CAKE
1½ cups flour
1 teaspoon baking soda
1 teaspoon baking powder
¼ cup sugar
¼ teaspoon salt
1 egg, beaten
⅔ cup sour milk
1 cup blueberries
¼ cup melted butter or
    margarine

TOPPING
2 tablespoons butter
2 tablespoons flour
½ cup dark brown sugar
1 teaspoon baking powder
⅓ cup chopped nuts
¼ teaspoon cinnamon

CAKE: Mix all ingredients until well moistened. Put in well-greased 9-inch square pan. Add topping. Bake in 350° oven for 20-25 minutes.

TOPPING: Mix butter, flour, sugar and baking powder until crumbly. Add nuts and cinnamon; mix thoroughly. Sprinkle on top of batter.

Note: Great served with cranberry juice and lots of hot coffee.

Yield: 9 servings.

Beer Bread

3 cups self-rising flour
2 tablespoons sugar
1 (12 ounce) can beer at
    room temperature

Raisins or sunflower seeds
    (optional)

In large bowl, stir flour and sugar. Add beer and beat by hand 25 strokes. Add raisins, if desired; place in greased 8½x4½x2½-inch loaf pan. Bake at 350° for approximately 1 hour and 15 minutes. Serve while warm; may be toasted.

Note: 1 cup self-rising flour equals 1 cup all-purpose flour plus 1 teaspoon baking powder and ½ teaspoon salt.

Yield: 1 loaf.

Cherry Coffee Cake

3 cups flour
1¼ cups sugar
¼ teaspoon salt
1½ teaspoons baking soda
1½ teaspoons cinnamon
1¼ cups vegetable oil

3 eggs
1½ teaspoons almond flavoring
1 (20 ounce) can cherry
   pie filling
1½ cups chopped walnuts
Confectioners' sugar

Butter 13x9x2-inch pan and place in the refrigerator or freezer to firm the butter. In a large bowl, blend all ingredients except the pie filling and walnuts. Add the pie filling and walnuts and mix well. Batter will be thick. Pour into prepared pan. Bake at 325° for 70-80 minutes or until a cake tester inserted in center comes out clean. Cool cake 15 minutes in pan; remove to wire rack and cool completely. Before serving, sprinkle top with confectioners' sugar. May be frozen.

Yield: 16 servings.

Rhubarb Coffee Cake

1½ cups brown sugar,
   firmly packed
⅔ cup vegetable oil
1 egg
1 teaspoon vanilla
2½ cups flour, sifted
1 teaspoon salt

1 teaspoon baking soda
1 cup milk
1½ cups chopped rhubarb
¾ cup sliced almonds, divided
½ cup sugar
1 tablespoon butter, softened

Grease and flour two 9x1½-inch round pans. Mix brown sugar, oil, egg and vanilla. Combine flour, salt and baking soda. Add to the egg mixture alternately with milk. Stir in rhubarb and ½ cup almonds. Pour into pans. Mix sugar, butter and ¼ cup almonds; sprinkle on batter. Bake in 350° oven for 40-45 minutes.

Yield: 12-16 servings.

Orange Nut Coffee Cake

CAKE

2 large oranges
1½ cups seedless raisins
1 cup walnuts
3 cups flour, sifted
1½ teaspoons baking soda
1 teaspoon salt
1½ cups sugar
¾ cup shortening

1¾ cups milk
3 eggs

TOPPING
½ cup orange juice
½ cup sugar
1 teaspoon cinnamon
½ cup chopped nuts

CAKE: Remove seeds from oranges. Grind together oranges, pulp and rind; strain, reserving juice for topping. Add raisins and walnuts. Set aside. Sift together flour, baking soda, salt and sugar. Add shortening; blend well. Add 1¼ cups milk, mixing well. Add eggs and another ½ cup milk. Beat until batter is well-blended. Fold orange-raisin mixture into batter. Pour batter into a well-greased and lightly floured 9x13x2-inch pan. Bake at 350° for 45-50 minutes or until cake tests done.

TOPPING: Drip orange juice over warm cake. Combine sugar, cinnamon and walnuts. Sprinkle over cake. Decorate with orange slices if desired.

Yield: 12 servings.

Corn Bread

1 cup flour
1 cup yellow cornmeal
1 tablespoon baking powder
2 eggs

1 teaspoon salt
3 tablespoons sugar
1 cup sour cream
¼ cup melted butter

Mix first 7 ingredients together. Add melted butter. Pour into 8x8x2-inch greased pan and bake in 375° oven for 25 minutes or until golden brown. Delicate but firm.

Yield: 12-16 servings.

Sour Cream Cheese Coffee Cake

2½ cups flour
1 cup sugar, divided
¾ cup butter or margarine
½ teaspoon baking powder
½ teaspoon baking soda
¼ teaspoon salt
¾ cup sour cream

2 eggs
1 teaspoon almond extract
1 (8 ounce) package cream
  cheese, softened
½ cup jam or preserves
½ cup sliced almonds

Grease and flour 9-inch springform pan. In large bowl, combine flour and ¾ cup of sugar. Cut in butter with pastry blender until mixture resembles coarse crumbs. Reserve 1 cup crumb mixture. To remaining crumb mixture, add baking powder, baking soda, salt, sour cream, 1 egg and extract; blend well to form batter. Spread batter over bottom of pan and thinly coat 1-inch up sides. In another bowl, combine cream cheese, ¼ cup sugar and 1 egg; blend well. Pour over batter in pan. Spoon jam over cheese filling. Sprinkle reserved crumb mixture over top; sprinkle with almonds. Bake at 350° for 55-60 minutes or until golden brown. Center will be soft. Cool at least 15 minutes before serving.

Note: Stir the jam or preserves before spooning over cheese layer.

Yield: 8-10 servings.

Cranberry Nut Bread

2 cups flour, sifted
1 cup sugar
1½ teaspoons baking powder
1 teaspoon salt
½ teaspoon baking soda
¼ cup shortening

1 teaspoon grated orange peel
¾ cup orange juice
1 egg, well beaten
1 cup fresh coarsely chopped
  cranberries
½ cup chopped nuts

Sift together dry ingredients. Cut in shortening. Combine peel, juice and egg. Add to dry ingredients, mixing just to moisten. Fold in berries and nuts. Turn into greased 9x5x3-inch pan. Bake in 350° oven for one hour. Cool. Remove from pan. Wrap and store overnight.

Yield: 1 loaf.

Lemon Bread

BREAD
2 eggs
1 cup sugar
6 tablespoons margarine
1½ cups flour
½ teaspoon salt
1 teaspoon baking powder

½ cup milk
½ cup chopped walnuts
1 teaspoon lemon rind

TOPPING
½ cup sugar
Juice of 1 lemon

BREAD: Beat eggs, sugar and margarine together. Sift flour. Add salt and baking powder to sifted flour. Add dry ingredients to egg mixture, alternately with milk. Fold in nuts and lemon rind. Spoon batter into 2 lightly greased 8½x4½x2½-inch loaf pans. Bake at 350° for 45 minutes. Remove from oven and make cuts in top of bread with knife.

TOPPING: While still hot, combine ingredients and pour over bread. Topping will be absorbed in bread.

Yield: 2 small loaves.

Pear Nut Bread

1 (16 ounce) can pear halves
2 cups sifted flour
1 teaspoon baking soda
1 teaspoon baking powder
½ cup sugar
½ teaspoon ginger

1½ teaspoons grated lemon rind
½ cup chopped nuts
⅔ cup pear syrup
1 egg
2 tablespoons lemon juice
2 tablespoons butter, melted

Drain pears; reserve syrup and one-half of the pears. Chop remaining halves. Put dry ingredients in bowl. Combine remaining ingredients and pour over dry ingredients. Stir until blended. Pour into greased 8½x4½x2½-inch loaf pan. Garnish with reserved pears, sliced. Bake in 350° oven for 1 hour. Store in airtight container overnight.

Yield: 1 loaf.

Zucchini Bread

2 cups shredded raw zucchini
2 cups sugar
1 cup oil
3 eggs
1 teaspoon vanilla
¼ teaspoon baking powder
1 teaspoon baking soda
1 teaspoon ginger

1 teaspoon cloves
1 teaspoon cinnamon
3 cups flour or 2 cups flour
   and 1 cup oatmeal
½ teaspoon salt
1 cup chopped nuts
   and/or raisins

Combine all ingredients and mix well. Bake in 2 greased 8½x4½x2½-inch loaf pans or two 1-pound coffee cans at 350° for 1 hour.

Yield: 2 loaves.

Irish Soda Bread

4 cups sifted flour
¼ cup sugar
1 teaspoon salt
1 teaspoon baking powder
2 tablespoons caraway seeds
¼ cup butter or margarine

2 cups raisins
1⅓ cups buttermilk
1 egg, beaten
1 teaspoon baking soda
1 egg yolk, beaten

Sift flour, sugar, salt and baking powder in bowl. Stir in caraway seeds. Cut in shortening until mixture resembles coarse meal. Stir in raisins. Combine buttermilk, egg and baking soda. Add to flour mixture; stir enough to moisten mixture. Knead lightly, on floured surface, until dough is smooth. Shape into a ball and put in a greased 2-quart round casserole. Using a sharp knife, cut a 4-inch cross about ½-inch deep in center of dough. Brush with egg yolk. Bake in a 375° oven for 1 hour or until tester comes out clean. Cool for 10 minutes before removing from casserole. Cool before cutting. To serve, cut loaf in half, place cut side down; thinly slice each half.

Yield: 1 loaf.

Berry Patch Muffins

2 cups flour
1 tablespoon baking powder
½ teaspoon salt
1 tablespoon cinnamon
1¼ cups milk
2 egg whites, lightly beaten

½ cup margarine or butter,
   melted
1½ cup berries: strawberry,
   blueberry or raspberry
1 cup sugar

Stir flour, baking powder, salt and cinnamon together; make well in center. Add milk, egg whites and shortening. Combine; add berries and sugar, stirring quickly. Spoon batter into greased muffin tins. Bake at 375° for 20 minutes.

Yield: 20 muffins.

Bran Muffins for Busy Bakers

8 teaspoons baking soda
1 quart buttermilk
4 eggs
1½ cups vegetable oil
2½ cups sugar or half white,
   half brown
1 tablespoon salt

1½ teaspoons cinnamon
½ teaspoon cloves
5½ cups flour
1 pound raisins
1 cup chopped dates
2 cups all-bran cereal
2 cups bran flakes

In a large container, with tight-fitting cover, mix ingredients in order, blending well after each addition. Refrigerate overnight. Spoon batter into greased muffin tins, filling ⅔ full. Bake at 375° for 15-18 minutes or until tested done.

Note: This batter will keep 8-10 weeks stored in refrigerator. Fresh muffins can be made daily.

Yield: 8 dozen muffins.

Bran Muffins – For Your Heart's Sake

2 cups 100% bran cereal
1¼ cups lowfat plain yogurt
½ cup skim milk
¼ cup margarine, melted
¼ cup egg substitute or
   2-3 egg whites
1 cup flour

⅓ cup light brown sugar,
   packed
1 tablespoon baking powder
1 teaspoon cinnamon
1 apple, peeled, cored and
   chopped
¾ cup raisins

Mix cereal, yogurt, milk, margarine and egg; let stand 5 minutes. In large bowl, mix flour, sugar, baking powder and cinnamon. Add bran mixture, stirring until just blended. Stir in apple and raisins. Spoon into 12 greased muffin cups. Bake in 400° oven for 20 minutes or until tested done. Serve warm.

Yield: 12 muffins.

Cranberry Muffins

1 cup chopped fresh cranberries
¾ cup sugar, divided
1 teaspoon grated orange peel
1 egg, beaten

½ cup orange juice
2 tablespoons oil
2 cups biscuit baking mix

Mix cranberries, ½ cup sugar, and orange peel; set aside. Combine egg, ¼ cup sugar, orange juice, and cooking oil; add all at once to biscuit mix. Stir just until moistened. Fold in cranberry mixture. Fill greased muffin pans ⅔ full. Bake in 400° oven for 20-25 minutes.

Yield: 18 muffins.

Healthy Heart Scones

1⅓ cups oat flour
1⅓ cups unbleached flour
3 tablespoons brown sugar
2 teaspoons sesame seeds
2 teaspoons cream of tartar
1 teaspoon baking soda

7 tablespoons well-chilled
  margarine
⅓ cup skimmed milk
½ cup dried currants, dried
  diced apricots or frozen
  raspberries
2 teaspoons skimmed milk

Put first six ingredients into a large mixing bowl; cut in margarine. Mix in the ⅓ cup milk. Add fruit; mix thoroughly. Knead lightly to combine ingredients. Pat into circle ½-inch thick. Use a 2½-inch fluted cutter to cut scones. Brush with the remaining 2 teaspoons milk. Place on greased baking sheet. Bake at 375° for 15-20 minutes until golden.

Note: Scones' dough should not be worked too much.

Yield: 8-12 scones.

English Tea Scones

2 cups flour
⅓ cup sugar
1 tablespoon baking powder
1 teaspoon baking soda
½ teaspoon salt

6 tablespoons butter
  or margarine
1 egg, slightly beaten
½ cup raisins or currants
½ cup milk
1 egg (for wash)

Sift dry ingredients together. Cut in butter until mixture resembles coarse crumbs. Add raisins. Add egg and milk, stir until dough follows fork around bowl. Turn out on a floured surface. Knead gently about 15 times. Divide into 2 balls, pat flat to 1-inch thickness and cut into wedges, 4 wedges each. Can also be patted out and cut with a biscuit cutter. Brush tops with slightly beaten egg. Bake on greased baking sheet at 425° for 12-15 minutes.

Note: Do not overwork dough.

Yield: 8 servings.

Apple Danish

PASTRY
3 cups flour
½ teaspoon salt
1 cup margarine
½ cup milk
1 egg yolk

FILLING
6 cups sliced apples
1½ cups sugar

¼ cup melted butter
2 tablespoons flour
1 teaspoon cinnamon
1 egg white

GLAZE
1 egg white, slightly beaten
   with water
½ cup confectioners' sugar

PASTRY: Combine flour and salt. Cut in margarine until mixture resembles coarse crumbs. Combine egg yolk with milk. Add to flour mixture. Stir until dough leaves sides of pan. Divide in half. Roll half of dough into a 15x10-inch rectangle. Transfer to greased 15½x10½x1-inch pan (jelly roll pan).

FILLING: Combine all ingredients except egg white and spoon over pastry. Roll remaining dough into a 15x10-inch rectangle. Place over filling. Brush with egg white. Bake in 375° oven for 40 minutes or until golden brown. Partially cool.

GLAZE: Mix ingredients and drizzle over warm pastry. Cut into squares.

Yield: 15-20 pieces.

Easy Rhubarb Jam

5 cups cut rhubarb
   (½-inch pieces)
1 cup crushed pineapple,
   drained

5 cups sugar
1 (3 ounce) package
   strawberry jello

Combine fruits with sugar in heavy saucepan. Stir over low heat until sugar dissolves. Cook over medium heat for 20 minutes until clear and thick. Remove from heat. Stir in jello and seal with paraffin at once in jelly jars.

Yield: 6-7 jars.

Pumpkin Pecan Muffins

3½ cups flour	2 cups cooked pumpkin
2 teaspoons baking soda	4 eggs, beaten
1½ teaspoons salt	1 cup oil
3 cups sugar	⅔ cup water
2 teaspoons cinnamon	½ cup chopped pecans
2 teaspoons nutmeg	or walnuts
1 teaspoon allspice	1 cup dates or raisins

Combine flour, baking soda, salt, sugar, cinnamon, nutmeg and allspice in large mixing bowl. Make a deep well in center. Add pumpkin, eggs, oil, water, pecans and raisins; mix just enough to moisten all ingredients. Pour into greased muffin tins. Bake at 350° for 20 minutes or until done. Cool 10 minutes before removing from pan. Continue cooling on rack. Wrap and store in refrigerator or freezer.

Yield: 28-30 muffins.

Praline Biscuits

½ cup butter	Cinnamon
½ cup brown sugar,	2 cups biscuit baking mix
firmly packed	⅓ cup applesauce
36 pecan or walnut halves	⅓ cup milk

Put 2 teaspoons butter, 2 teaspoons brown sugar and 3 nut halves in each of 12 muffin cups. Sprinkle cinnamon in each cup. Heat in oven until melted. Mix remaining ingredients until a dough forms; beat 20 strokes. Spoon onto mixture in muffin cups. Bake in 450° oven for 10 minutes. Invert immediately onto a heat-proof serving plate.

Yield: 12 biscuits.

Barm Brack Bread
Irish Freckle Bread

1 cake yeast or 1 package
    active dry yeast
¼ cup water, heated to 105-115°
1 cup milk
½ cup butter or margarine,
    melted
3 eggs, beaten

⅔ cup sugar
5 cups flour
1½ cups currants
1 grated lemon rind
1 teaspoon salt
⅓ cup chopped candied
    citrus peel

Soften yeast in water and add next 5 ingredients. Let rise until double in bulk. Add remaining ingredients. Mix well. Put in a well-greased 9-inch loaf pan and let rise 1 hour. Bake in a 350° oven for 50 minutes. Brush with melted butter.

Yield: 1 loaf.

Italian Herb Bread
for the Bread Machine

1¼ cups water
2 tablespoons olive oil
2 tablespoons sugar
1 teaspoon salt
⅛ teaspoon cayenne pepper

¼ teaspoon paprika
½ teaspoon savory
½ teaspoon thyme
3½ cups bread flour
2¼ teaspoons active dry yeast

Measure ingredients into 2-pound bread pan and insert into machine. Select "white bread, dry milk" setting. When finished, cool bread on rack before slicing.

Yield: 1 loaf.

Oatmeal Molasses Bread

1 cup water	2 teaspoons salt
1 cup milk	½ cup molasses
3 tablespoons butter	1 package active dry yeast
1 cup old-fashioned rolled oats	4½-5 cups white flour

Combine water, milk and butter in saucepan and bring to boil. Add oats and cool to lukewarm. Add salt, molasses and yeast. Beat for 2 minutes. Add flour. Knead approximately 10 minutes and place in large greased bowl. Cover with hot damp cloth. Put bowl in warm place until mixture is double in size. Then punch down and divide into two loaves. Put into 8½x4½x2½-inch greased loaf pans and let rise again. It will rise faster this time. Bake at 375° for 30-40 minutes.

Note: To hurry the rising, heat oven to 200°; turn oven off. Put bowl of dough in oven. On rack below, place a couple of pans of boiling water. The warm oven and the steam from the water will help the rising. Makes wonderful toast!

Yield: 2 loaves.

Walnut Rolls

2 tablespoons margarine	1 tablespoon coarse salt
⅔ cup milk	1 cup chopped walnuts
⅓ cup buttermilk or yogurt	4 cups flour, divided
1 (1 ounce) yeast cake or	1 egg, beaten
package active dry yeast	½ teaspoon cardamom (optional)

Melt margarine in milk; remove from heat and add buttermilk. Add yeast cake plus the salt and cardamom. Add yeast. If you use dry yeast, dissolve in ¼ cup 110° water. Add flour, reserving ½ cup. Add nuts. Knead dough well. Cover and let stand at room temperature one hour. Remove to floured surface. Knead again using reserved flour. Shape into 20 or 24 balls. Place on greased cookie sheet. Let stand 40 minutes longer. Brush with beaten egg. Bake in preheated 350° oven, 15-18 minutes. Serve warm.

Note: Excellent for breakfast or afternoon tea served with a mild cheese. These may be shaped into larger rolls; if so, check baking time. If served with cheese or cold cuts, omit cardamom.

Yield: 20-24 rolls.

Orange Rolls

ROLLS

1 cup lukewarm milk
¼ cup shortening
1 teaspoon salt
¼ cup sugar
1 package active dry yeast
1 egg, lightly beaten
3 cups flour
2 tablespoons melted butter

3 tablespoons sugar
1 tablespoon grated orange rind

SYRUP
⅓ cup sugar
2 tablespoons water
½ cup orange juice

ROLLS: Mix first 4 ingredients until shortening is soft. Add yeast to mixture and stir until yeast is dissolved. Add egg and flour; mix with hands. Put mixture on lightly floured board. Cover and let stand 10 minutes. Knead until smooth. Place in greased bowl, turn out and return to bowl greased side up. Cover with a damp cloth and let rise until mixture is doubled in size, approximately 2 hours. Punch down and roll into a rectangle. Spread mixture of butter, sugar and orange rind on the rectangle. Roll tightly; cut into slices. Place in 2 well-greased 9-inch cake pans and let rise until they are doubled in size. Bake at 425° for about 10 minutes. Remove pans from oven and slowly pour hot syrup over rolls. Return to oven and bake 10 minutes more. Remove from pans while hot to prevent sticking.

SYRUP: Boil sugar and water; simmer 5 minutes. Remove from heat and add orange juice.

Yield: Approximately 18 rolls.

Cranberry Butter

1 cup cranberries
1½ cups confectioners' sugar

½ cup cold butter
1 tablespoon lemon juice

Mix ingredients together in food processor until berries are well chopped. Keep refrigerated. Serve with warm rolls.

Yield: 3 cups.

Olibollen
Dutch Doughnuts

½ cup milk
2 teaspoons brown sugar
1 teaspoon salt
¼ cup warm water (105-115°)
1 package active dry yeast
1 egg, lightly beaten
1½ cups flour

⅛ teaspoon nutmeg
½ teaspoon cinnamon
¾ cup seedless raisins
½ cup chopped candied
   orange peel
1 quart vegetable oil
Confectioners' sugar

Scald milk; stir in brown sugar and salt; cool to lukewarm. Measure warm water into large warm bowl; stir in yeast and dissolve. Stir egg, flour, nutmeg and cinnamon into the milk mixture. Beat rigorously until batter is elastic and falls in sheet from spoon. Stir in raisins and orange peel; mix well. Cover; let rise in warm place until doubled in bulk, about one hour. When doubled, do not stir down. Meanwhile, heat oil to 350°. Using two spoons, shape dough in 1-inch balls; drop immediately into hot oil. Dip spoons in hot oil each time before shaping dough. Fry doughnuts about three minutes or until golden brown, turning once. Drain on paper towels. Cool and roll in confectioners' sugar.

Yield: 2 dozen.

Feather Light Pancakes

4 eggs, separated
1 tablespoon sugar
½ cup cottage cheese
½ cup sour cream

¾ cup flour or ¼ cup each bran,
   cornmeal and wheat flour
½ teaspoon baking soda
¼ teaspoon baking powder
½ teaspoon salt

Beat egg whites until stiff but not dry; add sugar gradually. Separately, beat egg yolks well. Gradually fold in cottage cheese and sour cream. Sift dry ingredients. Fold into batter. Fold in beaten egg whites. Drop by spoonful onto lightly greased griddle and cook twice as long as regular pancakes. Serve with bacon and maple syrup or with fruit and whipped cream.

Yield: 9-12 small pancakes.

Pretzels

1 tablespoon honey
1½ cups warm water (110°)
1 package active dry yeast
1 teaspoon salt
4 cups flour

2 tablespoons baking soda
6 cups water
1 egg, beaten
Kosher salt

Add honey to water; sprinkle in yeast; stir until dissolved. Add salt. Blend in flour. Knead the dough. Place in a large bowl and let rise until doubled. Cut dough into pieces. Roll them into ropes and twist into pretzel shapes. In a large pot, boil 6 cups water and baking soda. Drop 4 pretzels at a time into boiling water and cook for one minute. Transfer to a lightly greased cookie sheet. Brush with egg. Sprinkle with kosher salt. Bake at 425° for 12-15 minutes or until brown.

Note: From the 5th century until the early 20th, pretzels were considered Lenten food and only served from Ash Wednesday through Good Friday. The shape symbolized 2 arms, crossed in prayer.

Yield: Varies with size.

Fluffy Today/Thin Tomorrow Flapjacks

2 cups flour
1 teaspoon baking soda
1 tablespoon sugar
½ teaspoon salt

2 cups buttermilk
1 egg
1 tablespoon oil

Sift dry ingredients twice. Beat egg in buttermilk. Mix wet and dry ingredients lightly with fork. Mix in oil. Either cook immediately in butter or skillet greased with piece of bacon for fluffy flapjacks or let stand in refrigerator overnight before cooking for thinner flapjacks.

Yield: 4-6 servings.

Double Fruit Pancakes

PANCAKES
2 cups flour, sifted
¼ cup sugar
4 teaspoons baking powder
1 teaspoon salt
2 eggs, separated
2 cups milk
2 tablespoons butter or
　margarine, melted
1 cup chopped fresh cranberries

½ cup finely chopped apple

CIDER SAUCE
1 cup brown sugar
1 cup cider
1 tablespoon butter
½ teaspoon lemon juice
¼ teaspoon cinnamon
Dash nutmeg

PANCAKES: Sift together dry ingredients. Combine beaten egg yolks and milk. Add to dry ingredients; stir well. Stir in shortening, cranberries and apple. Fold in stiffly beaten egg whites. Let batter stand a few minutes. Bake on hot griddle using ⅓ cup batter for each pancake. (Use spatula to spread batter evenly.) Serve with butter and warm syrup or cider sauce.

CIDER SAUCE: Mix all ingredients together. Bring to boil. Cook 30 minutes.

Yield: 12 pancakes.

Fresh Cranberry Waffles

1¾ cups sifted all-purpose flour
¼ cup sugar
2½ teaspoons baking powder
½ teaspoon salt
2 egg yolks, beaten

1¼ cups milk
2 tablespoons oil
1 cup fresh cranberries,
　chopped
2 egg whites, stiffly beaten

Sift together flour, sugar, baking powder and salt. Combine egg yolks, milk and oil. Add to dry ingredients; mix well. Stir in berries. Fold in egg whites. Bake in hot waffle iron. Serve with Cider Sauce (See Double Fruit Pancakes for recipe).

Yield: 12 waffles.

Fruit Cream Cheese Pancake

1 (8 ounce) package cream
   cheese, softened
½ cup sour cream
3 tablespoons orange flavored
   liqueur or orange juice
3 tablespoons sugar
½ cup flour

¼ teaspoon salt
½ cup milk
2 eggs, beaten
1 tablespoon margarine
2 cups strawberries, peach
   slices or blueberries
¼ cup toasted slivered almonds

Combine cream cheese, sour cream, liqueur and sugar, mixing until well-blended. Chill. Combine flour, salt, milk and eggs; beat until smooth. Heat 10-inch oven-proof skillet in 450° oven until very hot. Add margarine to coat skillet; pour in batter immediately. Bake on lowest rack at 450° for 10 minutes. Reduce heat to 350°; continue baking 10 minutes or until golden brown. Fill with fruit; top with cream cheese mixture. Sprinkle with nuts. Serve immediately.

Yield: 6-8 servings.

Country Griddlecakes

⅔ cup flour, sifted
⅓ cup yellow cornmeal
1½ teaspoons baking powder
⅓ teaspoon baking soda

¼ teaspoon salt
⅓ pound bulk pork sausage
2 eggs, separated
⅔ cup milk

Sift flour again with cornmeal, baking powder, soda and salt. Crumble sausage and fry until done. Drain; reserve 2 tablespoons drippings. Beat egg yolks; combine with milk; add dry ingredients and mix well. Add sausage and drippings; beat until thoroughly blended. Fold in stiffly beaten egg whites. Drop by tablespoons on moderately hot, lightly greased griddle. Serve with butter, warm syrup and baked apple rings.

Yield: 16 medium size pancakes.

Spoon Bread

4 cups milk	1¾ teaspoons salt
1 cup cornmeal	4 eggs, well beaten
2 tablespoons butter or	
margarine	

Mix milk and cornmeal; scald and cook 5 minutes in top of double boiler or until the consistency of thick mush. Add butter and salt. Slowly fold in eggs. Pour into a greased 1½-quart baking dish. Bake at 400° for 45 minutes. Serve at once in dish in which baked. Serve with butter and bacon and/or fried apples.

Yield: 4-5 servings.

Hot Apple Oatmeal

4 cups milk	½ teaspoon cinnamon
½ cup brown sugar	2 cups rolled oats
2 tablespoons butter	2 cups chopped apples
½ teaspoon salt	1 cup raisins

Combine the milk, sugar, butter, salt and cinnamon in an oven-proof pot and bring to a boil. Remove from heat and stir in the oats, apples and raisins. Bring mixture to a simmer, place in a 350° oven; cook uncovered for 30 minutes.

Yield: 4 servings.

Granola

1½ pounds (9-11 cups) quick	1 cup vegetable oil
cooking rolled oats	⅔ cup maple syrup or brown
1 cup wheat germ	sugar
1 cup shredded coconut	⅓ cup water
1 cup chopped nuts (peanuts,	1 teaspoon salt
walnuts, sesame or	
sunflower seeds)	

Mix thoroughly; spread on 2 cookie sheets. Bake at 300° for 1 hour, stirring every 15 minutes. Keeps well in a covered container if the kids don't find it.

Yield: 12 cups.

The Soup, Salad & Sandwich Collection

COOKSTOVE
Ransom and Co., Albany, New York
Cast iron and sheet metal c. 1846
Gift of Mrs. Dorothy M. Francis, 1975. 39.1-11

This cookstove was called Granger's Patent Air
Tight, and the firebox is similar to those found on
column parlor stoves of the period. Instead of
columns on either side, however, there are two
boiling holes, and the flue leads to a large sheet
iron oven.

Cold Peach Soup

5 large fresh peaches, skinned
¼ cup sugar
1 cup sour cream
¼ cup sherry

2 tablespoons orange juice
   concentrate
Juice from 1 large lemon
Additional peach slices
Strawberries

In a food processor or blender purée peaches with sugar until smooth. Mix in sour cream, sherry, orange and lemon juice; blend again until smooth. Refrigerate overnight and serve in chilled sherbet glasses with either fresh peach slices or strawberries as garnish.

Yield: 6-8 servings.

Melon Soup

1 (8 ounce) package softened
   pineapple cream cheese
2 cups cantaloupe chunks

1 cup honeydew chunks
1 cup orange juice
¼ teaspoon salt

Purée all ingredients until smooth. Chill before serving.

Yield: 4 servings.

Strawberry Soup

1 quart strawberries
   (reserve 3-4 for garnish)
1½ cups sugar

¾ cup sour cream
1 cup half-and-half
1½ cups dry white wine

Prepare berries; purée with sugar in blender. Strain into a 3-quart bowl. Whisk in sour cream, then half-and-half and wine. Chill. Serve in well-chilled sherbet glasses, garnishing each with a half strawberry.

Yield: 6-8 servings.

Cucumber-Yogurt Soup

2 medium cucumbers, peeled,
   seeded and sliced
1 cup water
½ cup chopped onion
½ teaspoon salt
Dash of pepper

2 cups chicken broth, divided
¼ cup all-purpose flour
2 whole cloves
1 cup plain low-fat yogurt
2 teaspoons dried whole
   dill weed

Combine first 5 ingredients in a saucepan; bring to a boil over medium heat. Reduce heat, cover, and simmer until cucumbers are tender. Spoon mixture into the container of an electric blender; process until smooth. Set aside. Gradually add ½ cup chicken broth to flour in a saucepan; cook over low heat 1 minute, stirring constantly. Gradually add remaining 1½ cups broth and cucumber purée. Add cloves; simmer 5 minutes, stirring constantly. Chill well. Remove cloves. Stir in yogurt and dill weed.

Yield: 4 cups.

Gazpacho

4 cups skinned, seeded,
   chopped ripe tomatoes
¾ cup chopped onion
1 (10¾ ounce) can beef
   consommé
1 (10¾ ounce) can beef bouillon

1½ cups chopped green pepper
1 teaspoon paprika
1 clove garlic, minced
½ cup lemon juice
¼ cup olive oil

Combine all ingredients and let stand at room temperature for one hour to blend flavors. Chill at least two hours but better if made a day ahead.

Yield: 6 servings.

Carrot Soup

4 tablespoons vegetable oil
1½ cups sliced and
   chopped carrots
1 large onion, chopped
1½ teaspoons grated fresh
   ginger root
1½ teaspoons grated orange rind

6 cups chicken stock
1½ cups half-and-half (whole
   milk may be substituted)
4 tablespoons chopped fresh
   parsley (reserve 1 tablespoon
   for garnish)

In a heavy skillet, sauté first 3 ingredients for 5 minutes. Add ginger root, orange rind and parsley. Use enough chicken stock to cover above and simmer for 30 minutes until carrots are tender. Remove from heat and purée. Add remaining stock and half-and-half. Reheat or chill. Garnish.

Yield: Over 2 quarts.

Carrot Leek Soup

1 medium leek, thinly sliced
4 teaspoons low-fat margarine
6 medium carrots, sliced
2 medium potatoes, peeled
   and cubed

3 (14 ounce) cans chicken broth
2 cups skim milk
⅛ teaspoon pepper

In large saucepan, sauté leek in margarine until tender. Add carrots, potatoes and broth. Bring to a boil. Reduce heat; cover and simmer until vegetables are tender. Cool to room temperature. Remove vegetables with slotted spoon to blender or food processor. Add enough liquid to cover. Blend until smooth. Return to pot. Stir in milk and pepper. Heat through again before serving.

Yield: 8-10 servings.

Lentil Soup

4 cups water or vegetable stock
1 onion, sliced
2 stalks celery, sliced
2 carrots, chopped
1 cup lentils
¼ teaspoon celery seed

1 bay leaf
1 teaspoon marjoram
½ teaspoon chili powder
½ teaspoon garlic powder
¼ cup chopped fresh parsley

Bring stock to a boil; add vegetables. Bring to a boil again. Add the lentils. Simmer 45 minutes covered. Add celery seeds and bay leaf. Simmer 10 minutes more. Add remaining seasonings, simmer 5 minutes more. Remove bay leaf. Garnish with parsley.

Yield: 4 servings.

Peasant Bean Soup

¼ cup butter or margarine
1 large onion, finely minced
4 cloves garlic, finely minced
1 pound bulk spicy
    sausage meat
1 (20 ounce) can each red and
    white kidney beans, drained

2 cups beef or chicken broth
1 (28 ounce) can crushed
    tomatoes
¼ cup whiskey
Pepper to taste

Heat butter until foamy. Sauté onion and garlic until tender. Add sausage, breaking into small pieces as it cooks. Add remaining ingredients and simmer, covered, for about 1½ hours.

Yield: 5-6 servings.

Union Street Lunch's Bacon-Bean Soup

1 pound navy beans
1 tablespoon salt
2 quarts water
1 pound bacon
Bacon drippings
2 cups diced carrots
2 cups diced celery
2 cups diced onions

1 (28 ounce) can of crushed
  tomatoes
1 quart chicken broth or
  three (10 ounce) cans
  of chicken broth
5 chicken bouillon cubes
¼ cup brown sugar
Black pepper to taste

Soak beans overnight in cold water. Bring beans and salt to a boil in 2-quarts of water. Simmer for 1½ hours. Cook bacon crisp; add to beans along with bacon drippings and next 7 ingredients; allow to simmer for ½ hour. Season with pepper to taste. Serve with a sandwich for a great warm-up on a chilly day.

Yield: 4 quarts.

Cream of Broccoli Soup

1½ pounds fresh broccoli or
  2 (10 ounce) packages
  frozen broccoli
½ cup chopped onion
2 tablespoons margarine
1 cup pared and diced potato

2 (13¾ ounce) cans chicken
  broth
½ teaspoon salt
Dash cayenne pepper
⅛ teaspoon nutmeg
1 cup light cream

Trim outer leaves and tough ends from broccoli. Cut stalks into short pieces. Cook broccoli 5 minutes. Drain. Using large saucepan, sauté onion in margarine until soft but not brown. Add the next 4 ingredients. Heat to boiling, simmer 15 minutes. Add broccoli, simmer 5 more minutes. Place in blender; blend until smooth. Return to pan; add cream and nutmeg. Garnish with broccoli florets.

Yield: 6-8 servings.

Brother James' Cabbage Soup

6 cups finely chopped cabbage
1 cup finely diced bacon
¾ cup finely chopped onions
¼ cup flour
4 cups chicken broth
½ cup finely diced carrots
1⅓ cups finely diced potatoes
Salt and freshly ground
    pepper to taste

1 teaspoon whole caraway
    seeds, crushed
1 tablespoon white wine
    vinegar
½ teaspoon sugar (optional)
1½ cups heavy cream
¼ cup finely chopped fresh dill

Cover cabbage with boiling water and cook one minute. Drain. Cook the bacon in a casserole or small kettle until rendered of fat. Add the onions and cook, stirring, until the onions are wilted. Sprinkle with flour and stir. Add the broth, stirring rapidly with a whisk. When the mixture simmers, add the cabbage, carrots, potatoes, salt, pepper, caraway seeds, vinegar and sugar. Cook, stirring often from the bottom, about 30 minutes. Stir in the cream and simmer five minutes. This is a very rich and thick soup that may be thinned with a little milk. Serve in hot soup bowls; sprinkle with fresh dill or dillweed.

Yield: 8 servings.

Cream of Celery Soup

4 tablespoons butter
    or margarine
2 garlic cloves, minced
1 cup coarsely chopped onion
¼ cup flour
10 cups chicken broth

12 cups celery, trimmed and cut
2 teaspoons salt
Several grinds fresh pepper
1 teaspoon fresh ground nutmeg
1 cup heavy cream

Heat butter in large saucepan and add garlic and onion. Cook until wilted. Sprinkle with flour and stir to blend. Add broth, slowly stirring. Add celery, salt, pepper and nutmeg. Simmer until celery is cooked, 15-20 minutes. Purée mixture in blender and return to pan. Add cream and stir while re-heating.

Note: Freezes well.

Yield: 3 quarts.

Cream of Mushroom Soup

¼ cup butter
⅓ cup flour
¼ cup finely chopped onion
¼ cup finely chopped celery
1 small clove garlic, minced
¼ teaspoon white pepper
Pinch of mace

1½ pounds mushrooms, thinly
   sliced — not chopped
1 quart chicken or turkey stock
1 cup heavy cream
¼ cup dry sherry
¼ cup minced parsley
Salt to taste

Melt butter in 3-quart heavy saucepan over medium heat. Add flour; stir with whisk until smooth. Cook 3 minutes, stirring continuously. Do not brown. Add onions, celery, garlic, pepper and mace. Cook over medium heat, stirring occasionally, until celery and onions are softened. Add mushrooms, stirring with a wooden spoon to avoid breaking; cook until soft. Add stock; bring to boil. Reduce heat and simmer for 5 minutes. Add cream, sherry, parsley and salt. Reheat.

Yield: 6 servings.

French Onion Soup Gratiné

¼ cup butter
3 large onions, sliced
1 teaspoon sugar
1 tablespoon flour
2½ cups water

½ cup red wine
2 (10½ ounce) cans beef broth
1 loaf French bread
4 slices of provolone cheese

In 4-quart saucepan over medium heat, sauté onions and sugar for 10 minutes in hot butter. Stir in flour until well-blended. Add water, wine and undiluted beef broth; heat to boiling. Reduce heat to low. Cover and simmer 10 minutes. Cut four 1-inch thick slices of bread; save remaining bread to eat with soup. Toast the bread slices in 325° oven until lightly browned. Ladle soup into four 12-ounce oven-proof bowls and place 1 slice toasted bread on top of each with cheese slice. Place bowls on jellyroll pan for easier handling. Bake in 425° oven 10 minutes or until cheese is melted.

Yield: 4 servings.

Pea Soup

2 tablespoons butter
1 tablespoon chopped onion
2 cups frozen peas
2 lettuce leaves, torn
1 small carrot, sliced thin
½ teaspoon salt

1 teaspoon sugar
2 cups chicken broth
1 cup heavy cream
Garlic powder and pepper
    to taste

Sauté onions in butter for 5 minutes. Add next 6 ingredients. Cook until vegetables are soft, about 20 minutes. Remove and purée in food processor or blender. Add cream and heat slowly. Add garlic powder and pepper.

Yield: 4-6 servings.

Basque Potato Soup

1 pound Italian sausage, sliced
½ cup chopped onion
2 (1 pound) cans tomatoes
4 Idaho potatoes, peeled
    and diced (6 cups)
1 cup diagonally sliced celery
2 tablespoons chopped
    celery leaves

1½ cups water
2 beef bouillon cubes
1 tablespoon lemon juice
1 bay leaf
2 teaspoons salt
½ teaspoon dried thyme
¼ teaspoon pepper

Brown the sausage over medium heat in a large pot. Add the onions; cook 5 minutes. Add the remaining ingredients and bring to a boil; reduce heat and simmer, uncovered, for 40 minutes, or until potatoes are tender.

Yield: 4 quarts.

Potato and Leek Soup

1 medium diced white onion	6 tablespoons flour
¼ cup melted butter	3 cups chicken broth
1 teaspoon sweet basil	3 cups half-and-half
Dill weed, thyme, and fresh	8-10 medium red potatoes,
ground pepper to taste	unskinned, thinly sliced
1 medium bunch fresh leeks	

In saucepan on medium heat, sauté onion in butter until translucent. Mix in spices. Wash leeks thoroughly, discard root and cut off halfway up the stalk. Slice leeks into about ¼-inch thick slices. Add to pan and sauté 5 minutes more. Mix in flour and cook for another 2 minutes. Add stock and half-and-half. Simmer 15 minutes stirring every 3-4 minutes. Add potatoes and simmer for an additional 30 minutes.

Note: Substitute whole milk for half-and-half for fewer calories. May also be puréed and served cold garnished with chopped chives.

Yield: 6-8 servings.

Cheddar-Potato Soup

¼ cup butter	1 cup thin strips of green and
1½ cups diced celery and	red peppers
onion, mixed	2 cups cooked, diced potatoes
2 cloves garlic, chopped	2 tablespoons white wine
½ cup flour	1 teaspoon dry mustard
3 quarts chicken stock or broth	4-5 dashes hot pepper sauce
3 cups shredded sharp	4-5 dashes Worcestershire sauce
Cheddar cheese	1 tablespoon soy sauce or tamari
2 cups heavy cream	

Melt butter over medium heat. Add celery, onions and garlic. Sauté until tender but not browned. Stir in flour. Cook 5 minutes. Add stock and simmer for ½ hour. Stir in cheese over low heat. Add cream, peppers and potatoes and simmer for additional 10 minutes. Do not boil. Add remaining ingredients. Keep warm until serving.

Yield: 16 servings.

Cheese Soup

¼ cup butter or margarine
½ cup flour
1½ cups chicken broth
½ cup finely chopped onion
½ cup finely chopped carrots
½ cup finely chopped
    fresh parsley

½ cup finely chopped chives
1 pound sharp Cheddar,
    shredded
1 (12 ounce) can beer, at
    room temperature

Cook butter and flour until golden brown. Whisk in chicken broth; add onions, carrots, parsley and chives; cook 20 minutes. Stir in cheese and beer. Serve soup hot with bowls of hot buttered popcorn.

Yield: 4 servings.

Avgolemono Soup
Traditional Greek Soup

4 tablespoons uncooked rice
5 cups chicken or lamb broth
4 eggs

Juice of 2 lemons
Salt to taste

In a large saucepan, cook rice in broth for 25 minutes. In a separate bowl, combine eggs and lemon juice; beat for 2 minutes. Remove the broth from heat; whisk in the egg mixture. Divide the soup among 4 bowls and serve immediately. The soup should be creamy but not too thick.

Yield: 4 servings.

Autumn Soup

1 onion, chopped
2 tablespoons chopped leeks,
   white part only
2 tablespoons butter
2 cups chicken broth
2 cups canned pumpkin
1 (10¾ ounce) can celery soup

½ teaspoon sugar
½ teaspoon mace
¼ teaspoon nutmeg
Salt and pepper to taste
1 cup half-and-half
Sour cream
Fresh parsley

Sauté onion and leeks in butter until transparent. Stir in broth, pumpkin and celery soup. Heat thoroughly. Purée mixture in blender. Pour into 2-quart pan and add sugar, mace, nutmeg, salt and pepper. Return to stove and slowly add half-and-half. Garnish with a dollop of sour cream and parsley.

Yield: 6 servings.

Queen Victoria Soup

1 small onion, peeled
   and chopped
2 tablespoons butter
1 cup finely diced celery
½ pound mushrooms,
   finely chopped
4 cups chicken broth

½ cup diced, cooked
   chicken breast
½ cup diced, cooked ham
2 tablespoons quick-cooking
   tapioca
1-2 cups light cream
Salt and pepper to taste

Sauté onion in butter until soft but not brown. Add celery and mushrooms; stir gently over low heat for a few minutes. Add remaining ingredients except cream, salt and pepper. Simmer for 15-20 minutes. Stir in cream. Heat and season to taste.

Yield: 5-6 servings.

Farmers' Soup/Stew

2 tablespoons olive oil
½ pound slab bacon,
  rind removed and cut
  into ½-inch cubes
6 medium carrots, halved
  lengthwise and cut
  into ½-inch lengths
3 medium onions, diced
  into ¼-inch pieces
4 cloves garlic, minced
2 leeks, cut into ½-inch slices
  using 3 inches of green part
1 head cabbage, cored and
  cut into 1-inch pieces
1-2 russet potatoes,
  peeled and diced

½ cup dried green split peas
8 cups defatted chicken broth
1 cup chopped Italian
  parsley, divided
2 teaspoons dried thyme
1 teaspoon dried tarragon
Salt and pepper to taste
4 medium zucchini, diced
  into ½-inch pieces
¾ pound Swiss chard or
  spinach, cut crosswise
  into 1-inch pieces
6 plum tomatoes, peeled,
  seeded and diced

Heat oil in large heavy pot over medium heat. Add bacon; cook, stirring 10-12 minutes. Add carrots, onions, garlic and leeks. Cook over low heat 15 minutes to wilt vegetables, stirring occasionally. Add cabbage, potatoes and split peas to vegetables. Cook 10 minutes over low heat. Add broth, seasonings and ½ cup parsley. Bring to boil, lower heat and simmer covered for 30 minutes. Add zucchini and Swiss chard; cook 10 minutes longer. Add tomatoes and remaining ½ cup parsley. Cook 5 minutes more. Serve piping hot. Delicious when made with fresh garden vegetables for that first cool day of fall.

Yield: 8 servings.

Pasta e Fagioli

1 cup chopped onion
1 small clove garlic, chopped
2 tablespoons oil
2 chicken bouillon cubes
4 cups water
1 (8 ounce) package
   small shell pasta
1 (1 pound) can tomatoes,
   chopped

1 (1 pound) can cannelloni
   beans
1 bay leaf
1 teaspoon salt
¼ teaspoon pepper
½ teaspoon oregano
1 teaspoon fresh or dried
   parsley

Sauté onion and garlic in oil. Add bouillon cubes with water. Cover; bring to boil and stir in shells. Cook until almost tender. Drain. Stir in tomatoes and beans with liquid, bay leaf, salt, pepper, oregano and parsley. Bring to boil. Cook 10 minutes, stirring frequently. Remove bay leaf before serving.

Yield: 4-6 servings.

Italian Barley Soup

1½ quarts rich beef stock
2 cups water
¾ cups barley
1 cup chopped celery
1 cup grated carrot
1 cup chopped yellow onion
4 cloves garlic, crushed
½ cup red wine
1 piece lemon peel,
   about 1x½-inch

A little salt and lots of pepper
½ tablespoon basil
¼ tablespoon oregano
½ cup fresh chopped parsley
2 bay leaves
½ tablespoon rosemary
2 tomatoes, peeled and chopped
¼ cup tomato paste
Freshly grated Parmesan or
   Romano cheese

Bring the stock and water to a boil. Add the barley and simmer lightly. Add the celery, carrot, onion, garlic, wine, lemon peel, pepper and salt; simmer covered for 2 hours. Stir often or the barley will stick to the bottom of the pot. Add the herbs, tomatoes and tomato paste. Continue cooking, covered, for 1 more hour, for a total cooking time of 3 hours. Stir in a handful of grated cheese before serving.

Yield: 8 servings as an entrée.

Garden Vegetable Soup

2 tablespoons margarine or
  vegetable oil
1 cup sliced carrots
1 cup sliced celery, with
  some of the tops
1 cup chopped onion
1 clove garlic, crushed
9 medium tomatoes,
  skinned and chopped
1 teaspoon dried oregano,
  crushed, or 1 tablespoon
  fresh, snipped

1 teaspoon dried basil,
  crushed, or 1 tablespoon
  fresh, snipped
2 teaspoons salt
¼ teaspoon pepper
1 (13¾ ounce) can beef broth
1 cup cut green beans
2 cups thinly sliced zucchini
¼ cup chopped parsley
½ cup grated Parmesan cheese

Melt margarine in Dutch oven; sauté carrots, celery, onion and garlic for 5 minutes. Add tomatoes, oregano, basil, salt and pepper. Cook 15 minutes. Add beef broth and green beans. Cook 30 minutes. Add zucchini and parsley; cook another 20 minutes. Serve with grated Parmesan cheese.

Note: Freezes well.

Yield: 8 cups.

Sweet Potato Soup

1 large onion, diced
2 large carrots, peeled and diced
4 cloves garlic, peeled
  and sliced
3 tablespoons butter
1 Granny Smith apple, peeled,
  seeded and diced

4 tablespoons curry powder
5 large sweet potatoes, peeled
  and chunked
4 cups chicken stock or water
½ cup heavy cream
Salt and pepper to taste

Sauté the onions, carrots and garlic for a few minutes in butter, then add apples. When vegetables are soft, add the curry powder and cook 5 minutes. Add the sweet potatoes and chicken stock. Cover and simmer for about 1 hour or until potatoes are soft. Purée the soup in a blender or food processor in small batches, then return to pot. Stir in heavy cream and season with salt and pepper.

Yield: 12 servings.

Meatball Soup

MEATBALLS
1 beaten egg
1 teaspoon salt
⅛ teaspoon pepper
½ cup bread crumbs
½ teaspoon oregano
1 pound ground beef
2 tablespoons margarine

SOUP BASE
½ cup chopped onions

2 tablespoons margarine
2 medium carrots, diced
2 stalks celery, thinly sliced
1 medium potato, diced
1 (13 ounce) can tomatoes
2 (10½ ounce) cans beef broth
4 cups water
1 bay leaf
1 small zucchini, sliced
Parmesan cheese

MEATBALLS: Mix first 6 ingredients and shape into small balls. Brown in margarine. Set aside.

SOUP BASE: In a large pot, sauté onions in margarine. Add next 7 ingredients. Bring to a boil and simmer 30 minutes. Add meatballs and zucchini; simmer 30 minutes. Serve topped with Parmesan cheese.

Yield: 8 servings.

Peruvian Shrimp and Corn Chowder

⅓ cup chopped green onions
   (use some stem for color)
1 clove garlic, minced
¼-½ teaspoon cayenne pepper
1 generous tablespoon butter
   or margarine
2 (10¾ ounce) cans of cream
   of potato soup

1 (3 ounce) package of cream
   cheese, softened
1 soup can of milk
1 pound frozen cleaned
   medium or large raw shrimp
1 (8 ounce) can whole kernel
   golden corn, undrained
Salt and pepper

In a small fry pan, sauté onions with garlic and cayenne pepper in butter until tender. Combine soup, cream cheese, and milk in a saucepan. Blend in onions, garlic, and cayenne pepper. Add shrimp and corn. Bring to a boil over medium to high heat, stirring often. Reduce heat and simmer for about 6-8 minutes, stirring occasionally. Use salt and pepper according to taste. Shake a little cayenne pepper on top for color.

Yield: About 7 cups.

Minestrone

3 pounds marrow bone
with lots of meat
4 quarts water
2 teaspoons salt
1 cup dried red kidney beans
1½ tablespoons olive oil
3 slices bacon, diced
1 cup coarsely chopped onions
3 cloves garlic, crushed
½-¾ cup chopped fresh
parsley
2 (6 ounce) cans tomato paste
2 teaspoons sage leaves
1 teaspoon dried basil or
2 tablespoons chopped
fresh basil

1 teaspoon freshly ground
pepper
2 cups coarsely shredded
cabbage
1½ cups sliced carrots
1½ cups sliced celery
1 medium zucchini, sliced
1 (9 ounce) package frozen
green Italian beans
1 (15 ounce) can chick peas
¾ cup shell macaroni or
Acini di pepe, cooked
1 (10 ounce) package frozen
green peas

Place soup bones, water, red beans and salt in large cooking pot. Boil slowly 2½-3 hours. Cool. Remove bones and fat. Skim soup. Return meat to pot. Heat oil in skillet; add bacon and brown lightly. Add onions and garlic. Cook 5-6 minutes over low heat. Add parsley, stirring and cooking one minute more. Add to soup pot. Mix tomato paste with sage, basil, pepper and add to pot. Boil for a few minutes. Add cabbage, carrots, celery and zucchini. Cover and simmer over low heat for 30 minutes. Add green beans and chick peas. Cook 15 minutes. Add green peas and macaroni; cook 2 minutes. May be served with grated Romano cheese and crusty French bread.

Note: Divide into containers. Freeze or have a party!

Yield: 6½ quarts.

Country Herb Soup

¾ pound pinto beans	½ teaspoon dried rosemary
1 quart water	½ teaspoon celery seeds
1 pound ham, cut into	¼ cup dark brown sugar
½-inch cubes	½-1 tablespoon chili powder
2¾ cups tomato juice	1 teaspoon salt
1 quart chicken stock	1 bay leaf, crumbled
3 medium onions, chopped	½ teaspoon dried thyme
3 cloves garlic, chopped	½ teaspoon dried basil
¼ cup chopped green pepper	½ teaspoon dried marjoram
3 tablespoons chopped	¼ teaspoon curry powder
fresh parsley	4 whole cloves
1 teaspoon dried oregano	1 cup dry sherry
½ teaspoon ground cumin	1-2 scallions, chopped

Soak pinto beans overnight in water. Combine all ingredients except sherry and scallions. Simmer partially covered for 3 hours, stirring every ½ hour. Add sherry just before serving. Sprinkle each serving with chopped scallions.

Yield: 6-8 servings.

Oyster Bisque

1 tablespoon butter	Salt and freshly ground
1 tablespoon flour	pepper to taste
1 quart milk, scalded	1 quart oysters, ground,
½ cup finely chopped celery	with liquid included
1 small green pepper, seeded	Worcestershire sauce to taste
and finely ground	

Melt butter in a saucepan; blend in flour. Gradually whisk in milk; bring mixture to boil, stirring constantly. Add celery, green pepper, salt and pepper. Add oysters; heat through but do not boil. Add Worcestershire sauce.

Yield: 4 servings.

Cranberry Soufflé Salad

1 envelope unflavored gelatin
2 tablespoons sugar
¼ teaspoon salt
1 cup water
½ cup mayonnaise
2 tablespoons lemon juice
1 teaspoon grated lemon rind

1 (16 ounce) can whole
   cranberry sauce
1 orange or apple, peeled and
   diced, or 1 (8½ ounce) can
   pineapple tidbits, drained
¼ cup chopped walnuts

Mix gelatin, sugar and salt thoroughly in a small saucepan. Add water; stir constantly over low heat until gelatin is dissolved. Remove from heat; stir in mayonnaise, lemon juice and rind. Blend. Quick chill in refrigerator freezer for 10-15 minutes or until firm at edge but soft in center. Beat until fluffy; fold in remaining ingredients. Turn into 4-cup oiled mold and chill until firm. Unmold and garnish with salad greens; serve with mayonnaise.

Yield: 6-8 servings.

Lemon Cream Cheese Salad

2 cups boiling water
1 (6 ounce) package lemon
   gelatin
3 tablespoons sugar (optional)
1 (8 ounce) package cream
   cheese, softened
1 (20 ounce) can crushed
   pineapple, drained

2 cups chopped apples
   (Winesap, Red or
   Golden Delicious)
2 stalks celery, diced
½ cup coarsely chopped
   walnuts
Lettuce

Dissolve gelatin and sugar in water. In separate bowl, at medium speed, beat cream cheese until fluffy. At low speed, slowly add gelatin mixture; beat until smooth. Stir in remaining ingredients except the lettuce. Pour into 13x9x2-inch pan or 9-cup oiled mold. Cover and chill for 4 hours or overnight. Serve on lettuce.

Yield: 12 servings.

Red Crest Tomato Aspic

2 boxes strawberry jello
3 cups tomato juice
1½ tablespoons horseradish
2½ teaspoons scraped onion

½ cup thick chili sauce
¼ teaspoon Worcestershire
   sauce
Salt to taste

Dissolve jello in boiling tomato juice. When dissolved, stir in other ingredients and pour into 3-cup oiled mold.

Yield: 3 cups.

Seafoam Delight

1 (28 ounce) can pears
   (reserve juice)
1 (3 ounce) package
   lime gelatin
1 cup whipping cream

1 (8 ounce) package
   cream cheese
1 tablespoon mayonnaise-type
   salad dressing
Sliced almonds (optional)

Heat 1 cup juice from pears until boiling. Dissolve gelatin in juice. Refrigerate. When partly congealed, beat in blender. Purée pears in blender. Add cream cheese and blend. Add salad dressing and blend. Whip cream separately. Add gelatin. Fold mixtures together. Pour into mold and let set. When ready to serve, unmold and garnish with almonds if desired.

Yield: 6-8 servings.

Green Bean Salad

2 pounds small fresh
   green beans
2 tablespoons sesame
   seeds, toasted

2 tablespoons fresh lemon juice
1½ teaspoons vegetable oil
1 teaspoon salt
Freshly ground pepper

Wash and trim beans. Cook approximately 4 minutes. Drain and refresh under cold water. Drain. Toss with remaining ingredients.

Yield: 6-8 servings.

24-Hour Bean Salad

1 (16 ounce) can cut green beans
1 (16 ounce) can cut wax beans
1 (16 ounce) can dark red
kidney beans
1 (10 ounce) package frozen
lima beans, cooked
1 (4 ounce) jar chopped
pimiento

1 green pepper, thinly sliced
or 5 ounces frozen
diced pepper
1 medium onion, thinly
sliced, separated into rings
½ cup sugar
½ cup olive oil
½ cup cider vinegar

In large covered bowl, mix all above ingredients and chill. Stir occasionally. Cover, refrigerate over night. Take out of refrigerator 15 minutes before serving if oil is congealed. Stir before serving.

Yield: 8 servings.

Herbed White Bean Salad

1 pound small dry white beans
2 quarts water
1 teaspoon salt
2 medium tomatoes,
seeded and chopped
½ cup chopped red onion
½ cup quartered black olives

6 tablespoons olive oil
6 tablespoons white wine
vinegar
2 large garlic cloves, minced
1 tablespoon fresh basil or
1 teaspoon dried
Salt and pepper to taste

Rinse beans. Simmer in water and salt until tender, approximately 1¼ hours. Drain well. Cool. Combine beans with rest of ingredients, adjusting seasonings to taste. Best if made 1 or 2 days ahead.

Note: If beans are soaked overnight, cooking time may be shortened.

Yield: 12 servings.

Broccoli Salad with Basil Dressing

SALAD

2 bunches broccoli
1 small roasted red pepper or
    1 (2 ounce) jar pimientos,
    drained

DRESSING

2 tablespoons red wine vinegar
1 tablespoon lemon juice
¼ cup fresh basil leaves, minced
    (do not substitute dried)

1 clove garlic, minced
Pinch of salt
¼ cup grated Parmesan cheese
⅓ cup vegetable oil or
    half olive oil
Dash honey
Freshly ground black pepper
    to taste
Lettuce leaves for platter

SALAD: Trim broccoli florets, peel stems and cut into bite-size pieces. Steam the broccoli until tender but still crisp. Plunge into ice water. Drain and dry in a towel. Mix in bowl with the red pepper.

DRESSING: Mix vinegar, lemon juice, basil, garlic, salt and cheese. Drizzle oil while mixing until well-blended. Season with honey and pepper. The whole mixture may be made in a blender or food processor. Stir again before using. Toss dressing with broccoli/pepper mixture. Serve over salad greens. Broccoli can be marinated longer but do not arrange lettuce until ready to serve.

Yield: 4-6 servings.

Cottage Cole Slaw

½ cup cottage cheese
½ cup mayonnaise
3 tablespoons vinegar
1½ teaspoons onion juice
¾ teaspoon salt

½ teaspoon pepper
Caraway seed (optional)
6 cups finely shredded cabbage
2 cups diced apples
½ green pepper, chopped

Combine cottage cheese and mayonnaise. Add next 5 ingredients. Combine dressing with cabbage, apples and pepper.

Yield: 8 to 10 servings

Spicy Cole Slaw

1 cup vinegar
1 cup sugar
½ teaspoon turmeric
1 teaspoon celery seed
1 teaspoon mustard seed

1 teaspoon salt
1 large head cabbage, finely
　shredded
1 green pepper, chopped
1 onion, chopped

Mix vinegar, sugar and seasonings; bring to a boil. While hot, pour over vegetables, cool, refrigerate. Keeps well for 7 days.

Note: Cole Slaw must be one of the oldest and most popular American dishes. (James Beard)

Yield: 10-12 servings.

Cold Cauliflower Salad

1 cauliflower, bite-size pieces
¼ cup vinegar
½ cup olive or salad oil

½ cup stuffed olives, sliced
4 ounces blue cheese, crumbled
¼ cup green onion, chopped

Combine all ingredients; marinate at least 8 hours.

Yield: 8 servings.

Cucumber With Cumin and Yogurt
Middle Eastern

3 cups plain yogurt
2 cucumbers, peeled and
　sliced thin

1 small onion, minced
1 teaspoon ground cumin
Freshly ground pepper

Whip yogurt with a whisk. Fold in remaining ingredients and chill for 1 hour or more.

Yield: 3-4 servings.

Green Pea/Red Radish Salad

2½ pounds fresh peas,
   shelled or 1 (20 ounce) bag
   frozen peas
¾ cup water
¼ cup mayonnaise
1 tablespoon chopped parsley

1 tablespoon tarragon vinegar
¾ teaspoon salt
⅛ teaspoon pepper
1 bunch or 1 (6 ounce) bag
   radishes, chopped
Lettuce leaves

In 3-quart saucepan, over high heat, bring water to boil; add peas. Bring to boil. Reduce heat to low; cover and simmer 3-5 minutes until peas are tender. Drain; rinse under cold water to cool. Set aside. In large bowl, with whisk or fork, mix mayonnaise, parsley, vinegar, salt and pepper. Add peas and radishes, toss to coat. Cover and refrigerate to mellow. Serve on lettuce leaves in lined serving bowl or on individual plates.

Yield: 4-6 servings

Hot German Potato Salad

6 medium potatoes, boiled
   unpeeled
6 slices bacon, cooked crisp
   and crumbled
½ cup chopped onion

1 tablespoon flour
½ cup water
½ cup vinegar
½ teaspoon salt
1 tablespoon sugar

Peel and cube potatoes. Add bacon and onion. Add flour to bacon drippings in frying pan. Stir over heat for 1 minute. Add water, salt, vinegar and sugar. Cook until thickened and pour over potato mixture. Mix well and serve hot.

Yield: 4-6 servings.

Potato Salad Mold

1 envelope unflavored gelatin
2 tablespoons sugar
1 teaspoon salt
1¼ cups boiling water
¼ cup lemon juice
8 stuffed green olives, sliced
½ green pepper, cut into strips
3 hard-cooked eggs, chopped
4 cups diced cooked potatoes

1 cup diced celery
¼ cup diced green peppers
¼ cup diced pimiento
¼ cup chopped green onions
¼ cup chopped parsley
1½ teaspoons salt
1 cup mayonnaise
½ cup heavy cream, whipped

Mix gelatin, sugar and salt thoroughly; cover with the boiling water and stir to dissolve sugar. Add lemon juice. Pour thin layer of mixture into 1½-quart ring mold; chill. When gelatin layer is firm, place "flower" design on top with olive slices and green pepper strips. Combine remaining ingredients with rest of gelatin mixture. Spoon over gelatin in ring mold. Chill until firm. Invert on serving plate.

Yield: 8 servings.

Crunchy Red Potato Salad

3 pounds red potatoes
¾ cup Italian dressing
4 slices bacon
1 cup chopped celery

1 cup chopped onion
1 teaspoon crumbled
    fresh rosemary
Salt and pepper to taste

Scrub potatoes, cut into chunks; steam approximately 20 minutes, just until tender. Cool slightly, slice and toss with Italian dressing. Marinate overnight in covered non-metal container. Next day, cook bacon and crumble. Reserve 1 tablespoon bacon fat to sauté the onion and celery slowly for 4 minutes. Add to potatoes, along with bacon, rosemary, salt and pepper. Chill 3 hours or serve warm.

Yield: 4-6 servings.

Sweet Potato Salad

4 medium sweet potatoes,
    cooked and chilled
¾ cup crushed pineapple,
    drained
¾ cup miniature
    marshmallows

½ cup chopped roasted pecans
¼ cup celery, diced
2 tablespoons orange juice
½ cup mayonnaise
Mandarin orange sections
Lettuce

Peel chilled sweet potatoes and cut into small cubes. Add pineapple, pecans, marshmallows and celery. Mix orange juice with mayonnaise and add to salad. Toss gently. Serve on bed of lettuce and top with orange sections.

Yield: 4-6 servings.

Romaine-Spinach Salad

1 head romaine lettuce, torn
4 cups torn spinach
¼ cup sliced radishes
¼ cup sliced green or
    purple onion
4 slices bacon, cooked
    and crumbled
Raw mushrooms (optional)
2 hard-cooked eggs, sieved

1 clove garlic, crushed
1 teaspoon dry mustard
½ teaspoon salt
½ teaspoon pepper
1½ teaspoons minced fresh
    basil or ½ teaspoon
    dried basil
¼ cup white or wine vinegar
½ cup vegetable oil

Combine first 6 ingredients in a large bowl; toss gently. Combine eggs and remaining ingredients in a jar. Cover tightly and shake vigorously. Pour dressing over salad; toss gently. Serve immediately.

Yield: 8 servings.

Layered Spinach Salad

1 (10 ounce) package
  raw spinach
Sugar
6 hard boiled eggs, sliced
1 cup bacon bits
1 small head Boston lettuce
1 red onion, sliced in rings

1 (10 ounce) package frozen
  peas, thawed but not cooked
Mayonnaise-type salad
  dressing
1 (8 ounce) package shredded
  Swiss cheese
Paprika

Tear spinach leaves into bite-size pieces and cover bottom of 13x9x2-inch glass casserole. Sprinkle with sugar. Arrange sliced eggs on top. Sprinkle with bacon bits. Tear lettuce into bite-size pieces. Arrange over bacon bits. Cover with onion rings, then peas. "Frost" with salad dressing. Sprinkle with Swiss cheese. Dust with a little paprika for color. Cover. Refrigerate for at least 2-3 hours or overnight.

Note: May also "frost" with salad dressing combined with low-fat yogurt to decrease the fat content.

Yield: 12 servings.

Spinach-Pear Salad

½ tablespoon sugar
½ teaspoon salt
Freshly ground pepper
2 tablespoons balsamic
  vinegar
¼ cup vegetable oil
1 pound spinach, washed
  and stemmed

1 pound ripe pears,
  peeled and sliced
½ cup seedless grapes
1 small red onion,
  thinly sliced
⅓ cup chopped walnuts
1 cup bean sprouts

Combine first 5 ingredients for dressing. Assemble the spinach with fruit, onion, walnuts and sprouts. Add dressing and serve immediately.

Note: Other greens may be substituted for spinach.

Yield: 6-8 servings.

Variegated Salad

SALAD
2 Golden Delicious apples,
    peeled and chopped
2 tablespoons lemon juice
4 cups fresh spinach
4 cups red leaf lettuce
½ cup cashews, pecans
    or walnuts
½ cup crumbled blue cheese

½ cup sliced mushrooms
6 slices cooked bacon, crumbled

DRESSING
¼ cup red wine vinegar
⅓ cup olive oil
3 tablespoons steak sauce
1 clove garlic, crushed or
    1 teaspoon garlic powder

Pour lemon juice over apples. Wash and tear spinach and lettuce into bite-sized pieces. Add remaining salad ingredients. Combine dressing ingredients and shake. Pour over salad and toss.

Yield: 6-8 servings.

Parmesan Vegetable Tossed Salad

2 cups fresh broccoli florets
2 cups cauliflower florets
½ medium sweet onion,
    thinly sliced
3 tablespoons sugar
2½ tablespoons grated
    Parmesan cheese
¼ teaspoon salt

¼ teaspoon dried basil
1 cup mayonnaise
½ pound bacon, cooked
    and crumbled
½ large head lettuce, torn
1 cup seasoned croutons
1 (4 ounce) can sliced water
    chestnuts, drained

Combine broccoli, cauliflower and onion in large bowl. Combine sugar, cheese, salt, basil and mayonnaise. Mix well. Add to vegetables and toss. Refrigerate several hours or overnight. Add bacon, lettuce, croutons and water chestnuts just before serving.

Yield: 10-12 servings.

Mandarin Orange Salad

DRESSING
½ teaspoon salt
Dash of pepper
2 tablespoons sugar
2 tablespoons vinegar
¼ cup salad oil
Dash of red pepper sauce
1 tablespoon chopped
fresh parsley

SALAD
¼ cup sliced almonds
4 teaspoons sugar
¼ head iceberg lettuce
¼ head romaine lettuce
1 cup chopped celery
2 green onions with tops,
thinly sliced
1 (11 ounce) can mandarin
oranges

Mix all dressing ingredients; shake in tightly covered jar. Refrigerate.

Cook almonds and sugar over low heat, stirring constantly, until sugar melts and almonds are coated. Cool. Break apart and store at room temperature. Tear lettuce into bite-sized pieces. Toss with celery and onions. Refrigerate no longer than 24 hours. To serve, put greens in bowl; add drained oranges and almonds. Add dressing. Toss and serve.

Yield: 6-8 servings.

Chinese Chicken Salad

2 cups diced cooked chicken
1 (8 ounce) can bamboo shoots
(optional)
1 (8 ounce) can water chestnuts
1 cup diced celery
2 tablespoons minced onion

1 cup slivered almonds
2 (11 ounce) cans mandarin
oranges, drained
1½-2 cups mayonnaise
Chinese noodles

Mix and refrigerate overnight. Serve on Chinese noodles.

Yield: 4-6 servings.

Caesar Salad with Grilled Chicken

SALAD
1 head romaine lettuce
2 cloves garlic, peeled
  and chopped
2 tablespoons vegetable oil
3 slices bread, cubed
3 grilled chicken breasts,
  cut into pieces

DRESSING
2 cloves garlic, peeled
  and mashed

2 tablespoons lemon juice or
  cider vinegar
Pinch of salt
Pinch of pepper
3 tablespoons Parmesan
  cheese
½ teaspoon anchovy paste
½ teaspoon Dijon mustard
1 tablespoon oil

SALAD: Tear lettuce into bite-size pieces. Wash, drain and dry thoroughly. Sauté garlic in oil until light brown. Strain and discard garlic; sauté bread cubes in garlic oil until golden brown. Drain and keep warm.

DRESSING: Combine ingredients, adding oil in a fine stream and stirring constantly to blend well. Toss lettuce with dressing. Serve on chilled salad plate garnished with chicken, which may be either hot or cold.

Yield: 6 servings.

Taco Salad

1 pound lean ground beef
1 (16 ounce) can stewed
  tomatoes
1 (4 ounce) can chopped
  green chilies, drained
1 teaspoon beef flavor instant
  bouillon or 1 bouillon cube

¼ teaspoon hot pepper sauce
⅛ teaspoon garlic powder
1 medium head lettuce,
  shredded
1½ cups corn chips
1 medium tomato, chopped
1 cup shredded Cheddar
  cheese

In large skillet brown meat; pour off fat. Add stewed tomatoes, chilies and seasonings. Simmer uncovered 30 minutes. Place meat mixture on shredded lettuce in large bowl or on platter. Garnish with chopped tomato and corn chips. Sprinkle with cheese.

Yield: 4 servings.

Chicken and Pasta Salad

DRESSING
½ cup mayonnaise-type
   salad dressing
⅓ cup water
1 tablespoon barbecue or
   chili sauce
1½ teaspoons white vinegar
1½ teaspoons freeze dried
   chives, crumbled
¼ teaspoon garlic powder
¼ teaspoon black pepper

SALAD
1 pound chicken breasts,
   skinned and boned
3 cups uncooked pasta twists
   (rotini)
6 slices bacon, cooked
   crisp and crumbled
3 cups lettuce, cut in
   bite-size pieces
1 large tomato, coarsely
   chopped

Blend dressing ingredients in large salad bowl. Place chicken breasts in 6-quart pot. Add enough water to cover. Bring to boil; reduce heat to low and simmer until chicken is done. Remove to cutting board to cool. Skim and add water to liquid in pot to make 4 quarts. Bring to boil. Add pasta and cook 9 minutes until firm but tender. Drain well. Add hot pasta to dressing in bowl and toss to coat. Cut chicken in bite-size pieces and add to pasta. Add bacon, lettuce and tomato. Toss gently.

Yield: 4 servings.

Broccoli Salad

2 bunches broccoli, cut into
   bite-size pieces
1 bunch fresh scallions, white
   and green parts, cut up
½-¾ cup raisins, softened in
   boiling water

6 slices bacon, cooked crisp
   and crumbled
¼ cup sugar
1 cup mayonnaise
2 tablespoons vinegar
1-2 teaspoons lemon juice

Mix broccoli, scallions, raisins and bacon together; toss gently. Blend sugar, mayonnaise, vinegar and lemon juice thoroughly. Fold dressing into vegetable mixture. Cover and refrigerate 1-2 hours before serving.

Yield: 8-10 servings.

Chicken Waldorf Salad

6 chicken breast halves, boned,
   skinned and trimmed
2 teaspoons chicken stock base
2 cups water
2 apples, diced (put into
   water with lemon juice
   to prevent browning)

1 cup diced celery
⅓ cup mayonnaise (non-fat)
⅓ cup broken walnuts
⅓ cup golden raisins
Lettuce

Cook chicken, covered in water with chicken stock until done (about 15 minutes after boiling). Drain and reserve stock for later use. Chill, then dice chicken. Drain apples and add with celery to chicken. Toss together with mayonnaise; add nuts and raisins. Serve on bed of lettuce.

Note: For variety, other fruits may be added (diced pineapple, grapes, etc.) and turkey may be substituted for chicken.

Yield: 6 servings.

Tabbouleh Salad
Middle Eastern

5-6 bunches Italian parsley,
   chopped fine
2 bunches scallions, chopped
2 large tomatoes, chopped
¼ cup fine cracked wheat
   (bulgur #3)

¼-½ cup chopped fresh mint
   or 2 tablespoons dried
¼-½ cup olive oil
Juice of 4-5 lemons
Salt and pepper to taste
Romaine lettuce for serving

Parsley can be chopped in food processor; place on paper towels to absorb any moisture after chopping. Soak wheat in plenty of water for 10-15 minutes, change water 2-3 times by pouring off top water; replace; small particles will float. In a large bowl place parsley, tomatoes, scallions and mint. Remove wheat from water and squeeze dry; add to parsley. Add salt and pepper. Add about ¼ cup olive oil and about ½ of the lemon juice. Stir, taste. Tabbouleh should be moist and a little sour; keep adding oil and lemon juice until desired flavor is reached. Line serving bowl with lettuce leaves and mound salad in center. To eat, scoop a tablespoon of salad with a piece of lettuce.

Yield: 4-6 servings.

Fresh Seafood Salad

4 quarts water
1 pound peeled and
    deveined shrimp
1 pound sea scallops
1 pound cooked lobster meat
    or 1½ pounds prepared
    sea-legs
4 stalks celery, cut in
    1-inch pieces
1 pound seedless green
    grapes, halved

4 plum tomatoes, diced
1 bunch fresh dill,
    finely chopped
1 cup sour cream
½ cup mayonnaise
2 tablespoons Dijon-style
    mustard
Grated zest of 1 or 2 oranges
Salt and freshly ground
    pepper to taste
Water cress

Bring water to a boil; add shrimp and cook for 1 minute. Add scallops and cook only until water boils again. Drain and cool. Cut shrimp in half, crosswise. In a large bowl, gently toss seafood with celery, grapes, tomatoes and dill. Reserve some tomatoes and dill for garnish. In a small bowl combine sour cream, mayonnaise, mustard, orange zest, salt and pepper. Fold gently into seafood. Adjust seasoning. Cool. Serve in decorative bowl or individual scallop shells; sprinkle with a few pieces of tomato and dill. Garnish with water cress. Serve with French bread.

Yield: 6 if served as entrée or 10 as an appetizer.

Crabmeat Rice Salad

1 cup uncooked rice
2 small green peppers, chopped
1 (2 ounce) jar pimientos, cut
1 pound canned or cooked
    crabmeat, flaked

1 cup mayonnaise
1 teaspoon lemon juice
½ teaspoon curry powder
Salt, to taste

Cook rice according to package directions. Cool. Add green peppers, pimientos and crabmeat. Mix together remaining ingredients. Add to rice. Mix well. Serve cold.

Note: May also use 1 pound cooked chicken instead of crabmeat.

Yield: 5-6 servings.

Pasta Picnic Salad

1 (16 ounce) package
  spinach pasta
1 (8 ounce) bottle Italian
  dressing
½ cup mayonnaise
½ cup chopped fresh parsley
2 medium green peppers,
  chopped

1 pound cooked ham, diced
1 pound Swiss cheese, diced
3 small zucchini, diced
2 medium onions, thinly
  sliced and separated
1 (3 ounce) can black
  olives, halved
2-3 medium tomatoes, diced

Cook pasta according to package directions. Cool. Mix dressing, mayonnaise, parsley and green pepper. Combine with remaining ingredients. Toss with dressing mixture. Chill overnight.

Yield: 12-15 servings.

Tortellini Salad

2 (9 or 10 ounce) packages
  cheese-filled tortellini,
  fresh or frozen
5-6 tablespoons extra virgin
  olive oil
2 sweet red peppers, roasted
  and peeled, or 4 roasted
  halves from jar

⅓ cup coarsely chopped oil-
  packed sun-dried tomatoes
½ cup sliced ripe or
  Kalamata olives
½ cup chopped fresh
  basil leaves
Salt and freshly ground
  pepper to taste
3-4 tablespoons lemon juice

Cook tortellini according to package directions. Drain. Rinse gently with cold water and drain well. Transfer to large bowl and toss with 5 tablespoons oil. Cut peppers into ¼-inch lengthwise strips. Add to pasta, along with tomatoes, olives, basil, and salt and pepper. Add lemon juice and remaining tablespoon of oil if needed. Cover and refrigerate until a few minutes before serving.

Note: Excellent for picnics.

Yield: 4 main course servings or 8 first course servings.

Crunchy Noodle Salad

DRESSING
½ cup oil
3 tablespoons sugar
3 tablespoons apple cider
   vinegar
1 package seasoning from
   noodle package
   (listed below)

SALAD
½ medium head cabbage,
   shredded, or 1 (10 ounce)
   package shredded cabbage

5 scallions, chopped
   (use entire scallion)
1 (4 ounce) package sliced
   almonds, toasted until
   light brown
1 (4 ounce) package small
   dry-roasted sunflower
   seeds (not toasted)
1 (3 ounce) package Ramen
   noodles, Oriental flavored,
   white, wavy, reserving
   seasonings

DRESSING: Mix 4 ingredients well.

SALAD: Combine cabbage and scallions. Break noodles into small pieces while still in package wrapping. Combine uncooked noodles with almonds and sunflower seeds. Just before serving, mix 3 groups together: shredded cabbage, scallions; nuts, seeds, noodles; and salad dressing. Excellent with barbequed chicken.

Yield: 6-8 servings as a side dish.

Marinated Carrots

1 pound carrots, scraped
Juice of 1 large lemon
1 tablespoon wine vinegar
1 teaspoon Dijon-style mustard
6 tablespoons olive or
   vegetable oil

1 garlic clove, split part way
2 tablespoons finely
   chopped chives
Salt and pepper to taste

Cut carrots in ¼ inch slices. Cook in boiling salt water for 3-5 minutes or until barely tender. Drain well. Combine lemon juice, vinegar and mustard. Slowly whisk in oil. Add garlic, chives, salt and pepper. Add carrots while they are still warm. Stir to coat. Cover and refrigerate until well-chilled, stirring occasionally. Remove garlic before serving. Can be served several days later; more flavorful the longer marinated.

Yield: 4-6 servings.

San Diego Relish

¾ cup cider vinegar
½ cup salad oil
1 cup sugar
1 tablespoon water
1 teaspoon salt
1 (11 ounce) can white
  corn, drained
1 (16 ounce) can tiny
  peas, drained

1 (16 ounce) can French style
  green beans, drained
1 (4 ounce) jar pimiento,
  drained and chopped
½ cup finely chopped onion
½ cup finely chopped celery
½ cup finely chopped
  green pepper

Bring first 5 ingredients to a boil. Cool. Add other ingredients. Pour into 2-quart jar and refrigerate. Marinate overnight. Keeps well in refrigerator. May be used as a relish or served as a salad on lettuce.

Yield: 2 quarts.

Garlic Pickles

1 quart Kosher whole pickles,
  drained, discard brine
4 cloves garlic, divided

1 cup water
1 cup sugar
1 tablespoon white vinegar

Quarter pickles lengthwise. Put 2 thinly sliced cloves of garlic in bottom of jar; add pickles. Place remaining garlic, thinly sliced, on top. Bring water, sugar and vinegar to a quick boil. Pour into jar. Cover and refrigerate; shake jar each day for 5 days.

Yield: 1 quart.

Rags (Quick Pickles)

2 cucumbers
Salt
1 cup water

1 cup vinegar
1½ cups sugar
1 tablespoon mustard seeds

Cut cucumbers lengthwise into strips approximately ½" thick. Sprinkle with salt; let stand one hour or more; pour off liquid. Boil vinegar with water, sugar, and mustard seeds. Pour over cucumber strips. Ready to eat when cool.

Yield: Varies depending on size of cucumbers.

Creamy Anchovy-Dill Salad Dressing

½ (1¾ ounce) can anchovy
  fillets, drained
1 tablespoon freshly squeezed
  lemon juice
2 tablespoons grainy
  Dijon mustard

⅓ cup buttermilk
2 tablespoons chopped
  fresh dill
1 scallion, minced

In small bowl, crush anchovies with a spoon in lemon juice until smooth. Blend in mustard, buttermilk, dill and scallion.

Yield: ½ cup.

Creamy Citrus Salad Dressing

2 tablespoons orange juice
2 tablespoons lemon juice
2 tablespoons honey
1½ teaspoons grated
  orange rind

½ teaspoon salt
½ teaspoon dry mustard
⅛ teaspoon paprika
1 cup sour cream or
  plain yogurt

In bowl, blend first seven ingredients; fold in sour cream. Cover and chill.

Yield: 1¼ cups.

Fruit Salad Dressing

1 cup salad oil
⅔ cup very fine granulated sugar
1 teaspoon dry mustard
1 teaspoon paprika
1 teaspoon celery seed

¼ teaspoon salt
⅓ cup honey
⅓ cup vinegar
1 tablespoon lemon juice
1 teaspoon minced onion

Mix all ingredients well in blender.

Yield: 2 cups.

Low-Cal Salad Dressing

¼ cup cider vinegar
¼ cup olive oil
1 packet granulated sugar
  substitute

1 clove fresh garlic, crushed
  (optional)

Blend ingredients. Pour over salad and toss.

Note: No salt, no sugar, always gets compliments.

Yield: 4 servings.

Balsamic Vinaigrette Salad Dressing

2 shallots
1 clove garlic
⅓ cup balsamic vinegar

2 tablespoons fresh parsley
Salt and pepper to taste
1 cup virgin olive oil

Combine all ingredients except oil in blender. Add oil slowly, blending well. May be refrigerated up to 3 weeks.

Yield: 1½ cups.

"Hot" Vinaigrette Salad Dressing

3 cups vegetable oil
1 cup red wine vinegar
Dash of Worcestershire sauce
1 tablespoon chopped garlic
1 tablespoon black pepper

1 tablespoon chili powder
½ cup fresh basil or
  1 tablespoon dried
2 pinches oregano

Put all ingredients in a large container, mix well and refrigerate to use as needed.

Yield: 1 quart.

Raspberry Vinaigrette Salad Dressing

⅓ cup raspberry vinegar
½ teaspoon salt
½ teaspoon white pepper
1 tablespoon sugar
1 tablespoon chopped
    fresh parsley

1 tablespoon chopped
    fresh chives
1 cup oil (½ vegetable blended
    with ½ olive)

Put vinegar in mixing bowl. Add salt, pepper and sugar; mix until well-blended. Add herbs; continue mixing. Add oil slowly, continuing to mix until thoroughly blended.

Yield: 1½ cups.

Hudson Valley Vegetarian Sandwich
A Luncheon Gallery Favorite

1 fresh eggplant, sliced
3 eggs
Chopped fresh basil to taste
Salt and pepper to taste
Vegetable oil

1 (14 ounce) can pimentos
1 pint alfalfa sprouts
Focaccia bread, sliced
    and toasted

Beat eggs with basil, salt and pepper. Dip eggplant into egg mixture; sauté in oil. Place 3 slices of eggplant, a piece of pimento and some sprouts in each sandwich. Serve warm or at room temperature.

Yield: 3-4 sandwiches.

Gourmet Tuna Spread

1-2 apples (Granny Smith or
    Golden Delicious)
1 (6½ ounce) can albacore tuna
    in water, drained

Vanilla yogurt
Mayonnaise

Peel, slice and finely chop apples. Combine with flaked tuna. Add equal parts yogurt and mayonnaise until desired consistency is reached.

Yield: 2-3 sandwiches.

Tuna Sandwiches with Lemon Butter

TUNA MIXTURE
1 cup canned tuna
½ cup chopped cucumber
1 tablespoon grated onion
2 teaspoons lemon juice
¼ cup chopped green pepper
½ cup chopped celery
Salt, pepper and paprika, to
    taste
¼ cup mayonnaise, or more, to
    moisten

LEMON BUTTER
¼ cup butter, softened
Grated peel of 1 lemon
1½ tablespoons lemon juice
1 tablespoon grated onion

6 slices bread

Combine ingredients for each mixture separately. Spread tuna on bread buttered with lemon butter.

Yield: 3 sandwiches.

Best 'Wurst Sandwich

½ pound liverwurst
1 (8 ounce) package cream
    cheese, softened
3 hard-cooked eggs, chopped

3 tablespoons mayonnaise
½ teaspoon chopped chives
Salt and pepper
12-16 slices bread

Remove skin from liverwurst. Add remaining ingredients except bread. Cream thoroughly. Add more mayonnaise, if needed, to spread easily.

Yield: 6-8 sandwiches.

Stuffed Franks

½ cup crushed corn chips
⅓ cup finely chopped onion
¼ cup tomato sauce
1 teaspoon Worcestershire
sauce

1 cup shredded American
cheese
10 frankfurters
10 frankfurter rolls

Combine corn chips, onion, tomato sauce, Worcestershire sauce and cheese; mix well. Slit frankfurters lengthwise to make a pocket. Spoon cheese mixture into each slit. Place frankfurters in a 13x9x2-inch baking pan. Bake uncovered at 350° for 20 minutes or until cheese is melted. Serve in rolls.

Yield: 10 servings.

Lemon-Cucumber Tea Sandwiches

6 tablespoons unsalted butter,
room temperature
Grated zest of 1 lemon
1 tablespoon lemon juice
with pulp
12 thin slices white or
whole wheat bread,
crusts trimmed

1 small cucumber, peeled and
thinly sliced
Very fine granulated sugar
Freshly ground black pepper
to taste

Cream butter with zest and lemon juice in small bowl. Spread light film of butter on each slice of bread. Cover half the bread slices with a thick layer of cucumber. Sprinkle lightly with sugar and pepper. Cover with remaining buttered bread slices. Cut each sandwich into four triangles.

Yield: 24 tea sandwiches.

Grilled Salmon Sandwich

1 (7½ ounce) can salmon,
   flaked
2 tablespoons horseradish
1 tablespoon lemon juice
¼ cup mayonnaise

Salt and pepper to taste
6 slices bread, crusts removed
8 ounces pasteurized
   processed cheese spread
½ cup milk

Mash salmon, discarding skin and bones. Combine with horse-radish, lemon juice, mayonnaise and salt and pepper. Spread between bread slices. Grill in buttered skillet on both sides until brown. Melt cheese with milk in double boiler and pour sauce over each sandwich. Serve immediately.

Yield: 3 sandwiches.

Reuben Sandwich Casserole

1 (27 ounce) can sauerkraut,
   drained well
3 medium tomatoes, sliced
½ cup butter or margarine
1 (8 ounce) bottle Thousand
   Island dressing

½ pound corned beef, thinly
   sliced
½ pound Swiss cheese, grated
1 (8 ounce) can refrigerated
   biscuits
4 crisp rye crackers, crushed
¼ teaspoon caraway seed

Grease a 13x9x2-inch pan. Spread sauerkraut on bottom; add tomato slices; dot with butter. Pour Thousand Island dressing over all and cover with corned beef. Sprinkle cheese on top. Bake at 425° for 15 minutes. Separate rolls and place atop casserole; sprinkle crackers and caraway seeds on top. Bake at 425° for 15-20 minutes.

Yield: 8 servings.

LOMBARDO'S RED
Lori Lawrence
Oil on canvas, 1989
Gift of Mrs. Georgina H. Williams, 1991.1

Lori Lawrence has worked in the Albany area since 1975, and has
exhibited her work throughout the east coast. "Lombardo's Red" depicts
a lively gathering inside Lombardo's Restaurant, an Albany landmark
established in 1918. The colorful painting evokes the intimate social
atmosphere of a family restaurant, and includes portraits of some of
Lombardo's regular clientele, including the artist and her husband.

Cheddary Ham 'n Eggs Casserole

8 slices bread
6 thick slices boiled ham,
   cut into pieces or
   1½ pounds sausage meat,
   browned and drained
2 cups grated mild
   Cheddar cheese

4 eggs
2½ cups milk, divided
1 teaspoon salt
¾ teaspoon dry mustard
1 (10¾ ounce) can cream of
   mushroom soup

Remove crusts, butter bread and cube. Place in a buttered 13x9x2-inch pan. Cover with meat. Top with grated cheese. Beat eggs with 2 cups milk, salt and mustard. Pour over meat and cheese. Refrigerate overnight. Before baking, dilute soup with ½ cup milk. Pour over casserole. Bake in a 300° oven for 1½ hours or until set.

Yield: 8-10 servings.

Cheese Soufflé

¼ cup butter or margarine
¼ cup flour
1 cup milk
1½ cups grated sharp
   Cheddar cheese

4 eggs, separated
½ teaspoon salt
Dash of pepper

Melt butter in top of double boiler over low heat; blend in flour. Stir milk in slowly. Cook; stir until thickened and smooth. Keep heat low. Add cheese; stir until melted and the sauce is smooth. Remove from heat. In small bowl, beat egg yolks slightly. Add small amount of hot sauce slowly, stirring rapidly. Stir in remaining hot sauce. Add salt and pepper. Set aside. In large bowl, beat egg whites just until stiff peaks form. Gently fold cheese mixture into egg whites. Pour into buttered soufflé dish or 1½-quart casserole. Place in pan of hot water. Bake at 350° for 40-60 minutes or until firm to touch. Serve immediately.

Yield: 4 servings.

Old-fashioned Baked Eggs

1½ cups milk
2 cups bread cubes,
   crusts removed
3 eggs, slightly beaten
1½ cups grated sharp
   Cheddar cheese

1 teaspoon salt
Pinch of pepper
1 tablespoon melted butter
   or margarine
3 tablespoons grated onion
⅛ teaspoon dried basil

Mix all ingredients together. Bake in buttered 9x9x1½-inch pan for 25-30 minutes at 350°. Serve with bacon, sliced ham or sausage.

Yield: 4 servings.

Deviled Eggs with Mushrooms

12 eggs, hard-cooked
1 pound mushrooms,
   chopped and sautéed
1 teaspoon salt
¼ teaspoon each, pepper
   and paprika

½ teaspoon curry powder or
   1 (4½ ounce) can deviled ham
2 cups thin white sauce
¾ cup buttered bread crumbs,
   firmly packed
⅓ cup grated Cheddar cheese

Cut eggs in half lengthwise; remove yolks and put them through a sieve. Add seasonings to sieved yolks, along with some of the mushrooms and just enough white sauce to hold mixture together. Refill egg whites and press the halves together. Place in buttered 9-inch square pan and cover with remaining white sauce mixed with remaining mushrooms. Sprinkle with buttered crumbs mixed with cheese and bake at 400° until thoroughly heated and brown, about 20 minutes.

Yield: 6 servings.

Scrambled Eggs-Fines Herbes

½ cup butter or margarine
¼ cup flour
2 cups whole milk
16 eggs

¼ cup butter or margarine
Fines Herbes: Traditionally a
mixture of parsley, chives,
tarragon and chervil

Melt ½ cup butter; add flour and stir until smooth. Gradually add milk and cook until thickened. Set aside. Beat eggs and add herbes. Heat large skillet; add ¼ cup butter. When melted, add eggs. As eggs cook and begin to set, stir in white sauce. This will keep eggs moist up to 4 hours if kept over low heat.

Yield: 8 servings.

Pecan French Toast

4 eggs
⅔ cup orange juice
⅓ cup milk
¼ cup sugar
¼ teaspoon nutmeg
¼ teaspoon vanilla

½ loaf Italian bread, cut in
1-inch slices
⅓ cup butter or margarine,
melted
½ cup pecan halves
2 tablespoons grated
orange peel

Using whisk, beat eggs, orange juice, milk, sugar, nutmeg and vanilla. Place bread with edges touching in single layer in 13x9x2-inch pan. Pour egg mixture over bread. Cover and refrigerate overnight, turning once. Pour melted butter into 11x17x2-inch pan. Arrange bread slices in single layer in pan. Sprinkle with orange peel and pecans. Bake at 400° for 20-25 minutes until golden. Serve immediately with maple syrup and butter.

Yield: 4 servings.

Angel Hair Pasta with Broccoli

1 bunch fresh broccoli
¼ cup light olive oil
4 tablespoons unsalted
   butter, divided
2 scallions, cut into
   ¼-inch pieces

1 garlic clove, peeled and
   crushed
2 tablespoons white wine
1 pound angel hair pasta
Grated Parmesan cheese
   to taste

Cut broccoli into florets. Peel and chop the stems into bite-size pieces. Cook broccoli in boiling water for 3-4 minutes until crispy but tender. Drain. In a saucepan, heat oil and 3 tablespoons butter over medium heat. In a skillet, melt remaining 1 tablespoon butter and sauté the scallions and garlic for 2 minutes. Add wine and cook 5 minutes. Add melted butter and oil, then the broccoli. Keep hot while you cook the pasta in a large pot of salted boiling water until it is *al dente,* about 30 seconds. (Angel hair cooks very quickly.) Drain and toss with the broccoli mixture and Parmesan cheese.

Yield: 4 servings.

Mexican Lasagna

1 pound lean ground beef
1 (16 ounce) can refried beans
2 teaspoons dried oregano
1 teaspoon ground cumin
¾ teaspoon garlic powder
12 uncooked lasagna noodles
2½ cups water
2½ cups picante sauce or salsa

2 cups sour cream or yogurt,
   drained
¾ cup finely sliced
   green onions
1 (2.2 ounce) can black olives,
   drained and sliced
1 cup shredded Monterey
   Jack cheese

Combine beef, beans, oregano, cumin, and garlic powder. Place four of the uncooked lasagna noodles in the bottom of a 13x9x2-inch baking pan. Spread half the beef mixture over the noodles. Top with four more noodles and the remaining beef mixture. Cover with remaining noodles. Combine water and picante sauce. Pour over all. Cover tightly with foil; bake at 350° for 1½ hours or until noodles are tender. Combine sour cream, onions and olives. Spoon over casserole; top with cheese. Bake uncovered, until cheese is melted, about 5 minutes.

Yield: 12 servings.

Cheesy Beef and Pasta in a Pot

2 pounds lean beef, ground
Vegetable oil
2 medium onions, chopped
1 garlic clove, crushed
1 (14 ounce) jar spaghetti sauce
1 (1 pound) can stewed tomatoes
1 (3 ounce) can sliced
   broiled mushrooms

8 ounces shell macaroni
1½ pints sour cream
½ pound sliced provolone
   cheese
½ pound mozzarella cheese,
   sliced thin

Cook ground beef in a little vegetable oil in a large, deep frying pan until brown, stirring often with a fork. Drain off any excess fat. Add onions, garlic, spaghetti sauce, stewed tomatoes and undrained mushrooms; mix well. Simmer 20 minutes or until onions are soft. Meanwhile cook macaroni according to package directions; drain and put ½ the pasta into a deep casserole. Cover with half the tomato-meat sauce. Spread half the sour cream over sauce. Top with slices of provolone cheese. Repeat, ending with slices of mozzarella cheese. Cover casserole. Bake at 350° for 35-40 minutes. Remove cover; continue baking until mozzarella melts and browns slightly.

Yield: 8-10 servings.

Mushroom-Rice-Nut Casserole

⅓ cup regular long grain rice
⅔ cup water
3 onions, chopped
3 cloves garlic, minced
1 pound mushrooms, sliced

¼ cup hazelnuts
2 eggs
1 cup half-and-half
Salt and pepper to taste

Boil rice in water 10-15 minutes. Let stand to cool. Sauté onions, garlic, mushrooms, and nuts. Add to rice. Beat eggs; add cream, salt and pepper. Mix with rice and vegetables. Pour into greased 8x4x2½-inch loaf pan or 1-quart ovenproof casserole. Bake in 300° oven for 1 hour.

Note: Best served with meats or fish that do not have gravy or sauce.

Yield: 4-6 servings.

No-Boil Lasagna

1 tablespoon vegetable oil
1 medium onion, chopped
1 clove garlic, minced
1 pound ground beef
2 (14 ounce) cans tomato sauce
1 (10 ounce) can undrained
    sliced mushrooms
½ cup water
1 teaspoon oregano
1 cup cottage cheese

½ cup grated Parmesan cheese
1 (10 ounce) package frozen
    chopped spinach
1 egg, slightly beaten
2 teaspoons vegetable oil
1 teaspoon salt
1 (6 ounce) package
    mozzarella cheese
½ package lasagna

Sauté onion and garlic in oil. Add ground beef and brown. Remove excess fat, stir in tomato sauce, mushrooms, water and oregano; bring to a boil and remove from heat. Combine cottage cheese, Parmesan cheese, thawed well-drained spinach, egg, oil and salt. Spoon ⅓ of tomato sauce mixture into 13x9x2-inch baking dish. Cover with ⅓ of lasagna. Repeat layering. Spread remaining cheese and spinach mixture over top and cover with remaining lasagna and sauce. Top with cheese slices, cover with foil and bake at 375° for 45 minutes. Uncover and bake until cheese starts to brown, about 15 minutes. Let stand for at least 10 minutes before serving.

Note: If substituting another sauce recipe, make sauce thinner than usual or thin with water; otherwise, lasagna will be dry.

Yield: 12 servings.

Baked Rice

1 cup uncooked long grain rice
¼ cup margarine
2 cups chicken broth

1 cup chopped fresh mushrooms
1 cup chopped water chestnuts
Pinch of saffron (optional)

Mix all ingredients in ovenproof 2-quart casserole. Bake covered for 1-1¼ hours. If dry, add a little water or chicken broth.

Yield: 5-6 servings.

Macaroni and Cheese, Welsh Style

4 tablespoons butter, divided
2 tablespoons flour
1 cup whole milk
1 teaspoon prepared
  brown mustard
½ teaspoon Worcestershire
  sauce

1 pound uncooked macaroni
10-12 ounces sharp Cheddar
  cheese, shredded
2 garlic cloves, cut in half
½ cup bread crumbs
2 tablespoons grated
  Romano cheese

In a double boiler, melt 2 tablespoons of the butter over hot water. Stir in the flour, making a paste. Stir in milk, a little at a time. Stirring constantly, bring to just below boiling and cook 2 minutes. Stir in mustard and Worcestershire sauce. Remove from heat. Cook the macaroni in boiling water until it is *al dente*. Drain. Butter a 2-quart casserole and rub with garlic. Starting with the white sauce, alternate the sauce, pasta and cheese. Top with a mixture of the bread crumbs and Romano cheese. Dot with 2 tablespoons of butter, cut into small pieces. Bake at 400° for about 45 minutes or until brown.

Yield: 8 servings.

New Age Fried Rice

¾ cup frozen tiny (early) peas
1 small onion, chopped
4-5 mushrooms, sliced
1 teaspoon olive oil
1 (8 ounce) carton egg substitute

2 cups cooked brown rice
1 tablespoon low sodium
  soy sauce
Pepper to taste
Chopped parsley

Cook peas according to package directions. Sauté onion and mushrooms in oil until golden. Stir eggs into onion/mushroom mixture. Cook until set; break into small pieces. Add rice, peas, soy sauce, pepper and heat through. Sprinkle with parsley.

Note: A great way to use leftover rice.

Yield: 2 servings.

Baked Tomato Macaroni

1 pound large elbow
   macaroni or penne
1 cup olive oil
9-12 garlic cloves, minced fine
1 cup chopped onion
1 tablespoon sugar

1 teaspoon crushed dried
   red chili pepper
¼ cup dried crumbled basil
2 tablespoons dried
   crumbled oregano
3 (28 ounce) cans tomatoes
Grated Parmesan cheese

Place the pasta in a large bowl. Pour olive oil over it and toss well. Let set for one hour. Pour pasta into a strainer; drain excess olive oil into a deep non-aluminum saucepan. Add the garlic, onion, sugar, chili peppers, basil, and oregano. Heat until oil gets very hot over moderate heat, 10 minutes. Remove from heat and cool to room temperature. Crush the tomatoes with your hands or food processor using metal blade and add to mixture. Preheat oven to 400°. Place pasta in a large non-aluminum roasting pan. Pour sauce over pasta and stir well. Bake uncovered in the center of the oven for 40 minutes, turning with a spatula every 10 minutes to ensure that pasta cooks evenly. Serve with Parmesan cheese.

Note: No, there is not a mistake in this recipe. The pasta actually bakes without being boiled first. Be generous with your seasoning and garlic, as baking reduces their pungency. You can make several batches of this crowd-pleaser and reheat it but don't try doubling the recipe in one pan.

Yield: 12 side dishes or 8 main dish servings.

Späetzle
German Egg Dumplings

2 cups sifted flour	⅔ cup milk
1½ teaspoons salt	4 eggs

Combine ingredients. Stir until mixture is blended; beat for 5 minutes. Pass mixture slowly through a coarse sieve held over a 4-quart saucepan of boiling salted water. Boil the späetzle for 8 minutes. When they rise to the surface, the späetzle are cooked. Drain. Rinse with cold water. Serve with beef rouladin, sauerbraten or Hungarian goulash.

Note: Späetzle are a favorite accompaniment for meats and vegetables.

OPTIONS:

• Lightly browned in butter before serving

• Pour ¼ cup melted butter over späetzle and, if desired, stir in ¼ cup warmed sour cream. Stir well.

• Sauté ½ cup chopped onions in ½ cup butter; stir until hot and thoroughly mixed.

Yield: 4-6 servings.

Barley Bake

4 tablespoons butter	6 cups chicken broth
1 cup chopped onion	2 teaspoons dried dill weed
2 cups barley, rinsed	

In a 3½-quart "rangetop-to-oven" casserole melt butter over moderate heat. Stir in onion and barley; cook, stirring frequently, about 5 minutes, until barley is tender. Add broth and dill; increase heat to moderately high and bring to a boil. Cover casserole and bake 1 hour and 15 minutes in a 325° preheated oven, until barley is tender. Fluff with a fork before serving.

Note: Good with roast lamb or veal.

Yield: 6-10 servings.

BASKET OF TOMATOES, LOUIS WORTHMAN

Harry Worthman (1909-1989)
Oil on canvas, 1946
AIHA Purchase, 1993.31

This informal portrait of Rensselaer County farmer Louis Worthman (1885-1979), was painted by his son, Harry Worthman. Worthman began his artistic career as a political cartoonist for the Knickerbocker Press. Later he moved to Texas, where he established himself as a portrait painter throughout the Southwest.

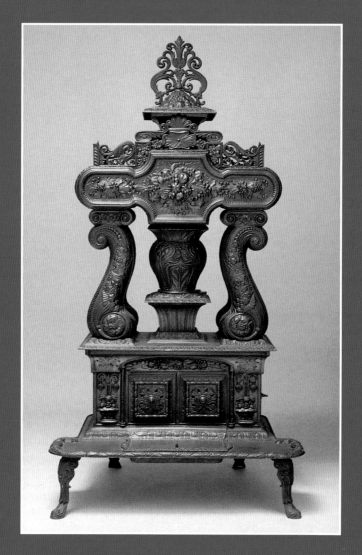

FOUR-COLUMN PARLOR STOVE

Johnson, Geer and Cox, Troy, New York
Patented 1844   Cast Iron
AIHA Purchase 1980.36

This elegant cast iron stove is part of the Albany
Institute's extensive collection of locally-made stoves.
Made during the 1840s, column stoves were used as
focal points in the parlor. These stoves became very
elaborate, often combining classical and American
symbols as part of their design.

FANCY SIDE CHAIR
Attributed to William Buttre, Albany, New York (1815-1818)
Ash, beech, tulip and rush
AIHA Purchase 1992.16

In 1815, William Buttre moved to Albany from New York City and opened a "fancy chair store" on State Street. With the industrialization of cabinetmaking, Buttre and the journeymen who worked in his shop assembled thousands of inexpensive chairs for the growing upstate market. The flat surfaces of these fancy chairs provided a natural base for painted neoclassical decorations.

REGENTS PUNCH BOWL

Porcelain, c. 1765

Gift of Colonel William Gorham Rice and his son William Gorham Rice, Jr.
U1972.25.1

This very large (22½" diameter) porcelain punch-
bowl with overglaze enamels was made in China
for export to America. The decorative patterns
include the familiar "famille rose" around the
outside rim, with large tree peonies symbolic of
springtime and love. Once used during the Great
Ball in the New York State Assembly Chamber
held in 1824 to honor Lafayette, it was later used
to serve punch at an annual party held for the
Board of Regents.

PRESENTATION PITCHER

Enoch Wood and Son,
Earthenware, c. 1824
AIHA purchase 1971.15

An unusually large (19" high) piece of historical
pottery, this pitcher is printed with scenes of the
War of 1812. Although the British were defeated in
that war, they wanted the American trade, so they
manufactured many pieces intended to appeal to
American patriotism. This pitcher, which belonged
to Horace Jones, a Troy merchant, was said to have
been used at the reception for General Lafayette in
1824. It also bears a picture of the Clermont sailing
up the Hudson River past West Point.

FRUIT IN A CLASSICAL SETTING
John Vanderlyn, Jr. (1805-1876)
Oil on canvas, c. 1854-1858
AIHA Purchase 1983.11

The window-sill setting is rather unusual for a
still-life painting of this period. The artist's knowledge
of this motif may have come from European examples,
or from his uncle, John Vanderlyn (1755-1852), noted
American portrait and history painter. Reflecting the
tastes of the well-to-do, the classical containers,
furniture, and architectural elements were all
fashionable at mid-century.

VIEW OF SHAKER CREEK

Richard Callner (1927-)
Watercolor and gouache, 1988
AIHA purchase, 1988.23.2

Callner's interpretation of the view
of Shaker Creek outside his studio
window reflects his mastery of
dazzling color, pattern and repetition
in a combination of still life, interior
views and exterior landscape.

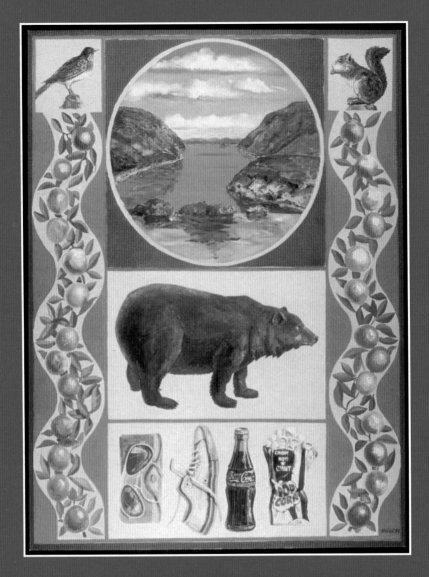

BEAR TOTEM

Don Nice (1932-)
Oil on canvas, 1984
AIHA Purchase, 1991.62.

This six-foot tall painting, recently purchased by the Albany Institute, reflects the concerns of Nice's generation of artists – abstract versus realism, and the illusion of space versus its denial in traditional two-dimensional representation. In "Bear Totem", Nice's juxtaposition of fruit and animals, signifying nature, with the lost sneaker, crumpled candy wrapper and other debris, has earned him a reputation as an "environmental" artist.

DINING TABLE

Unidentified New York cabinetmaker, c. 1749-1763
Gift of the heirs of Major John Taylor Cooper, 1899.1

This large mahogany oval-top masterpiece table of William and Mary design
was originally owned by Sir William Johnson (1715-1774), Superintendent of
Indian Affairs for British North America, and was presumably used by him
when conducting official business with the local Native Americans. Listed in
the 1774 inventory of his home, Johnson Hall, it was inherited by his son,
Sir John Johnson (1742-1830). After Sir John, a Tory, fled to Canada in 1776,
his property was sold at several venues by the State of New York. This table
was acquired by John Taylor, later Governor of New York, and descended in
his family.

Crabmeat Delight

2 tablespoons chopped
   green pepper
2 tablespoons butter
2 tablespoons flour
½ teaspoon dry mustard
¼ teaspoon salt
½ teaspoon Worcestershire
   sauce

¾ cup milk
1 cup grated cheese
1 cup stewed tomatoes,
   coarsely chopped
1 cup shredded crabmeat
Rice or patty shells

Sauté green pepper in butter for 2 minutes. Add next 4 ingredients and stir until blended. Gradually stir in milk. Add tomatoes and cheese; stir until cheese melts. Stir in crabmeat. Serve over rice or patty shells.

Yield: 2-3 servings.

Carolina Crabmeat Quiche

1 9-inch pie crust, unbaked
1 cup shredded Swiss cheese
5 large eggs
1½ cups half-and-half

½ teaspoon salt
⅛ teaspoon black pepper
½ cup sliced mushrooms
1 (6½ ounce) can crabmeat

Sprinkle cheese into pie crust. Beat eggs well and mix with half-and-half and seasonings. Pour over cheese. Add mushrooms. Sprinkle crabmeat over all. Bake 35 minutes at 350° or until knife inserted in center comes out clean. Cut in wedges.

Note: To cut calories, whole or 2% milk may be used.

Yield: 6 servings.

Fish Fillets – Quick and Easy!

To cook fish fillets, place on buttered cookie sheet. Preheat oven to its hottest. Run your hands under cold water and pat the fish fillets. Place fillets in hot oven and cook 3-4 minutes. They will be cooked perfectly!

Baked Crabmeat Salad

2 cups flaked crabmeat
½ cup diced cucumber
1 cup chopped celery
2 hard cooked eggs, chopped
¼ teaspoon salt
⅛ teaspoon pepper
¼ teaspoon Worcestershire
　sauce

¼ cup chopped ripe olives
Mayonnaise

TOPPING
⅔ cup dried bread crumbs
¼ cup melted butter
　or margarine

Combine ingredients and moisten with mayonnaise. Divide into 4 scallop shells. Top with dry bread crumbs blended with melted butter. Place shells on baking sheet. Bake at 350° for 30 minutes.

Yield: 4 servings.

Seafood Casserole

2 (10¾ ounce) cans cream of
　shrimp soup
3 tablespoons sherry
1 (4½ ounce) can mushrooms,
　drained

Butter
½ pound lump crab meat
½ pound bay scallops
½ pound cooked shrimp
6 slices American cheese

Stir together soup, sherry and mushrooms. Sauté scallops in butter for 3-5 minutes. Add shrimp and crab meat to scallops; fold gently into soup mixture. Place in 2-quart greased casserole. Refrigerate 3-24 hours. Bake, uncovered, for 1 hour in 300° oven. Cover with cheese for last 30 minutes. Serve over rice or in patty shells.

Yield: 6 servings.

Pasta with Bay Scallops

1 pound bay scallops
Juice of 1 lemon
¼ cup margarine
¼ cup oil
8 shallots, finely sliced
½ cup white wine
1 cup puréed canned
    plum tomatoes
12 ounces clam juice

½ teaspoon fennel or anise seed
Pepper and salt to taste
2 tablespoons margarine
1 pound capellini
1 tablespoon margarine
½ cup freshly chopped parsley
1 tablespoon finely chopped
    lemon zest

Marinate the scallops in lemon juice for ½ hour. In large skillet sauté shallots in oil and margarine until they begin to lose color. Add next 5 ingredients. Bring to a boil; reduce heat and simmer 10 minutes. Drain and sauté the scallops in the 2 tablespoons margarine over high heat for 1 minute. Add scallops to sauce and cook 2 minutes. Cook capellini according to package directions. Drain and return to same pot. Toss with margarine. Add sauce with scallops. Sprinkle with parsley and lemon zest. Sauce can be made the day before and refrigerated. Reheat before scallops are added.

Note: Use sea scallops cut into quarters or Nantucket Bay scallops.

Yield: 4 servings.

Garlic Shrimp with Linguine

½ cup butter or margarine
2 teaspoons minced garlic
1 pound large shrimp,
    shelled and deveined
¾ cup seeded and sliced
    red bell pepper
3 tablespoons chopped fresh
    basil or 1 tablespoon
    dried basil

2 tablespoons chopped fresh
    parsley or 1 tablespoon
    dried parsley
¼ teaspoon salt
¼-½ teaspoon coarsely
    ground pepper
½ pound spinach linguine,
    cooked and drained

Sauté garlic in butter or margarine for 1 minute. Add next 6 ingredients and sauté 2-3 minutes until shrimp are tender. Serve over linguine.

Yield: 4 servings.

Nantucket Bay Scallops and Saffron Risotto

2-3 tablespoons minced shallots
½ cup Italian tomatoes,
   drained and chopped
½ teaspoon saffron
1 cup dry white wine, divided
½ pound Nantucket Bay
   scallops, whole, or
   sea scallops, quartered

1 cup half-and-half
5 cups chicken broth
2 tablespoons unsalted butter
1 tablespoon olive oil
½ cup minced onion
1½ cups Italian Arborio rice
Fresh parsley

Combine shallots, tomatoes, saffron and ½ cup wine in a saucepan. Bring to a boil over medium heat. Add scallops and cook for 2 minutes but no longer. Remove scallops from liquid; set aside. Bring liquid to a boil and simmer until reduced by about one-half. Add cream. Continue cooking for 2-3 minutes until liquid is slightly thickened. Return scallops to pan; cover and set aside. Bring broth to simmer. Heat butter and oil in a large casserole over moderate heat. Add onion and sauté for 2 minutes until soft but not brown. Using a wooden spoon, stir in rice until grains have a glossy appearance. If not, add more butter or oil. Add remaining ½ cup wine, stirring constantly. Start adding simmering broth ½ cup at a time, stirring constantly. Wait until each portion of broth is nearly absorbed before adding next ½ cup of broth. After 18-20 minutes, as the rice is tender but still firm, add the scallop and cream mixture. Stir well to combine. Garnish with parsley and serve hot.

Note: For additional color, asparagus tips or very thinly sliced red pepper may be added halfway through the broth-adding step. Best served with salad and fresh bread.

Yield: 4 servings.

Shrimp à la Creole

3 heaping tablespoons flour	4 green bell peppers, chopped
¾ cup salad oil	1 (4 ounce) can Italian
1 large onion, chopped	tomato paste
4 pounds medium shrimp,	4-5 cups hot water, divided
cleaned and deveined	Salt and pepper to taste

In skillet, make a roux using flour and oil. Brown well. Add chopped onion and brown slightly. Add shrimp, salt and pepper, and stir, making sure shrimp does not stick to pan. Stir until shrimp is coated with onion mixture. Add green peppers and tomato paste, stirring for 15 minutes over moderate heat until each shrimp is coated. Slowly add 1 cup hot water. Lower heat and cook an additional 15 minutes, stirring well. Add 3-4 cups hot water. If water is added slowly, the rich gravy will cling to the shrimp. Cook 30 minutes.

Yield: 8-10 servings.

Shrimp and Artichoke Casserole

¼ cup butter	1 pound cooked and
¼ cup flour	deveined shrimp
¾ cup milk	1 (14 ounce) jar artichokes or
¾ cup heavy cream	1 package frozen
Salt and pepper to taste	artichokes, cooked
¼ cup dry sherry	¼ pound sliced, sautéed
1 tablespoon Worcestershire	mushrooms
sauce	¼ cup grated Parmesan cheese
	Paprika

Melt butter; add the flour and stir for one minute. Gradually add, while stirring constantly, milk, heavy cream, salt and pepper. Remove from heat; add sherry and Worchester sauce to cream sauce. In greased casserole, layer shrimp, artichokes and mushrooms. Pour sauce over layers. Sprinkle cheese and paprika over top. Bake 20-30 minutes at 350°.

Yield: 4-5 servings.

Shrimp and Scallops Gruyère

1 cup plus 3 tablespoons
   butter or margarine
1 cup flour
4 cups milk
1 pound processed Swiss
   Gruyère cheese, diced
¼ teaspoon garlic powder
2½ teaspoons salt
¼ teaspoon white pepper
¼ teaspoon dry mustard
1 tablespoon tomato paste
4½ teaspoons lemon juice
1½ pounds raw scallops
¾ pound mushrooms, sliced
1½ pounds cooked,
   cleaned shrimp

Make cream sauce in the top of double boiler with 1 cup butter, flour and milk. Add cheese to the sauce. Cook and stir until cheese melts. Add garlic powder, 2 teaspoons salt, pepper, mustard, tomato paste and 3 teaspoons lemon juice. Poach scallops for about 3 minutes in water containing the remaining lemon juice and salt. Add 1 cup of the broth to the cream sauce. Sauté mushrooms in remaining 3 tablespoons butter and add to sauce. Drain scallops and add with the shrimp to the sauce. Heat for 10-15 minutes.

Note: May be made the day before and reheated in double boiler before serving. Thin with a little milk if necessary. Serve with rice tossed with walnuts and diced green pepper or toast points.

Yield: 10-12 servings.

Hot Seafood Salad Supreme

1 (8 ounce) package
   frozen crabmeat
1 pound fresh shrimp,
   cooked and peeled
1 (8 ounce) can sliced
   water chestnuts, drained
1 cup diced celery
1 onion, thinly sliced
1 cup mayonnaise
3 slices bread

Mix the seafood, water chestnuts, celery and onion with mayonnaise. Break up bread and sauté in butter. Place seafood mixture in casserole; top with sautéed bread and bake at 325° for 30 minutes.

Yield: 5-6 servings.

Fettuccine with Shrimp and Snow Peas

1 pound medium raw shrimp
1 tablespoon finely minced
    fresh ginger root
3 large egg yolks
2 tablespoons rice wine vinegar
1 tablespoon lemon juice
½ cup olive oil
¼ cup heavy cream

2-3 tablespoons oriental
    sesame oil
2 tablespoons hot water
Salt and pepper to taste
½ pound snow peas
1 pound fettuccine
3-4 scallions, finely chopped

Boil shrimp 3-4 minutes; peel, devein and refrigerate. Combine next 4 ingredients in a blender at low speed. Add next 5 ingredients; blend. Blanch snow peas in boiling water 30-60 seconds; refresh under cold water; drain and pat dry. Recipe may be done ahead to this point and refrigerated. Cook fettuccine according to package directions. On a large platter, layer the fettuccine, shrimp, sauce, peas and scallions. Serve at room temperature.

Yield: 4-5 servings.

Italian Shrimp Pasta Toss

8 ounces fettuccine
¼ cup unsalted butter
1 cup broccoli florets
1 cup sliced carrots, ¼-inch thick
1 cup sliced fresh mushrooms
½ cup chopped onion
12 ounces medium fresh or
    frozen shrimp, shelled,
    deveined, rinsed

½ teaspoon finely
    chopped garlic
1 teaspoon dried basil leaves
½ teaspoon salt
¼ teaspoon pepper
1½ cups (6 ounces) shredded
    mozzarella cheese

Cook fettuccine according to package directions. Drain. Melt butter in 10-inch skillet. Add broccoli, carrots, mushrooms, onion, shrimp and garlic. Cook over medium heat for 5-7 minutes, stirring occasionally until vegetables are crisply tender and shrimp turn pink. Stir in basil, salt and pepper. Add fettuccine and cheese. Continue cooking for 2-4 minutes, tossing gently, until cheese is melted.

Yield: 6 servings.

Blend of the Bayou

1 (8 ounce) package cream
  cheese
6 tablespoons margarine,
  divided
1 large onion, chopped
2 stalks celery, chopped
1 bell pepper, chopped
1 pound shrimp, cooked,
  peeled and deveined

1 (10¾ ounce) can
  mushroom soup
½ pound fresh mushrooms
1 tablespoon crushed garlic
1 teaspoon hot pepper sauce
½ teaspoon red pepper
2 cups crabmeat
¾ cup rice, cooked
Grated sharp Cheddar cheese
Bread crumbs

Soften cheese and 4 tablespoons margarine in microwave or double boiler. (Do not boil; will separate.) Using a large skillet, sauté the onion, celery and pepper in 2 tablespoons margarine; add cheese mixture. Add the next 8 ingredients. Mix well. Place in 2-quart casserole and bake 20-25 minutes in a 350° oven. Sprinkle cheese and crumbs over top. Bake 5 minutes more.

Note: Freezes well but defrost before baking. Recipe can be doubled easily and baked in a lasagna pan.

Yield: 6-8 servings.

Herb-Roasted Orange Salmon

2 tablespoons olive oil
¼ cup fresh orange juice
Zest of one orange, finely grated
2 teaspoons minced garlic
2 teaspoons dried tarragon

Salt and coarsely ground
  pepper to taste
4 (8 ounces each) salmon
  fillets with skin
2 teaspoons freshly
  snipped chives

In a bowl, combine the olive oil, orange juice, orange zest, garlic, tarragon, salt and pepper. Add salmon fillets. Marinate for one hour at room temperature, turning once or twice. Preheat oven to 475°. Place salmon fillets, skin-side down, in an ovenproof dish and pour marinade on top. Bake for 7-8 minutes or until fish is just cooked through. Do not overcook. Fish should flake easily when tested with a fork. Carefully remove to a serving platter and sprinkle each fillet with ½ teaspoon chives.

Yield: 4 servings.

Psari Plaki
Greek Baked Fish

2 pounds fish fillets
   (haddock, bluefish,
   red snapper, etc.)
½ cup olive oil
5 scallions, chopped
2 cloves garlic, minced

2 cups chopped, peeled
   and seeded tomatoes
1 cup chopped fresh parsley
1 teaspoon dried oregano
1 cup white wine
2 onions, sliced into thin rings
Freshly ground pepper to taste

Place the fish in an oiled baking pan. Set aside. Heat the olive oil in a large skillet; add scallions and garlic and sauté gently for 5 minutes, until lightly browned. Add the tomatoes, parsley, oregano, wine and pepper. Cover and simmer for 10 minutes. Pour sauce over the fish. Top with onion rings. Bake at 375° for 20 minutes or until the fish flakes easily.

Note: Served traditionally on Palm Sunday.

Yield: 4 servings.

Smoked Salmon Fettuccine

3-4 ounces canned or
   packaged smoked salmon
3 tablespoons butter
1 tablespoon shallots or
   2 tablespoons green onions

1 cup heavy cream
Juice from ½ lemon
12 ounces hot, well-drained
   fettuccine or spaghetti

Melt butter in skillet. Add salmon and shallots and cook 2 minutes over low-medium heat. Add lemon juice and blend. Stir in cream slowly. Add the smoked salmon mix to pasta. Toss well and serve.

Note: This recipe may be enhanced by the following: garnish with parsley and tomato wedges; add a couple dashes of hot pepper sauce to salmon mixture; add a shot of scotch to sauce (with the alcohol cooked off); top with grated Parmesan cheese.

Yield: 2-4 servings.

Danish Fish Bake

1 cup water
1 (6 ounce) bottle clam juice
1 pound codfish or scrod,
   boned, cut-up
4 fillets of sole or flounder
½ cup shrimp, cooked
5 ounces mussels
¾ pound canned asparagus,
   drained, reserve liquid
¾ cup flour

½ cup half-and-half or
   whole milk
2 tablespoons margarine
½ teaspoon salt
2-3 tablespoons chopped
   parsley
2 tablespoons bread crumbs
¾ cup shredded mild cheese
   (optional)
½ cup margarine for topping

In a medium saucepan, bring water and clam juice to a boil; add codfish. Boil 2-3 minutes. Remove to shallow ovenproof baking dish. To same water add sole and boil 2 minutes; remove and add to codfish. In same water, add mussels; boil 2-3 minutes. Remove and add to codfish; discard liquid. Add shrimp. Arrange asparagus on top. In separate saucepan, mix flour and cream; whisk until smooth; heat. Add margarine, salt and asparagus liquid; whisk and bring to a boil. Remove from heat and add parsley. Pour over fish; sprinkle with cheese and bread crumbs; dot with margarine. Bake 20-25 minutes in a 350° oven. Serve with boiled potatoes.

Note: If using fresh or frozen asparagus, cook, reserving ¾ cup liquid.

Yield: 4-6 servings.

Fillet of Sole Marguery

4 fillets of sole or flounder
⅔ cup white wine, divided
1 tablespoon flour
2 cups heavy cream
1 pound cooked shrimp

½ pound fresh mushrooms,
   finely chopped
2 tablespoons butter
Salt

Place fillets in buttered pan; sprinkle with salt and pour ⅓ cup wine over fish. Bake 15-20 minutes at 375°, basting often. Remove fillets to platter. Thicken stock, in which fish has been baking, with flour. When well blended, add cream, shrimp and mushrooms that have been sautéed in butter. Add remaining wine. Pour mixture over fillets. Garnish with parsley and serve piping hot.

Yield: 4-6 servings.

Salmon Mousse

1 (15½ ounce) can red
   salmon, drained
2½ teaspoons fresh lemon juice
1 teaspoon salt
Dash cayenne pepper

1 envelope unflavored gelatin
½ cup cold water
2 tablespoons mayonnaise
¼ cup heavy cream

Drain salmon; discard bones and skin; mash as smoothly as possible. Combine salmon with next three ingredients. In top of double boiler, sprinkle gelatin over cold water and stir until dissolved. Add to salmon mixture. Whip heavy cream until it peaks and add with mayonnaise to salmon mixture. Pour into 1-quart greased mold and chill until firm. Unmold and serve with dill or egg sauce.

Yield: 4 servings.

Salmon Loaf with Celery Sauce

LOAF
1 (15½ ounce) can salmon,
   drained, discarding
   skin and bones
2 tablespoons butter
½ cup milk
1 cup cracker crumbs, divided
1 teaspoon onion flakes

¼ cup cream
2 eggs
Salt and pepper to taste

SAUCE
1 (10¾ ounce) can celery soup
½ cup milk
1 tablespoon minced parsley

LOAF: Flake salmon; add butter, milk, ¾ cup crumbs, onion flakes, cream, eggs, salt and pepper. Shape into loaf in greased 8x4x2½-inch pan. Sprinkle remaining ¼ cup cracker crumbs over top of loaf and dot with butter. Bake 45 minutes in 375° oven. Remove from pan and serve with hot sauce.

SAUCE: Heat celery soup mixed with milk and parsley.

Yield: 4-6 servings.

Tuna Cakes

CAKES
1 cup fresh bread crumbs
1 (6½ ounce) can tuna,
    drained and flaked
1 egg
1 teaspoon Worcestershire
    sauce
½ teaspoon dry mustard

¼ teaspoon salt
1 tablespoon vegetable oil

SAUCE
¼ cup mayonnaise
2 tablespoons chopped
    stuffed olives
¼ teaspoon dried dill weed

CAKES: Mix first 6 ingredients and shape into ½-inch thick patties. Sauté in the oil 4-5 minutes over medium heat until golden brown on both sides. Serve with dill sauce.

SAUCE: Mix mayonnaise, olives and dill weed.

Yield: 2 servings.

Cold Cucumber-Dill Sauce

¾ cup heavy cream or
    sour cream
2 tablespoons cider vinegar
    or lemon juice

¼ teaspoon salt
⅛ teaspoon paprika
1 large cucumber
2 teaspoons finely chopped dill

Beat heavy cream until stiff; add vinegar and seasonings. Pare, seed, cut finely, and drain the cucumber well. Add to the cream mixture with the dill.

Note: Chives can be substituted for the dill. Use sauce for fish or meat, preferably cold. Delicious with cold salmon.

Yield: 1½ cups.

Egg Sauce

2 tablespoons butter
2 tablespoons flour
1 cup light cream
2 hard-boiled eggs, crumbled
½ teaspoon salt
Dash of freshly ground pepper

1 tablespoon chopped
   fresh parsley
1 tablespoon chopped chives
1 teaspoon dry mustard
1 teaspoon brown sugar

Melt butter; add flour and cook 5 minutes over low heat, stirring until blended. Gradually add cream, stirring constantly. Simmer 10 minutes. Blend in remaining ingredients. If too thick, add more cream. Cook over low heat for 3 minutes. Serve hot over cauliflower, asparagus or fish.

Yield: 1½ cups.

Fish Sauce
A change from "Tartar" Sauce

1 clove garlic
1 teaspoon salt
½ cup tahini*

½ cup water
½ cup lemon juice,
   freshly squeezed

Mash garlic and salt, add tahini and mix well in blender or food processor. Gradually add water with machine on. Mixture will be thick. Add lemon juice. Sauce should be the consistency of smooth mustard. Serve with baked, grilled or fried fish or with grilled vegetables.

*Tahini is available in Greek, Italian or Middle Eastern stores. Keeps outside refrigerator for months.

Yield: 6 servings.

Marinade for Salmon Steaks

2 cloves garlic, crushed
⅓ cup soy sauce

1 tablespoon Dijon mustard
Juice from 1 lime

Mix all ingredients together. Marinate salmon for 2-4 hours, turning once. Broil in the usual manner.

Yield: Marinade for 4 salmon steaks.

Chicken and Pasta in Hot and Sour Peanut Sauce

1½ pounds boneless chicken, skinned and cut into strips
¼ cup vegetable oil
1 medium sweet onion, cut into strips
1 red pepper, cut into strips
½ pound fresh snow peas
½ cup peanut butter

1 dried chili pepper or hot pepper sauce to taste
¼ cup rice vinegar
2-4 tablespoons tamari or soy sauce
½ cup chicken broth
1 pound fettucini or vermicelli

In a wok or large skillet, heat oil until very hot. Add onions and chicken. Stir fry for 2 minutes. Add red peppers and snow peas; stir fry 2 more minutes. Add peanut butter, chili pepper, vinegar, and tamari. Stir until peanut butter blends in. Add broth and simmer 5 minutes. Cook pasta to desired doneness. Drain and place on serving plate. Pour mixture over pasta and serve immediately.

Note: All ingredients should be ready and measured before starting to cook.

Yield: 4 servings.

Pineapple Chicken Stir-Fry

2 whole chicken breasts, boned, skinned and cut into pieces
2 tablespoons oil
2 ribs celery, sliced
1 medium onion, sliced
2 tablespoons ketchup
1 tablespoon soy sauce

1½ tablespoons sugar
1 teaspoon salt
¼ cup hot pineapple juice
1 (7 ounce) can pineapple chunks, drained and juice reserved
Freshly grated ginger (optional)

Sauté chicken in oil, stirring occasionally, about 5 minutes. Add sliced onion and celery and sauté until transparent. Mix next 5 ingredients. Add to chicken breasts. Lower heat and simmer a few minutes. Add pineapple and heat.

Note: Recipe works well in a wok.

Yield: 4 servings.

Thai Curry Chicken with Vegetables

1½ pounds chicken breasts
2 tablespoons oil
1 teaspoon salt
1 teaspoon garlic powder
½ teaspoon ginger
½ teaspoon pepper
½ teaspoon cayenne pepper
1 tablespoon soy sauce
1 cup chicken broth

1 tablespoon curry powder
2 tablespoons rice wine vinegar
1 (14 ounce) can coconut milk*
1 (16 ounce) package
    San Francisco style frozen
    broccoli, carrots, water
    chestnuts and red peppers
5 cups hot cooked rice
Paprika

Skin, bone and cut chicken into 1-inch pieces. Heat oil over medium high heat in skillet or wok until hot. Stir in next 6 ingredients. Blend well. Add chicken; cook and stir 5-8 minutes or until coated with seasonings, lightly browned and no longer pink. Add chicken broth, curry powder, vinegar and coconut milk; stir. Bring to boil. Reduce heat; simmer uncovered 20-25 minutes, stirring occasionally. Add vegetables to skillet; bring to boil. Cook approximately 5 minutes or until vegetables are crisp-tender. Serve on rice. Sprinkle with paprika for color.

*Do not use cream of coconut.

Yield: 8 servings.

Poulet Blanchard

1 (4-5 pound) roasting
    chicken, cut up
Flour for dredging
Salt and pepper
2-4 tablespoons oil for frying
1 small onion, diced
1 stalk celery, diced

3-4 sprigs parsley, minced
1 clove garlic, minced
¼ teaspoon each thyme, sage,
    nutmeg and marjoram
1½ pounds fresh mushrooms,
    sliced, sautéed in butter
Milk or half-and-half

Prepare chicken for frying (dredge with flour, sprinkle with salt and pepper); fry in oil until golden brown. Place in 9x13x2-inch casserole. Add onion, celery, parsley and garlic; sprinkle with thyme, sage, nutmeg and marjoram; add mushrooms. Pour drippings from pan into casserole; add milk to cover. Bake, covered, in 350° oven for 1½ hours or until chicken is tender.

Yield: 8 servings.

Chicken Stew

1 tablespoon olive oil
1½ cups chopped onion
2 chicken breast halves,
   skinned, boned and cubed
3 cloves garlic, pressed
2 (16 ounce) cans non-fat
   chicken broth
1 quart water
2 carrots, chopped
2 stalks celery, chopped

3 russet potatoes, with
   skins, cubed
1 sweet potato, peeled
   and cubed
½ pound green beans, cut
   into 1-inch pieces
½ cup white wine
½ teaspoon dried thyme
Salt and pepper to taste

Sauté onions in hot oil 3-4 minutes. Add chicken and garlic. Cook 5 minutes, stirring constantly. Add remaining ingredients. Simmer for 30-40 minutes.

Note: Can thicken with 1 cup spinach rotelle added during last 10 minutes of cooking. Can be made ahead and reheated to serve.

Yield: 4-6 servings.

Mediterranean Chicken

2½-3 pounds meaty
   chicken parts
2 tablespoons cooking oil
1 (14½ ounce) can tomatoes,
   cut up, undrained
½ envelope onion soup mix
1 (6 ounce) jar marinated
   artichoke hearts, drained
   and quartered

½ cup pitted ripe olives, halved
¼ teaspoon cinnamon
¼ cup dry white wine (optional)
2¼ cups chicken broth or water
3 tablespoons margarine
   or butter
1½ cups couscous

Skin and rinse chicken. Pat dry. Sauté chicken in hot oil. Drain fat. Stir together the tomatoes and soup mix. Add to chicken in skillet. Bring to a boil. Simmer, covered, for about 35 minutes. Add artichokes, olives, wine, and cinnamon. Simmer, covered, 10 minutes or until chicken is no longer pink. Meanwhile, in a saucepan, bring broth and margarine to a boil. Stir in couscous. Cover; remove from heat. Let stand 5 minutes. Fluff with fork. Serve with chicken.

Yield: 6 servings.

Chicken Fricassee with Dumplings

3 pounds boned, skinned
   chicken breasts
⅓ cup flour
1 teaspoon dried marjoram
4 tablespoons butter or
   margarine, divided
2 medium onions, sliced
1 cup chopped celery
6 large carrots, scraped
   and halved
1 bay leaf
4 whole cloves

9 whole black peppercorns
1 (13 ounce) can salt-free
   chicken broth
1 cup water

DUMPLINGS
1½ cups biscuit mix
2 tablespoons chopped
   chives or parsley
1 egg, beaten
¼ cup milk
½ cup light cream

Wash chicken; dry with paper towel. Combine flour and marjoram; mix well. Dredge chicken in flour mixture, coating evenly. Shake off excess. Reserve leftover flour. Use 2 tablespoons hot butter in 6-quart Dutch oven to sauté chicken, a few pieces at a time, turning until lightly browned all over (about 15 minutes). Remove when browned. Continue browning the chicken, adding butter as needed. To drippings add onion, celery, carrots, bay leaf, cloves and peppercorns. Sauté and stir 5 minutes. Add broth and water; bring to a boil. Return chicken to Dutch oven. Bring to a boil; reduce heat; simmer, covered, for 40 minutes.

DUMPLINGS: In medium bowl, combine biscuit mix and chives; blend in eggs and milk. Drop batter by spoonful 2-3 inches apart onto chicken (not in liquid). Cook, uncovered, over low heat 10 minutes. Cover tightly; cook 10 minutes or until dumplings are light and fluffy. With slotted spoon lift dumplings to heated baking dish warmed in 200° oven. In small bowl, combine reserved flour (about 2 tablespoons) with light cream, stirring until smooth. Stir flour mixture gently into fricassee; simmer 5 minutes, or until mixture is thickened. Replace dumplings on top of fricassee; reheat gently, covered, 5 minutes.

Yield: 6 servings.

Hot Chicken Salad

4 cups diced cooked chicken
   or turkey
2 (10¾ ounce) cans cream
   of chicken soup
2 (10¾ ounce) cans cream
   of mushroom soup
2 cups diced celery
4 tablespoons minced onion
2 cups slivered almonds

1 cup mayonnaise
1 teaspoon salt
½ teaspoon pepper
2 tablespoons lemon juice
6 eggs, hard boiled
   and chopped
Corn flakes, crushed
Melted butter

Combine all the ingredients except last 2 and place in a 3-quart casserole. Cover with corn flakes in melted butter. Bake at 350° for 40 minutes.

Yield: 10-12 servings.

Chicken 'n Stuffing Casserole

1 (8 ounce) package
   stuffing mix, divided
½ cup melted butter
   or margarine
1 cup water
2½ cups diced cooked chicken
¼ cup green onion tops
   (optional)

½ cup chopped celery
½ cup mayonnaise
¾ teaspoon salt
2 eggs
1½ cups milk
1 (10¾ ounce) can
   mushroom soup
Grated cheese

Mix ½ package stuffing, butter, water and chicken and put in a 9x13x2-inch casserole. Mix the next 4 ingredients and layer over the first mixture. Top with remaining stuffing mix. Beat eggs; mix with milk and soup. Pour over casserole and refrigerate overnight. Remove from refrigerator one hour before baking. Bake uncovered in 350° oven for 40 minutes. Sprinkle with cheese and bake an additional 10 minutes.

Yield: 8 servings.

Chicken and Sausage with Rice

3 slices bacon, cut into
small squares
2 cups finely chopped onion
3 cloves garlic, minced
2 green peppers, cored,
seeded and chopped
1 pound Spanish or
Italian sweet sausage
½ pound Spanish or
Italian hot sausage
4 cups chicken stock, divided
Salt and freshly
ground pepper

12 stuffed green olives
1 tablespoon capers
1 teaspoon crushed whole
saffron or ½ teaspoon
powdered saffron
1 3-pound chicken, cut
into serving pieces
1 tablespoon paprika
¼ cup olive oil
2 cups uncooked rice
1 cup cooked green peas
Pimento for garnish

Sauté bacon, adding onion, garlic and green peppers. Sauté ½-inch lengths of sausages in a second skillet until meat is brown. Drain both skillets and combine mixtures in a 4-quart casserole; add ¼ cup stock. Add salt and pepper to taste, olives, capers and saffron. Sprinkle the chicken pieces with paprika. Sauté in olive oil until brown on all sides; add to the casserole. Rinse the rice in a collander; add to casserole. Add the remaining stock and cover. Bake 35-40 minutes at 400°, stirring once during the baking. If the rice becomes too dry, add more stock. When the rice is tender, uncover, and reduce oven heat to 300°. Add peas; cook 10 minutes. Garnish with pimento and serve with chilled dry white wine or cold beer.

Yield: 6-8 servings.

Pennsylvania Potato Dressing
for Poultry

3 cups hot mashed potatoes
½ cups soft bread crumbs
⅛ teaspoon pepper
1½ teaspoons sage

6 tablespoons melted butter
or margarine
2 tablespoons finely
chopped onion
1½ teaspoons salt

Combine all ingredients in order given and mix well.

Yield: Sufficient for a 5-pound chicken or duck.

Baked Orange-Pineapple Chicken

4 chicken breasts, skinned,
 boned and quartered
2 cups sour cream or
 strained yogurt
2 tablespoons lemon juice
1 teaspoon minced garlic
1 teaspoon paprika
1 teaspoon Worcestershire
 sauce

⅛ teaspoon pepper
1½ cups dry bread crumbs
¾ cup butter or margarine,
 melted and divided
2 (11 ounce) cans Mandarin
 oranges, drained
1 (20 ounce) can pineapple
 chunks, drained
¼ cup chopped fresh parsley

Combine sour cream, lemon juice and seasonings. Cover chicken pieces with mixture and refrigerate 4 hours. Remove from refrigerator and roll each piece in bread crumbs until coated. Place in greased shallow 9x13x2-inch baking pan. Pour ½ cup melted butter over chicken. Bake in 350° oven for 45 minutes. Mix remaining ¼ cup butter, fruit and parsley. Spoon over chicken. Bake 15-20 minutes more.

Yield: 6-8 servings.

Chicken Breasts Provençal
Microwave Recipe

8 chicken breasts, boned
 and skinned
2 medium zucchini, sliced
3-4 tomatoes, preferably
 plum tomatoes, sliced
5-6 green onions, chopped

2-3 tablespoons fresh parsley
3 tablespoons oil
2 tablespoons lemon juice
3 tablespoons chicken broth
Salt and pepper to taste

Place chicken breasts in microwave dish with zucchini and tomatoes. Sprinkle with remaining ingredients. Cover with clear plastic wrap and microwave 18-20 minutes.

Yield: 8 servings.

Stuffed Chicken Breasts with Proscuitto, Mozzarella and Sun-dried Tomatoes

3 whole chicken breasts, split,
  on the bone with skin
6 very thin slices proscuitto
6 ounces fresh mozzarella,
  sliced into 6 pieces
6 large or 12 small pieces of
  sun-dried tomato

Fresh thyme
6 fresh basil leaves or
  ½ teaspoon dried basil
Olive oil for drizzling
Freshly ground black pepper

Prepare the chicken breasts by loosening the skin gently to form a pocket. Place a slice of ham, cheese and tomato between the skin and the meat with a pinch of thyme and a basil leaf in each. Arrange on a baking sheet. (This can be done ahead.) When ready to bake, drizzle with a little olive oil and a bit of salt if desired. Grind pepper over the top. Bake at 375° for about 30 minutes or until the juices run clear when chicken is pierced. If you desire a really brown skin, place under the broiler for 1-2 minutes. Serve hot or at room temperature.

Yield: 6 servings.

Chicken Imperial

4-6 chicken breasts,
  boned and split
⅓ cup sherry, white wine
  or dry vermouth
2 tablespoons butter or
  margarine
1 teaspoon salt
1 teaspoon dried oregano
1 teaspoon curry powder

½ teaspoon dry mustard
½ teaspoon garlic powder
Dash pepper
¼ teaspoon paprika
2 teaspoons Worcestershire
  sauce
2-3 dashes hot pepper sauce
½ teaspoon dried rosemary

Arrange chicken breasts, skin side up, in large pan. Heat remaining ingredients together. Pour mixture over chicken; cover. Bake for 50 minutes in 375° oven, basting frequently with pan juices. Remove cover and bake an additional 10 minutes.

Yield: 4-6 servings.

Chicken in Phyllo

4 whole medium-size chicken
   breasts, boned and skinned
1 onion, chopped
2 tablespoons oil
3 cloves garlic, chopped
¾ pound mushrooms,
   chopped

Salt and pepper to taste
3 tablespoons chopped parsley
⅓ cup dry vermouth
½-1 cup margarine, melted
16 sheets phyllo dough
¼ cup bread crumbs

Sauté onions in oil; do not brown. Add garlic and mushrooms; sauté 3 minutes. Add salt, pepper, wine and parsley. Mix; set aside. Keep phyllo in closed plastic bag. Remove a few sheets at a time. (It dries out quickly.) Trim one-fourth off long end of sheets. Place 2 sheets on board or table. Brush with melted margarine; sprinkle with bread crumbs. Place 1 piece of chicken in middle of phyllo; cover with 2-3 tablespoons of sautéed vegetables that have been divided into 8 portions. Fold envelope style. Place on greased baking sheet with the seam down. Continue with remainder of chicken. Brush generously with melted margarine. Bake at 350° for 30-35 minutes. Serve immediately.

Note: Can be prepared several hours in advance and covered with wax paper and foil in refrigerator. Do not bake until serving time.

Yield: 8 servings.

Wine-Baked Chicken
and Artichoke Hearts

3 pounds chicken breasts,
   boned, skinned and split
2 (14 ounce) cans marinated
   artichoke hearts
1 (28 ounce) can tomato sauce

2 teaspoons dried oregano
2 teaspoons dried basil
3-5 cloves fresh pressed garlic
¾ cup white wine or sherry
Salt and pepper to taste

Arrange chicken in baking dish. Drain artichoke hearts. Arrange on chicken. Combine remaining ingredients. Pour over chicken. Bake at 400° for 45 minutes, basting frequently.

Note: Potatoes may be baked at the same time.

Yield: 6 servings.

Vintage Chicken

1 pound fresh mushrooms, sliced	Freshly ground pepper to taste
1 cup chopped green onions	1 tablespoon dried rosemary
4 tablespoons butter, divided	6 whole chicken breasts,
¾ cup flour	halved, boned and skinned
2-4 teaspoons garlic salt	2¼ cups dry white wine

Sauté mushrooms and onions in 2 tablespoons of the butter until soft. Set aside. Combine flour, garlic salt, pepper and rosemary. Dust chicken breasts lightly with flour mixture. Melt remaining 2 tablespoons of butter in a large skillet; brown chicken breasts on both sides. Set aside. Keep warm. Add wine, mushrooms and onions to the skillet, cooking and stirring to deglaze. Return chicken breasts to skillet. Cover. Cook for 15 minutes or until fork-tender.

Yield: 8 servings.

Chicken Breast Veronique

¾ cup butter or margarine	2 cups half-and-half
4-6 whole chicken breasts, split in half and skinned	½ cup dry white wine
	1⅓ cups diced ham
1 pound medium size mushroom caps, quartered	Salt and pepper to taste
	2 cups seedless green grapes
¼ cup flour	

Brown chicken breasts in butter. Set aside. Briefly sauté the mushrooms in same pan. Add flour and cream to make a roux. Gradually add the wine and stir thoroughly. Add ham, salt and pepper. Place chicken breasts in very large baking dish. Cover with sauce and bake 45-60 minutes in 325-350° oven depending on thickness of breasts. Spoon the grapes over the top for the last 10 minutes of baking.

Yield: 8-12 servings.

Chicken Casserole
with Avocado Garnish

4 whole chicken breasts, with
  skins, split in half
6 tablespoons butter, divided
4 tablespoons flour
1 cup light cream
1 cup chicken stock
Salt and freshly ground
  pepper to taste

½ cup freshly grated
  Parmesan cheese
2 dashes hot pepper sauce
½ teaspoon dried rosemary
½ teaspoon dried basil
¼ pound mushrooms, sliced
½ cup chopped toasted almonds
1-2 avocados

Steam the chicken breasts until tender. Cool, skin and bone. Melt 4 tablespoons of the butter until foamy; stir in flour and cook for 3 minutes. Slowly add the cream and chicken stock, stirring until smooth and thickened. Season with the salt, pepper, Parmesan cheese, pepper sauce and herbs. Set aside. Sauté mushrooms in remaining 2 tablespoons butter. Place chicken in a 2-quart casserole and top with mushrooms. Sprinkle with salt and pepper. Pour sauce over chicken mixture and bake, uncovered, at 350° for 25 minutes. Remove from oven. Sprinkle with almonds. Return to oven for 10 minutes. Peel and slice avocados lengthwise. Place on chicken before serving.

Yield: 4-8 servings.

Chicken Livers in Foil

1½ pound large chicken livers,
  cut in half
¼ cup melted butter

1 teaspoon salt
½ cup buttery crackers,
  crumbed

Dip livers in butter. Roll in crumbs mixed with salt. Separate pieces and place on a foil-lined jelly roll pan, 10½x15½x1-inch. Cover tightly with foil. Bake in 350° oven for 15 minutes. Uncover. Bake 10 minutes more. Serve immediately.

Note: Serve with scrambled eggs for brunch or with potatoes or rice and mushrooms with a salad for lunch.

Yield: 8 servings.

Grilled Turkey Breast

⅓ cup lemon juice
1 tablespoon Worcestershire
  sauce
2 teaspoons minced parsley
1 teaspoon freshly
  grated ginger

½ teaspoon salt
¼ teaspoon freshly
  ground pepper
1 fresh turkey breast
  (about 2-3 pounds)

Combine first 6 ingredients in a large plastic bag. Add turkey breast; seal tightly and marinate in refrigerator for several hours or overnight. Heat charcoal grill; move coals to grill turkey with indirect heat. Remove turkey from marinade and grill for 1 to 1½ hours or until meat thermometer registers 170°.

Yield: 4-6 servings.

Turkey-Cheese-Mushroom Timbale

6 eggs
2 cups milk
½ cup shredded sharp
  Cheddar cheese
6 round buttery crackers,
  crushed

½ teaspoon Worcestershire
  sauce
¼ teaspoon salt
¼ teaspoon pepper
2 cups diced cooked turkey
1 cup sliced mushrooms
Tomato slices

Whisk eggs and milk until well mixed. Add next 5 ingredients to egg mixture. Combine turkey and mushrooms; add to egg mixture. Pour into greased 2-quart oven-proof mold. Bake in preheated 350° oven for 20 minutes. Place 1 layer of sliced tomatoes over casserole and bake 10 minutes more. Invert on a heated serving plate. Serve immediately.

Note: Ingredients may be placed in a baked 9-inch pastry crust to serve as a quiche.

Yield: 8 servings.

Stuffed Turkey Rolls Florentine

ROLLS
10 slices cooked turkey,
   thinly cut
2 (10 ounce) packages
   frozen chopped spinach
1 (3¼ ounce) can pitted
   ripe olives
2 cloves garlic
10 slices pasteurized
   process cheese
Salt and pepper to taste

SAUCE
8 ounces sour cream
1 (10¾ ounce) can
   mushroom soup
1 teaspoon hot pepper
   sauce or to taste
1 teaspoon dried dill, thyme,
   basil or rosemary
1 cup shredded Monterey
   Jack cheese

ROLLS: Lay out turkey slices. Place thawed, drained spinach and olives down the middle of each slice. Squeeze garlic over each. Place cheese slice on each; salt and pepper, if desired. Roll up like crepes. Place in greased baking dish.

SAUCE: Mix all but cheese; pour over turkey rolls. Sprinkle with cheese. Bake at 350° for 15-20 minutes. Broil to brown, about 5 minutes.

Note: Parmesan cheese may be substituted for Monterey Jack; asparagus or broccoli for spinach.

Yield: 5-10 servings.

Roast Duckling

1 (5-6 pound) oven-ready
   duckling
1 onion

1 apple, quartered
½ cup water
2 oranges

Put onion and apple in the duck cavity. Place in roasting pan with water. Roast at 325° for 2½ hours. Remove fat from pan. Baste duck in the juice and grated rind of the oranges. Continue roasting for ½ hour. Cut duck into quarters, discarding onion and apple. Serve with applesauce.

Note: Duck will not be greasy since the apple and onion have absorbed the fat.

Yield: 4 servings.

Turkey Picadillo

2 teaspoons olive oil
1 medium onion, finely chopped
2 cloves garlic, minced
1 pound ground turkey,
  uncooked
1 (28 ounce) can crushed
  tomatoes
3 tablespoons tomato paste
⅓ cup golden raisins

1 tablespoon brown sugar
5 tablespoons white vinegar
1 teaspoon cinnamon
1 teaspoon cumin
½ teaspoon cayenne pepper
¼ teaspoon cloves
½ teaspoon salt
⅓ cup slivered almonds
  (optional)

Heat oil in large skillet over medium heat. Sauté onion and garlic until softened, about 5 minutes. Add turkey, breaking into small pieces; cook until meat is no longer pink. Add undrained tomatoes, tomato paste, raisins, sugar, vinegar, spices, and salt. Bring to boil. Reduce heat and simmer until thickened, about 30 minutes. Remove from heat and stir in almonds. Serve over rice or use to stuff bell peppers.

Yield: 4 servings.

Turkey Noodle Casserole

1½ pounds raw ground turkey
⅓ cup chopped onion
⅓ cup chopped green pepper
1 (15 ounce) can tomato sauce
½ teaspoon salt
¼ teaspoon pepper

1 (8 ounce) package
  wide noodles
1 (8 ounce) package
  Neufchâtel cheese, cubed
1 cup low-fat cottage cheese
½ cup low-fat plain yogurt
1 teaspoon poppy seeds

Sauté turkey, onion and pepper until meat is no longer pink. Drain; stir in tomato sauce, salt and pepper. Cook noodles, according to package directions, omitting salt. In small bowl, combine cheeses, yogurt and poppy seeds. Toss cheese mixture with hot noodles. Spoon meat mixture over center of ½ noodles in a 13x9x2-inch pan, leaving a 1½-inch border. Layer remaining noodles on meat, leaving border. Bake covered at 375° for 30 minutes. Uncover and bake 10-15 minutes or until casserole is browned.

Yield: 6-8 servings.

Duckling with Black Cherry Sauce

DUCKLING
1 4-6 pound Long Island
  duckling, quartered
1½ teaspoons salt
1 teaspoon pepper
2 teaspoons paprika

SAUCE
1½ cups port wine
1 whole clove

Pinch each of nutmeg,
  thyme and allspice
¼ teaspoon grated orange peel
½ cup bottled brown
  bouquet sauce
½ cup currant jelly
½ cup canned pitted
  black cherries
Juice of ½ orange
1 tablespoon butter

DUCKLING: Rub duckling with seasonings. Place in dry skillet, skin side down; cover tightly. Cook at 350° in electric skillet or over medium heat for 1 hour, turning at 20-minute intervals. Do not pour off fat during cooking.

SAUCE: Combine wine, spices and orange peel. Cook over medium heat until reduced by one-half. Blend in warm brown sauce. Add jelly, stirring until dissolved. Add cherries, orange juice and butter. Serve very hot sauce over duckling.

Note: Sauce can be made ahead and reheated.

Yield: 4 servings.

Beef Wellington with Mushroom Pâté

3 pounds trimmed fillet of beef
2 tablespoons cognac or
   other brandy
2 tablespoons freshly ground
   pepper, divided
6 slices bacon
¾ pound mushrooms, sliced

2 cloves garlic, mashed
2 tablespoons margarine
1 tablespoon oil
2-3 tablespoons chopped
   fresh parsley
1 sheet puff pastry, defrosted
1 egg, beaten (optional)

Rub fillet with cognac; season with pepper. Lay bacon diagonally over top. Place on a rack in a roasting pan; roast in a 450° oven 17-18 minutes for rare, 20-25 minutes for medium. Remove from oven and discard bacon. Cool to room temperature. Sauté mushrooms and garlic in margarine and oil, over medium heat for 5-6 minutes, stirring to prevent scorching. Add a little ground pepper and parsley. Cool. Let puff pastry come to room temperature; unfold and roll out on floured surface. Increase size by 20% lengthwise. Place mushroom mixture in a strip down the middle of pastry. Place beef over mushrooms; fold pastry around beef. It may not cover all the beef. Turn over on baking sheet with uncovered raw edges facing down; tuck in at each end to cover as much of the beef as possible. Make 3 small cuts on top diagonally. For a glossy crust, brush with the beaten egg before baking. Bake 30-35 minutes in 375° oven. Remove; let stand a few minutes before cutting.

SAUCE (optional): To the reserved pan juices, add ½ cup each of beef stock and sherry with 1 tablespoon chopped tarragon. Heat for 5 minutes.

Note: Mushroom stuffing is leaner than pâté de foie gras. The "pastry short cut" works for most except for those for whom there can be no "short cuts."

Yield: 4-6 servings.

Sirloin Tip Casserole

1 pound fresh mushrooms,
  sliced
3 medium onions, sliced
2 cloves garlic, minced
½ cup butter
2 pounds sirloin tip, cubed

2½ cups water
½ cup red wine
2 bouillon cubes
3 tablespoons soy sauce
3 tablespoons cornstarch

Sauté mushrooms, onions and garlic in butter in skillet. Remove with a slotted spoon to a 3-quart casserole. Add sirloin cubes to drippings in skillet. Sauté beef until brown. Add to casserole. Add remaining ingredients to skillet, stirring to deglaze. Cook until thickened, stirring constantly. Add to casserole. Chill overnight. Skim fat. Bake covered at 325° for 2 hours. Serve with noodles and a dollop of sour cream.

Yield: 6 servings.

Sour Cream Steak

3 pounds top round of beef,
  cut 1½ inches thick
3 tablespoons flour
2 teaspoons salt

2 tablespoons butter
4 medium onions, sliced thin
1 cup boiling water
1-1½ cups sour cream

Trim meat; pound in flour and salt. Pounding makes it more tender and shortens cooking time. Brown well in fat on both sides in hot frying pan. Transfer to oven-proof pan. Sauté onions and put on top of meat. Add boiling water to sour cream; mix well; cover meat. Bake 2½ hours in 350° oven or until meat is tender.

Yield: 4-6 servings.

Shaker Braised Flank Steak

3 pounds flank steak,
   cut 1½ inches thick
2 tablespoons flour
2 tablespoons butter
1 teaspoon salt
¼ teaspoon pepper
1 stalk celery, chopped

1 carrot, chopped fine
½ green pepper, chopped fine
2 medium onions,
   chopped fine
Juice of ½ lemon
½ cup ketchup

Score both sides of the meat diagonally. Dust with flour. Brown the meat on both sides in heated butter. Season with salt and pepper. Add vegetables, lemon juice and ketchup. Cover tightly and simmer gently for 1-1½ hours until meat is tender.

Yield: 6-8 servings.

Stir-Fry Steak Slices with Winter Radishes

1¼ pounds flank steak, very
   cold or partially frozen
1 tablespoon cornstarch
1 tablespoon soy sauce
1 tablespoon dry sherry
4 tablespoons oil, divided

½ pound winter radishes,
   peeled and sliced
4-5 scallions, sliced
½ teaspoon salt
½ teaspoon sugar

Cut meat into 1x1x¼-inch pieces. Mix cornstarch, soy sauce and sherry; mix in meat. Heat 1 tablespoon oil in skillet over high heat; add radishes, scallions, salt and sugar. Toss over high heat for 1-2 minutes. Remove from skillet; set aside. Heat remaining 3 tablespoons of oil in same skillet; add meat. Over high heat toss meat 1-2 minutes. Return vegetables to skillet and toss 1-2 minutes. A delicious stir-fry!

Yield: 4 servings.

Jewish Pot Roast

4-5 pounds beef brisket
¼ cup brown sugar
½ cup ketchup
¼ cup vinegar
1 tablespoon salt

2 cloves garlic, crushed
2 onions, sliced
4 carrots, bite-size pieces
2 cups water

Preheat oven to 375°. Place all ingredients in ovenproof casserole with a tight lid. Bake 2½-3 hours.

Yield: 6-8 servings.

Beef Stroganoff Dèja Vu

⅓ cup margarine
1 cup sliced onion
1 cup green pepper strips
1 clove garlic, crushed
2 tablespoons flour
1 tablespoon ketchup

½ teaspoon salt
1 (10 ounce) can condensed
  beef broth, undiluted
3 cups cooked beef strips
½ cup sour cream
¼ teaspoon dried dillweed

Sauté onion, pepper and garlic in margarine until onion is tender (about 5 minutes). Remove from heat. Stir in flour, ketchup and salt until well blended. Gradually add broth, stirring constantly. Add beef; bring to a boil. Reduce heat; simmer 5 minutes. (May be done ahead to this point.) Add sour cream and dill; heat to boiling. Serve over rice or noodles.

Note: A great way to use leftover London Broil or roast beef.

Yield: Serves 4.

Erster Sauerbraten

3 pounds beef, top round or
  brisket roast, floured
2 tablespoons oil
2 cups water
1½ cups sugar
2 cups cider vinegar
6-8 ginger snaps, broken

Salt and pepper
1 tablespoon mixed
  pickling spice in a bag
1 cup ketchup
1 onion, chopped
½ cup red wine
1 teaspoon beef extract

Brown floured roast in oil. Add water, vinegar and sugar. When hot, add remaining ingredients. Simmer for 2 hours or until tender. Before serving, thicken gravy with flour.

Note: Serve with egg noodles, potato dumplings or potato pancakes. Better if cooked day before serving.

Yield: 6-8 servings.

Zweiter Sauerbraten

3-4 pounds beef shoulder or
  rump roast
2 cups vinegar
2 cups water
Bay leaf
¼ teaspoon nutmeg

¼ teaspoon ginger
¼ teaspoon cinnamon
¼ teaspoon cloves
2 tablespoons flour
2 tablespoons butter

Heat liquid (enough to cover meat) with bay leaf until it boils. Add spices. Pour over meat in glass, crockery or plastic bowl. Cover and refrigerate. Turn daily for about 2 weeks. Cook in liquid in covered glass casserole or enamel roaster at 325° for 20-30 minutes per pound. Make gravy with flour browned in butter. Add 2 cups of the broth and whisk until thickened.

Note: The longer it sets, the better it gets. Venison may be substituted for beef.

Yield: 4 servings.

Beef and Sausage Stew

3 pounds stew beef
2½ pounds sweet sausage links
1 tablespoon oil
3 (4 ounce) cans mushrooms,
   reserving liquid
5 carrots, sliced

8-10 medium green
   peppers, sliced
2 stalks celery, sliced
2 (10¾ ounce) cans
   tomato soup
1 (12 ounce) can tomato paste
Salt and pepper to taste

Cube meat and brown in oil. Add water to reserved mushroom liquid to equal 2 soup cans and combine with remaining ingredients. Bring to boil and simmer about 3 hours.

Note: Stew may be frozen.

Yield: 15 servings.

Five Hour Stew

2 pounds lean stew beef,
   cut into chunks
1 large potato, cubed
2 stalks celery, cut into chunks
1 large onion, cut into chunks

1 large carrot, cut into chunks
2 (6 ounce) cans Bloody
   Mary Mix
2 tablespoons quick tapioca
Salt and pepper to taste

Mix first five ingredients in 3-quart casserole. Blend remaining ingredients and pour over meat and vegetable mixture. Cover and bake at 250° for 5 hours.

Yield: 8 servings.

Status Stew

2 pounds stewing beef, cubed
¼ cup butter
2 large onions, sliced
3 cloves garlic, sliced
1 tablespoon flour
¼ cup broken crispy bacon

2 teaspoons Worcestershire
   sauce
Salt and pepper to taste
Red Beaujolais wine to cover
12 tiny white onions, parboiled
½ cup sliced mushrooms

Brown beef cubes in butter with sliced onions and garlic. Add flour and mix. Add bacon, Worcestershire sauce, salt and pepper; cover with wine and simmer 2 hours. Skim off fat; add white onions and mushrooms; simmer 15 minutes more. Serve with rice or noodles.

Yield: 4-6 servings.

Twin Meat Loaves

1½ pounds ground beef
½ pound ground pork
¼ cup finely chopped onion
2 tablespoons finely
   chopped celery
2 teaspoons salt
½ teaspoon poultry seasoning
¼ teaspoon pepper
¼ teaspoon dry mustard

1 tablespoon Worcestershire
   sauce
4 slices soft bread, cubed
½ cup milk
2 eggs
½ cup dry bread crumbs
1 cup chili sauce
½ cup boiling water

In a large bowl, thoroughly mix meats. Stir in onion, celery and seasonings. In a small bowl, soak bread cubes in milk; add eggs. Beat with rotary mixer. Combine meat and egg mixtures. Form into 2 loaves; roll in bread crumbs. Place in greased shallow baking pan. Spread ½ cup chili sauce over each loaf. Pour boiling water around the loaves. Bake uncovered for 1 hour. Baste with liquid in pan at 15 minute intervals. Serve hot or cold.

Yield: 8-10 servings.

Surprise Beef Patties

1½ pounds ground round beef
   or beef/pork mixture
Salt and pepper
¼ cup cream
2 cups herbed bread cubes
1 small onion, chopped

1 tablespoon chopped parsley
3 tablespoons plus ¾ cup water
3 tablespoons salad oil
1 (10¾ ounce) can cream of
   mushroom soup

Combine meat, seasoning and cream. Form into 16 patties. Make a dressing of bread, onion, parsley and 3 tablespoons water. Place on 8 patties. Cover with remaining patties and press well into balls. Brown in hot fat. Add mushroom soup mixed with ¾ cup of water. Cover and bake in 350° oven 1 hour.

Note: May be frozen cooked or uncooked.

Yield: 4-8 servings.

Swedish Meatballs

⅓ cup chopped onion
2 tablespoons margarine
1 egg, beaten
½ cup milk
½ cup fresh bread crumbs
1¼ teaspoons salt
⅛ teaspoon pepper
½ teaspoon allspice

¼ teaspoon nutmeg
1½ pounds ground chuck
2 tablespoons oil
3 tablespoons flour
2 teaspoons sugar
Salt and pepper to taste
1 cup water
¾ cup light cream

Sauté onion in margarine. Combine egg, milk, and bread crumbs. Let stand 5 minutes. Combine with onion and spices; add meat, mixing well. Form small meatballs and sauté about 12 at a time in oil, transferring to casserole when browned. When all are done, add flour, sugar, salt and pepper to skillet; slowly add water and cream, cooking over low heat, stirring until thickened. Serve meatballs and gravy together or separately with noodles.

Note: May also be served as hors d'oeuvres.

Yield: Approximately 5 dozen small meatballs.

Grilled Salisbury Steaks

MEAT PATTIES

1¾ pounds finely ground
    lean beef chuck
2 tablespoons grated onion
2 tablespoons very finely
    chopped green pepper
1 clove garlic, mashed
1½ tablespoons finely
    chopped chives
1 tablespoon finely
    chopped parsley
Salt, pepper, paprika to taste
⅛ teaspoon powdered thyme

Flour
Olive oil

SAUCE
3 tablespoons butter
⅓ cup ketchup
1 tablespoon lemon juice
1 teaspoon Worcestershire
    sauce
½ teaspoon hot pepper sauce
1 teaspoon prepared mustard
Salt, pepper, mace to taste
2 tablespoons sherry

MEAT PATTIES: Combine beef, onion, green pepper, garlic, chives and parsley. Season with salt, pepper, paprika and thyme. Shape into 6 patties ¾-inch thick. Sprinkle with flour and brush with oil. Place on broiler rack 3 inches from flame. Broil 5 minutes or more on each side, depending on desired doneness.

SAUCE: While patties are broiling, melt butter with all ingredients except sherry. Blend well. Stir in sherry. Heat until hot, but not boiling. Serve on patties.

Yield: 6 servings.

Tailgaters' Loaf
A Picnic Special

1 loaf day-old Italian or
   French bread

HERB BUTTER
¼ cup melted butter
½ teaspoon thyme
½ teaspoon dill
½ teaspoon oregano
1 tablespoon minced parsley

STUFFING
1¼ pounds ground round steak

1 teaspoon salt
½ teaspoon pepper
½ medium onion, diced
1 teaspoon prepared mustard
1 tablespoon ketchup
1 tablespoon Worcestershire
   sauce
1 egg, beaten
1 teaspoon fresh ground pepper
½ cup bread crumbs, from loaf

Remove 2-inch thick slice from each end of bread and scoop out inside, leaving ¾-inch crust on all sides. Brush inside and each end with herb butter. Mix stuffing and pack into hollow loaf. Replace bread ends and wrap loaf loosely in foil. Bake at 350° for 1½ hours.

Note: Tarragon mustard may be thinned with mayonnaise as an optional sauce to be spread over slices as they are served. Pack hot to serve at room temperature or serve cold.

Yield: 6-8 servings.

Red Flannel Hash

2 cups chopped cooked roast
   beef or corned beef
2 cups chopped cooked
   potatoes
2 cups chopped cooked beets
¼ cup finely chopped onion

1 clove garlic, minced
1 teaspoon salt
¼ teaspoon pepper
¼ teaspoon dry mustard
6 slices bacon
½ cup light cream

Combine thoroughly all ingredients except the bacon and cream. Place in 9-inch square baking dish. Arrange bacon on top. Cover with cream. Bake in 350° oven for 45 minutes.

Yield: 6 servings.

Celebrity Chili

3 garlic cloves, minced
2 tablespoons vegetable oil
4 pounds round steak, ground
6 large onions, sliced
4 large green peppers, sliced
3 (1 pound) cans tomatoes
4 (1 pound) cans red kidney
  beans, drained

2 (6 ounce) cans tomato paste
¼ cup chili powder
1 teaspoon white vinegar
3 dashes cayenne pepper
3 whole cloves
1 bay leaf
Salt and pepper to taste

Cook garlic in oil until golden. Crumble meat and cook 10 minutes, breaking up to brown evenly. Pour drippings into another skillet and sauté onions and peppers until tender. Add to cooked meat with remaining ingredients. Cover; cook over low heat 1 hour. Top with grated cheese and serve with rice, tortillas or crackers.

Yield: 12 hearty servings.

Cold Corned Beef Loaf

1 (12 ounce) can corned beef
1 cup chopped celery
1 tablespoon minced onion or
  chives
4 hardboiled eggs, chopped
1 teaspoon Worcestershire
  sauce

1 tablespoon minced parsley
1½ cups undiluted beef
  bouillon
1 envelope unflavored gelatin
¼ cup cold water
6 tablespoons mayonnaise

Break up beef; add chopped celery, onion, hardboiled eggs, Worcestershire sauce and parsley. Heat bouillon; soften gelatin in ¼ cup cold water and add to bouillon. Pour over beef mixture; add mayonnaise and mix well. Put into an 8½x4½x2½-inch loaf pan. Chill 3-4 hours.

Yield: 5-6 servings.

Lamb Shanks

4 whole lamb shanks, trimmed
½ cup flour
¼ cup oil
1 tablespoon cornstarch
2 teaspoons salt
½ teaspoon dry mustard
¼ teaspoon pepper
¼ teaspoon ginger

¼ teaspoon cloves
¼ teaspoon onion salt
⅛ teaspoon garlic salt
½ teaspoon celery salt
1 teaspoon paprika
1 teaspoon minced parsley
3 cups chicken stock

Flour shanks; brown in oil. Place in large greased ovenproof casserole. Combine cornstarch and seasonings; add to pan drippings; blend. Gradually add stock. Cook over low heat until smooth and thickened. Pour over shanks. Bake covered at 350° for about 2½ hours, turning once. Serve with rice.

Yield: 4 servings.

Mrs. Lynch's Irish Stew

4 shoulder lamb chops
2 tablespoons oil
Flour
Salt and pepper
2 cups chicken broth
4 cloves garlic, chopped

2 dashes Worcestershire sauce
⅛ teaspoon rosemary
¼ cup vermouth or white
    wine or ½ can of beer
12 baby carrots
4 small onions

Trim fat and cut chops into pieces, leaving meat on bones; toss lamb in seasoned flour. Brown in oil; set aside. Add remaining ingredients except carrots and onions to pan. Simmer 10 minutes. Add lamb and vegetables. Simmer 1 hour or until tender. Serve with new boiled potatoes, biscuits or dumplings. Flavor improves if made a day in advance.

Yield: 2-4 servings.

Lamb Meatballs en Brochette

MEATBALLS

⅔ cup evaporated milk
1 egg
1 cup soft bread crumbs
½ teaspoon salt (optional)
½ teaspoon garlic salt
¼ teaspoon pepper
¼ teaspoon crumbled tarragon
¼ teaspoon savory
1½ pounds ground lamb
   shoulder

12 large fresh pineapple chunks
6 plum tomatoes
2 cucumbers, cut in ½-inch slices

BROWN LEMON SAUCE

½ cup lemon juice
½ cup salad oil
¼ cup water
2 tablespoons dark brown sugar
1 tablespoon soy sauce
¼ teaspoon ground ginger

SAUCE: Mix ingredients together.

MEATBALLS: Beat milk and egg together. Add bread crumbs, salt, garlic salt, pepper, tarragon, savory, and lamb. Mix well. Shape into 18 meat balls, about 1½ inches. Chill several hours. Place meat balls on skewers. Grill 4-5 inches from heat brushing with brown lemon sauce for about 8-10 minutes on each side. Place the pineapple, tomatoes and cucumbers on separate skewers and broil 5 minutes on each side.

Note: Lamb balls may be placed in a shallow pan with sauce poured over them and broiled in oven. Turn meat balls once or twice. Add pineapple, tomatoes and cucumbers for quick broiling to remain crisp and firm.

Yield: 6 servings.

Moussaka

1½ pounds eggplant
Salt and pepper

MEAT SAUCE
1 tablespoon oil
1 cup finely chopped onion
2 teaspoons finely
   minced garlic
1½ pounds ground beef or lamb
¼ teaspoon cinnamon
Salt and pepper to taste
¼ cup dry red wine
½ cup beef broth

1¼ cups canned crushed
   tomatoes, divided

CREAM SAUCE
1 tablespoon butter
2 tablespoons flour
1 cup milk
Salt and pepper to taste
1 egg yolk

ASSEMBLING
⅓ cup cooking oil
½ pound feta cheese, crumbled

Trim ends off eggplant. Cut into 12 slices of equal thickness. Sprinkle with salt and pepper. Set aside.

MEAT SAUCE: Heat oil in skillet. Add onions and garlic. Cook until onions are wilted; add meat, breaking up lumps. Add salt, pepper and cinnamon. Add wine, broth and 1 cup tomatoes. Stir. Bring to boil; cover and simmer 10 minutes.

CREAM SAUCE: Melt butter in saucepan. Add flour, stirring with whisk. Add milk, stirring rapidly. Season with salt and pepper. Stir in remaining tomatoes. Simmer 5 minutes. Stir in egg yolk and remove from heat.

ASSEMBLING: Heat 1 tablespoon cooking oil in non-stick pan. Pat eggplant slices dry; sauté all slices 45 seconds on each side. Add oil as needed. Arrange 4 slices in bottom of 2½-quart baking dish. Spoon ⅓ meat sauce over eggplant. Continue layering, ending with meat sauce. Spoon cream sauce over all. Sprinkle cheese over top and bake 15 minutes. If desired, broil until cheese is browned. More spices may be added if desired.

Note: Reduce fat by baking eggplant slices in microwave oven for 4 minutes or in conventional oven, covered, for 10-15 minutes.

Yield: 6 servings.

New England Lamb Stew

3 pounds lean shoulder of
   lamb, cut in 2-inch pieces,
   free of bone
Flour
Salt and pepper
Dry mustard
¼ cup butter
¼ cup grated onion

Boiling water
1 cup cider or apple juice
3 large onions, sliced
2 carrots, diced small
1 tablespoon celery seed
3 tablespoons ketchup
3 tablespoons chopped
   parsley

Dredge lamb in flour seasoned with salt, pepper and dry mustard. Melt butter in deep skillet. Add onion and meat. Sauté over medium heat until well browned. Add boiling water and cider to cover meat. Simmer, covered, 30 minutes. Add onions, carrots, celery seed, and more salt if needed. Simmer, uncovered, 1 hour. Add more water and/or cider, if necessary, to keep meat barely covered with liquid. Cook until meat is tender and most of liquid has been absorbed. Add ketchup and parsley. Heat 5 minutes. Serve with new potatoes, scrubbed, boiled and rolled in butter. Sprinkle with chopped chives.

Yield: 8 servings.

Bobotie
Ground Beef or Lamb Curry Casserole

2 pounds ground beef or lamb
1 slice bread, broken up
3 eggs, beaten
1 cup milk
2 tablespoons oil
1 large onion, finely chopped

2 tablespoons curry powder
1 teaspoon salt
½ teaspoon pepper
Juice of 1 lemon
1 small apple, chopped
2 tablespoons raisins

Soak bread in beaten eggs and milk. Set aside. Brown meat in oil. With slotted spoon, transfer to baking dish. Sauté onion in remaining oil. Add curry powder, salt, pepper and lemon juice. Bring to a boil; pour over meat. Drain bread, reserving liquid. Add bread to meat mixture. Stir in apple and raisins; smooth top and pour egg mixture over meat. Bake 30-40 minutes at 350°. Serve with rice and mixed green salad.

Yield: 6-8 servings.

Roast Loin of Pork with Rhubarb

ROAST
4-5 pound loin of pork,
   boned and tied
Olive oil
Salt and pepper
1 small onion, sliced
1 cup white wine

½ teaspoon rosemary

BAKED RHUBARB
3 pounds rhubarb
Butter
Juice of 1 orange
¾ cup sugar

ROAST: Brush pork with oil and sprinkle lightly with salt and pepper. Place on rack in roasting pan, fat side up. Add onion, wine and rosemary. Roast in 350° oven, allowing 35 minutes per pound, basting occasionally with pan juices until well done. Carve into ¾-inch slices and overlap on a bed of baked rhubarb. Skim excess fat from pan and strain juices into a sauceboat. If desired, sauce may be thickened with a little potato flour or arrowroot mixed to paste with orange juice or water.

BAKED RHUBARB: Wash rhubarb, but do not peel; cut into ½-inch pieces. Put into buttered baking dish with orange juice and sugar. Bake in 300° oven for 30 minutes or until tender. If necessary, sweeten with a little more sugar.

Yield: 8-10 servings.

Pork Tenderloin Fillets

1 pound pork tenderloin
Salt and pepper to taste
2 tablespoons butter
1 onion, sliced
1 tomato, peeled and sliced

1 tablespoon flour
¼ cup beef stock
1 tablespoon sour cream
¼ cup white wine

Slice pork into fillets ¾-inch thick; pound lightly and season well. Sauté on both sides in butter over high heat with onion and tomato. Reduce heat and simmer 20-30 minutes. Remove fillets; keep warm. Add flour to fat to form gravy, thinning with stock. Add cream and wine; strain and pour over fillets.

Yield: 4 servings.

Tourtière
Pork Pie

CRUST
1 cup shortening
1 teaspoon salt
3 cups flour
⅔ cup water

FILLING
2 pounds pork, fat removed,
   ground or cut into
   ½-inch cubes

1 pound ground beef
1 cup hot water
¼ teaspoon nutmeg
¼ teaspoon allspice
2 teaspoons salt
½ cup chopped onion
¼ teaspoon pepper
3 cups fresh bread crumbs

CRUST: Cut half the shortening into flour mixed with salt; cut in second half. Mix well. Stir in water to make pastry dough. Line 10-inch pie pan with half the dough, rolled.

FILLING: Mix all ingredients; place in pastry-lined pan. Top with remaining rolled pastry; crimp edge. Cut a few slits in top. Bake for 1½ hours at 325° or until nicely browned.

Note: Make as individual meat pies or as turnovers. May be served hot but is also good cold with pickles and beer.

Yield: 6-8 servings.

Apple-Brandy Pork Chops

6 thick cut pork chops
3 apples, peeled, cored
   and sliced
1 large onion, chopped

½ cup brandy
½ cup consommé
1 tablespoon sugar
¼ teaspoon cinnamon

Place chops in a 13x9x2-inch baking pan. Cover with apples and onion. Pour brandy and consommé over top. Sprinkle with cinnamon and sugar mixture. Cover with aluminum foil. Bake at 400° for 1 hour. Remove foil and bake approximately 30 minutes or until brown.

Yield: 6 servings.

Nectarine Pork Chops

4 pork chops, ½-inch thick
1 tablespoon salad oil
¾ cup chicken broth
½ cup orange juice

1 small onion, chopped
2 ribs celery, sliced
2 nectarines, peeled and sliced

Trim fat from chops. Heat oil in large skillet. Brown chops about 5 minutes on each side. Pour off drippings and wipe out skillet. Return meat to skillet and pour in broth and juice. Add onion. Heat to boiling. Cover, reduce heat and simmer for 30 minutes. Add celery and nectarines; cook uncovered an additional 10 minutes or until chops are tender.

Yield: 4 servings.

Easy Marinated Spareribs

4-5 pounds meaty spareribs
1 cup soy sauce
1 cup orange marmalade
3 garlic cloves, minced

1 teaspoon dried ginger
⅛ teaspoon ground
    black pepper

Marinate ribs in mixture of remaining ingredients for 12 hours; turn meat several times. Arrange ribs on a rack in a roasting pan; roast in 350° oven for 1½ hours, basting frequently with marinade until golden brown and very tender. Cut into serving pieces and serve hot.

Yield: 6 servings.

Fresh Asparagus and Ham Pie

1 8-inch baked pie crust	¼ cup mayonnaise
3 tablespoons margarine, melted	2 cups diced cooked ham
1 tablespoon cornstarch	1 pound asparagus, cut and cooked
¾ teaspoon salt	1 tablespoon lemon juice
⅛ teaspoon pepper	¼ cup grated Parmesan cheese
1 cup milk	

Mix margarine and cornstarch. Stir in salt, pepper and milk; bring to a boil for about 1 minute. Stir in mayonnaise; add ham. Toss hot asparagus with lemon juice. Layer ½ asparagus, then ½ ham mixture; repeat with remaining halves. Cover with cheese; broil 2-3 minutes, 3 inches from heat.

Note: A delicious "eggless" brunch dish!

Yield: 4 servings.

Ham-Chicken Bake

½ cup chopped onion	1 (4 ounce) can sliced undrained mushrooms
2 tablespoons butter or margarine	1 (5 ounce) can sliced water chestnuts, drained
3 tablespoons flour	1 (6 ounce) can artichokes (water packed), drained and quartered
½ teaspoon salt	
¼ teaspoon pepper	
1 cup light cream	2 cups cubed cooked chicken
2 tablespoons dry sherry	1 cup cubed cooked ham
	½ cup shredded Swiss cheese

Sauté onion in butter until tender but not brown. Blend in flour, salt and pepper. Stir in cream, sherry and mushrooms. Cook until thickened, stirring frequently. Add water chestnuts, artichokes, chicken and ham. Pour into shallow 1½-quart baking dish. Top with Swiss cheese. Bake for 30 minutes at 400° or until hot and bubbly.

Yield: 6 servings.

Ham and Cheese Ring

2 tablespoons parsley flakes
2 tablespoons finely
  chopped onion
2 tablespoons prepared mustard
1 tablespoon margarine
1 teaspoon lemon juice
¾ cup shredded Swiss cheese

1 (6 ounce) can chunk ham,
  drained and separated
1 cup chopped broccoli,
  cooked and drained
1 (8 ounce) can crescent
  roll dough
Grated Parmesan cheese

Combine parsley, onion, mustard, margarine and lemon juice in large bowl; blend well. Add Swiss cheese, broccoli and ham. Mix lightly and set aside. Separate crescent dough into 8 triangles; place dough, points toward the outside, in a circle with bases overlapping on cookie sheet or pizza pan. Center opening should be about 3 inches in diameter. Spoon ham filling in ring over bases of triangles. Fold points of triangle over filling and tuck under bases of triangle at center of circle. Sprinkle with Parmesan cheese. Bake 25-30 minutes at 350° until golden brown. A luncheon favorite!

Yield: 4-6 servings.

Ham Loaf with Pineapple Sauce

LOAF
1½ pounds lean ground pork
1 pound ground ham
½ cup cracker crumbs
2 eggs, beaten
½ cup milk
Dash paprika
½ teaspoon Worcestershire
  sauce

½ teaspoon dry mustard
Salt and pepper to taste
2 tablespoons finely
  chopped onions

SAUCE
½ cup crushed pineapple
¼ cup brown sugar
½ teaspoon dry mustard

Mix all loaf ingredients together in one bowl. Mix sauce ingredients in bottom of 9x5x3-inch loaf pan. Pack ham mixture firmly on sauce. Bake at 350° for 2 hours. Remove from pan and invert.

Yield: 6-8 servings.

Stuffed Ham Rolls
with Creamed Chicken Sauce

16 slices boiled ham

STUFFING
2 cups cooked rice, cooled
4 tablespoons chopped
   fresh parsley
¾ cup chopped almonds
¼ cup melted margarine
   or butter
Salt and pepper to taste
Dash of poultry seasoning

CREAMED CHICKEN
SAUCE
¼ cup butter
¼ cup flour
1½ cups chicken broth
1 cup heavy cream
1 egg, beaten
½ cup sherry
⅓ cup Parmesan cheese
2 cups cubed cooked chicken

STUFFING: Mix all ingredients and spread over ham slices; roll slices and secure with toothpicks. Place in 9x13x2-inch baking dish.

CREAMED CHICKEN SAUCE: Melt butter over low heat; add flour, stirring until smooth. Gradually add broth and cream, stirring constantly. Bring to boil, stirring until thickened. In a small bowl, stir a small amount of hot sauce into beaten egg. Return to sauce in pan; add sherry and cheese. Simmer 5 minutes; add chicken. Pour over ham rolls. Bake at 350° for 15 minutes or until heated through.

Yield: 8 servings.

Baked Sausage with Apples

4 large pork sausage links
4 apples

5 tablespoons dark
   brown sugar

Pierce the sausages with a fork and brown on all sides. Place in oven-proof casserole. Core, peel, and slice apples; place on top of sausages. Sprinkle brown sugar on top. Cover with foil. Bake 1 hour at 350°.

Yield: 2-4 servings.

Zucchini Sausage Bake

1 pound Italian sausage meat
5 tablespoons flour, divided
6 cups sliced zucchini
½ cup chopped onion
2 tablespoons butter
1 pound cottage cheese
¼ cup grated Parmesan cheese
2 eggs, well beaten
½ teaspoon garlic salt
 or powder
1 cup shredded Cheddar
 cheese

In large skillet, brown sausage, breaking into small pieces. Toss with 1 tablespoon flour. Spread on bottom of 11x7x2-inch pan. In same skillet, cook zucchini and onions in butter until tender, not brown. Toss with remaining flour. Spoon half of zucchini mixture over meat. In medium bowl, mix cottage cheese, Parmesan cheese, eggs and garlic salt. Spoon evenly over zucchini; top with remainder of squash and Cheddar cheese. Bake 30-35 minutes at 350°.

Note: May be prepared ahead of time and baked before serving.

Yield: 4-6 servings.

Chuck Wagon Calico Beans

1 pound bacon, diced and fried
1 pound hamburger,
 crumbled and fried
½ pound sausage meat,
 crumbled and fried
1 (40 ounce) can kidney
 beans, drained
1 (15 ounce) can lima
 beans, drained
1 (15½ ounce) can chick
 peas, drained
3 (11 ounce) cans pork &
 beans, undrained
1 large onion, diced
½ cup brown sugar
½ cup ketchup
2 tablespoons white vinegar
2 tablespoons prepared mustard

Combine ingredients and heat at 350° for 30-45 minutes. Flavors blend nicely when made a day ahead; may also be frozen.

Yield: 16-20 servings.

Spanakopeta

2 pounds fresh spinach,
  thoroughly washed
1 (15 ounce) container
  ricotta cheese
12 ounces feta cheese
¼ cup rice, uncooked
Pepper to taste

1 teaspoon nutmeg
6-7 green onions, sliced
3 tablespoons oil
6 eggs, well beaten
½ cup margarine, melted
16 sheets phyllo dough

Wash spinach well. Drain (use vegetable spinner, if available). Cook, in 3 batches, 2-3 minutes in microwave oven on high or in skillet. Drain after cooking. Coarsely chop on cutting board and drain. Mix cheeses, rice, salt, pepper and nutmeg. Sauté onions in oil. Add chopped spinach and cook 3-4 minutes. Do not brown. Add to cheese mixture; add eggs. Heat oven to 350°. Grease 13x9x2-inch pan or 10-inch square pan. Brush each sheet of phyllo with melted margarine. Place 8 sheets in bottom of pan. (Keep phyllo covered with a damp towel.) Place filling on top. Smooth top. Repeat with 8 sheets phyllo, brushing each sheet with margarine. With sharp knife, cut into squares or pie shape, especially the top layer. Bake 30-40 minutes. Best served immediately but can be reheated.

Note: Filling may be made in advance. Three 10-ounce packages frozen chopped spinach may be substituted for 2 pounds fresh spinach.

Yield: 6-8 servings.

Apricot Sauce for Ham

½ cup canned apricots,
  drained and sliced
2 tablespoons honey

¾ cup white wine
Juice and grated rind from
  one large orange

Heat ingredients together until warmed through. Serve immediately.

Yield: 1 cup.

Quesadillas with Three Cheeses

2 tablespoons olive oil
1½ cups thinly sliced onion
1½ cups red or green bell
  pepper strips
3 garlic cloves, minced
8 ounces Cheddar cheese,
  shredded
½ cup whipped cream cheese

6 tablespoons grated
  Parmesan cheese, freshly
  grated if possible
¼ teaspoon ground cumin
¼ teaspoon crushed red
  pepper flakes or to taste
6 (8-inch) flour tortillas
Tomatoes, lime slices and
  parsley for garnish

Heat olive oil in small non-stick pan; add onion, pepper and garlic; cook until tender-crisp (3-4 minutes). Set aside. Using fork, stir remaining ingredients, except tortillas, together. Preheat oven to 450°. On half of each tortilla, spoon vegetable mixture; top with cheese mixture. Fold over other half of tortilla and gently press to close. Arrange on baking sheet and brush with remaining 2 teaspoons oil. Bake 5 minutes or until cheese is melted. Garnish or serve with salsa, sour cream and/or guacamole.

Yield: 6 servings.

Spicy Cherry Glaze for Ham

1 (16 ounce) can sour pitted
  cherries in heavy syrup
1 envelope onion-mushroom
  or onion soup mix
½ cup brown sugar

2 tablespoons cornstarch
½ teaspoon cinnamon
½ teaspoon allspice
¼ teaspoon cloves

Drain and coarsely chop cherries, reserving 1 cup syrup. In small saucepan, mix soup, sugar, cornstarch, cinnamon, allspice and cloves. Stir in reserved syrup and cherries. Bring to a boil; simmer, stirring constantly until sauce is thickened, about 5 minutes. Baste ham frequently during baking.

Yield: About 2 cups. Enough for a 5-pound canned ham.

Apples Under Glaze

6 large baking apples
12 raisins, plumped in water
1 tablespoon grated orange rind
1 cup orange juice
¾ cup brown sugar

Pinch of salt
2 tablespoons Cointreau or
   other orange liqueur
½ cup roasted shaved
   almonds (optional)

Core apples. Pare about ⅓ down from stem end. Fill holes at bottoms with raisins. Place apples, pared ends up, in buttered baking dish. Combine orange rind, juice, sugar, and salt in saucepan. Bring to boil. Pour over apples. Bake at 350° about 45 minutes or until just tender, basting often with orange syrup from pan. About 5 minutes before apples are done, pour 1 teaspoon Cointreau over top of each apple. Scatter almonds on top, if desired. Serve plain as an accompaniment to a main dish, such as pork or poultry, or with whipped cream as a dessert.

Yield: 6 servings.

Baked Pineapple

½ cup butter or margarine,
   softened
½ cup sugar
2 tablespoons flour

2 eggs
1 (20 ounce) can crushed
   pineapple, drained
5 slices white bread, cubed

Cream together butter, sugar and flour. Add eggs and stir until smooth. Add pineapple. Fold in bread. Put in 1½-quart greased casserole. Bake at 350° for 30 minutes.

Note: Wonderful as a side dish with ham, pork or turkey.

Yield: 6 servings.

Cranberry Relish

2 cups cranberries
1 unpeeled orange,
   cut in eighths and seeded
3 tablespoons sugar

Pinch of salt
2-3 tablespoons orange
   flavored liqueur

Chop cranberries and orange together; mixture should not be mushy. Place in bowl and stir in remaining ingredients.

Yield: 2 cups.

Liver Baked with Onion and Herbs
Shaker Manifesto

1 large onion, sliced
2 tablespoons butter, melted
¼ cup hot water
6 ½-inch thick slices calves' liver
2 tablespoons flour, seasoned
   with salt and pepper

1 tablespoon chopped parsley
2 teaspoons thyme
2 tablespoons thick chili sauce
1 tablespoon brown sugar
2 tablespoons butter

Place onion in oven-proof 2-quart shallow casserole; pour the butter and water over it. Cover and bake in a 350° oven for 30 minutes. Dredge liver in flour; arrange over onion; sprinkle with parsley and thyme; dot with chili sauce, sugar and butter. Bake covered for 30 minutes at 350° and uncovered until liver is browned.

Yield: 6 servings.

Guzek's Osso Buco

4 veal shanks, cut 1¼-inch
   to 1½-inch thickness
Flour
⅓ cup olive oil
Salt and pepper to taste
1 onion, chopped
1 garlic clove, crushed
1 carrot, sliced
Pinch of thyme
½ cup white wine
Grated cheese

Dredge veal in flour. Heat several tablespoons oil in heavy skillet and brown veal well on all sides. Season with salt and pepper. Transfer veal and liquid to Dutch oven.

Add more oil to skillet. In hot oil sauté onion, garlic and carrot over medium heat for 5 or 6 minutes. Stir in thyme. Add wine; simmer until wine is almost evaporated. Pour mixture over veal and simmer about 1½ hours, covered, until veal is tender. Remove veal to platter. Keep hot. Reduce liquid in Dutch oven and serve as sauce over rice or buttered pasta. Top with grated cheese.

Yield: 4 servings.

Veal Loaf

2 pounds ground veal
Salt, pepper, garlic powder,
   parsley to taste
¾ cup flavored Italian
   bread crumbs
½ cup grated Romano cheese
1 teaspoon grated lemon peel
2 tablespoons ketchup
2-3 eggs or equivalent
   egg substitute

Mix all ingredients thoroughly. Pack in 9x9x3-inch loaf pan and bake 1½ hours at 350°. Serve hot or cold.

Note: May be frozen and baked later.

Yield: 6-8 servings.

Veal Parmigiana

TOMATO SAUCE
2 tablespoons olive oil
½ cup chopped onion
1 clove garlic, crushed
1 (1 pound) can Italian
　　tomatoes, undrained
2 teaspoons sugar
½ teaspoon dried oregano
¼ teaspoon dried basil
¼ teaspoon pepper

VEAL
1 pound thin veal scallopini
2 eggs, beaten
1 cup dry bread crumbs
½ cup olive oil, divided
1 (8 ounce) package
　　mozzarella cheese, sliced
¼ cup grated Parmesan cheese

SAUCE: Sauté onion and garlic in hot oil until golden brown, about 5 minutes. Add tomatoes, sugar, oregano, basil and pepper. Mix well, mashing the tomatoes. Bring to a boil. Simmer covered 10 minutes.

VEAL: Wipe veal with damp paper towels. Dip in eggs, then in bread crumbs, coating lightly. In large skillet heat about ¼ cup oil. Add veal a few pieces at a time and cook until golden brown, 2 or 3 minutes on each side. Add oil as needed. Place veal in 11x7x2-inch baking pan to cover bottom in a single layer. Add some tomato sauce, mozzarella and Parmesan cheese. Repeat the layers, ending with Parmesan cheese. Cover with foil. Bake 30 minutes at 350° or until bubbly.

Yield: 4 servings.

Veal Julienne

1½ pounds veal steak, cut into
½-inch strips
4 tablespoons butter or
margarine, divided
½ cup water
1 teaspoon dried basil
1 medium green pepper, diced
1 cup thinly sliced onions
1 (6 ounce) can sliced
mushrooms, drained

1 (15 ounce) can tomato sauce
½ cup halved or chopped
water chestnuts
Few drops hot pepper sauce
1 teaspoon Worcestershire
sauce
Salt and pepper to taste
½ cup dry sherry
1 cup sour cream or
drained yogurt

Brown veal strips slowly in 2 tablespoons butter, stirring often to prevent burning. Add water and basil; simmer 20 minutes. Meanwhile, sauté green pepper and onions in remaining butter until soft but not brown; add to veal with mushrooms, tomato sauce and water chestnuts; mix well. Simmer 15 minutes longer. Stir in hot pepper sauce, Worcestershire sauce, salt, pepper and sherry. Simmer 5 minutes. Lower heat; stir in sour cream slowly. Serve with parsley rice, lima beans and a green salad!

Note: Can be made ahead, except for adding sour cream, and reheated gently at serving time.

Yield: 6 servings.

Elegant Calves' Liver

1 2-inch thick slice of
calves' liver
Soybean or olive oil
¼ teaspoon garlic powder
¼ teaspoon oregano
¼ teaspoon rosemary

¼ teaspoon cracked pepper
¼ teaspoon hickory
smoked salt
1 cup sliced onions,
Bermuda or Vidalia
Butter or oil

Rub liver with oil and cover one side with mixed spices to form a thick crust. Broil 5 minutes; turn and cover other side with spices; broil 5 minutes more. Meanwhile cook sliced onion in oil until tender in microwave or sauté in skillet. Serve liver covered with onions.

Yield: 2 servings.

Veal Stew – A Taste of Italy

3 tablespoons margarine
2 tablespoons oil
1½ pounds veal, cut into
   1½-inch cubes
¾ cup coarsely chopped onion
3-4 garlic cloves,
   coarsely chopped
1 tablespoon flour
½ cup dry white wine or ¼
   cup white vermouth

1 cup canned Italian plum
   tomatoes with juice
1-2 sprigs fresh rosemary, or
   1½ teaspoons dried
4-5 fresh sage leaves, or
   2-3 teaspoons dried
3 tablespoons chopped
   parsley
1 tablespoon each oil
   and margarine
½-¾ pound mushrooms

Heat oil and margarine in large skillet. Brown veal in 2 or 3 batches (to ensure even browning) over medium to high heat. Remove when done. To same skillet, add onions and garlic; sauté a few minutes over medium heat. Return meat to skillet; sprinkle with flour, stirring to coat meat. Add wine; let bubble a little. Add tomatoes and juice. Add herbs. Simmer, covered, for one hour or until meat is tender. Cut mushrooms into 2 or 3 pieces each. In small skillet, brown mushrooms in the additional oil and margarine. Add to meat; simmer an additional 5 minutes. Serve over pasta, rice or noodles.

Note: Fresh, skinned, chopped tomatoes may be used with water added to equal one cup to replace Italian plum tomatoes.

Yield: 4 servings.

Veal Scallopini with Peas

1½ pounds veal scallopini
Salt and pepper
Flour
¼ cup olive oil

½ cup white wine
1 (9-10 ounce) package petite
    peas, cooked according to
    package directions

Pound veal slices until flat. Sprinkle salt, pepper and flour on both sides and sauté in olive oil until browned. Add wine; simmer over low heat until wine has almost evaporated and liquid has thickened slightly. Remove meat to a hot platter. Add peas to sauce and heat together. Pour over meat and serve.

Yield: 6 servings.

Venison Pot Roast

4 pound venison roast
½ cup vinegar
2 tablespoons salt
2 cloves garlic, sliced
Cold water
Salt to taste
2 tablespoons flour
Oil

2 cloves garlic, minced
1 large onion, sliced
2 tablespoons sugar
1 tablespoon Worcestershire
    sauce
1 teaspoon mustard
¼ cup vinegar or lemon juice
1 (16 ounce) can tomatoes

Allow venison to stand overnight in marinade made of vinegar, 2 tablespoons salt and sliced garlic added to water sufficient to cover venison. Dry and season with salt; roll in flour and brown in hot oil in skillet. Place in crock pot. Add remaining ingredients; cover and cook slowly 8 to 10 hours.

Yield: 10-12 servings.

The Vegetable Collection

EAST SIDE of MARKET STREET (now BROADWAY) FROM MAIDEN LANE SOUTH, ALBANY, NEW YORK

James Eights (1798-1882)
Watercolor on paper, c. 1850
Bequest of Ledyard Cogswell, Jr., 1954.59.68

The market was an important meeting place
for farmers, tradesmen, and their customers.
The covered market stalls are at the center of
the picture, with the First Dutch Reformed
Church at the right. The Institute collection
includes many sketches and watercolors by
James Eights, a noted Albany scientist and
medical doctor. Painted from memory in 1850,
the scenes record Albany as it looked in 1805.

Green Beans in Olive Oil
Middle Eastern

2 pounds green beans, cleaned
  and cut into 1-inch pieces
½ cup olive oil
3 large onions, chopped
3-4 cloves garlic, chopped

½ bunch cilantro, chopped
  (green coriander)
4 whole tomatoes, peeled and
  seeded or 1 (9 ounce) can
  Italian tomatoes, drained
Salt and pepper to taste

In a large skillet on medium to high heat, sauté onions in olive oil until golden brown, stirring frequently. Add garlic and cilantro; sauté 3 minutes longer. Add beans; sauté a few minutes more. Cover skillet; turn heat to low. Cook approximately 15 minutes stirring often. Add tomatoes, salt and pepper. Cover and cook on low heat for 35-40 minutes; should be well cooked, not crunchy. Serve at room temperature.

Yield: 4 servings.

Lemon-Walnut Green Beans

⅓ cup chopped walnuts
2 pounds fresh green beans,
  cut in half
¼ teaspoon salt
3 tablespoons butter
  or margarine
⅓ cup sliced green onions

1 tablespoon finely chopped
  fresh rosemary or
1 teaspoon dried rosemary
1 tablespoon lemon juice
1 tablespoon grated lemon rind
Garnishes: lemon slices,
  fresh rosemary sprigs

Spread walnuts on an ungreased baking sheet; bake at 300° for 10 minutes stirring several times. Set aside. Sprinkle beans with salt. Steam 8-12 minutes or until crisp-tender. Plunge green beans into cold water to stop the cooking process; drain and set aside. Melt butter in a large skillet over medium heat; add onions, and sauté about 3 minutes, stirring constantly. Add beans, walnuts, rosemary and lemon juice; cook until thoroughly heated, stirring constantly. Sprinkle with lemon rind and garnish, if desired. Serve immediately.

Yield: 8 servings.

Sweet and Sour Bean Casserole

6-8 slices of bacon, cut
    into pieces
1 onion, sliced
2 (15 ounce) cans butter beans
1 (15 ounce) can lima beans
1 (15 ounce) can kidney beans

1 (15 ounce) can pork
    and beans
½ cup cider vinegar
¾ cup dark brown sugar
½ teaspoon dry mustard
½ teaspoon garlic salt

Cook bacon in skillet until soft. Remove from pan. Sauté onion in bacon drippings until soft. Drain all beans except pork and beans. Put in 3-quart casserole. Combine vinegar, sugar, mustard and garlic salt in saucepan. Cook 10 minutes. Mix with beans in casserole. Stir in bacon. Cover and bake 1 hour at 350°.

Note: May be made in advance.

Yield: 10-12 servings.

Busy People's Beans

1 pound dried pea beans
6 cups warm water
3 tablespoons molasses
3 tablespoons brown sugar

1 medium whole onion
1 teaspoon dry mustard
¼ pound well-smoked bacon or
    leftover ham or ham bone

Wash beans. Put all ingredients in pan. Cover and barely bring to boil. Cook on low heat 6-8 hours.

Yield: 6-8 servings.

Broccoli Puff

4 eggs, beaten
½ cup milk
Dash of pepper

1 (10 ounce) package frozen
    chopped broccoli, cooked
    and drained
½ cup grated Parmesan cheese

Combine eggs, milk and seasoning. Stir in broccoli and cheese. Pour into greased 9-inch pie plate. Bake at 350° for 20-25 minutes or until set.

Yield: 4-6 servings.

Lenticchie in Umido
"Stewed" Lentils

1½ cups brown lentils
1 large scallion or a small leek
1 teaspoon dried marjoram
2 tablespoons extra virgin
    olive oil

1 cup red wine
1 teaspoon fennel seeds
Freshly ground pepper

Wash and pick over lentils. Soak overnight in cold water. Drain. Finely chop the scallion or leek. Place in saucepan and sauté with marjoram in olive oil until golden. Add the lentils, wine, fennel and pepper. Cover and cook over low heat for about 30 minutes.

Note: Serve with a green salad and fruit.

Yield: 4 servings.

Vegetarian Cholent

½ cup dry white northern beans
½ cup dry kidney beans
½ cup dry lima beans
2 tablespoons vegetable oil
    or margarine
3 large onions, diced

3 garlic cloves, diced
½ cup barley
3 large unpeeled potatoes,
    cut into chunks
½ pound mushrooms, sliced
1 (15 ounce) jar spaghetti sauce

Pick the beans over carefully, rinse and put in a large bowl. Cover with cold water and soak overnight. Heat oil in a 4-quart pot. Sauté the onions and garlic until soft, about 10-15 minutes. Add barley and drained beans. Cover with water 2 inches above ingredients. Cover pot, bring to a boil and simmer gently for 30 minutes over a low heat. Add remaining ingredients. Cook 30 minutes more. Place the mixture in a 6-quart casserole, cover and bake at 200° overnight.

Note: For a large crowd, bake a double batch in a turkey roaster. Do not freeze this dish.

Yield: 10-12 servings.

Broccoli-Cheese Casserole

2 pounds broccoli florets
¼ cup butter
¼ cup flour
¾ cup beef bouillon
1 cup half-and-half

2 tablespoons lemon juice
½ teaspoon salt (optional)
2 tablespoons sherry
½ cup grated Cheddar cheese
½ cup slivered almonds

Steam florets 4-5 minutes until just tender. Arrange in 11x7x2-inch casserole. Melt butter in skillet over low heat. Add flour; stir to blend. Slowly add bouillon, stirring to prevent lumps. Slowly add half-and-half, again stirring to prevent lumps. Carefully stir in lemon juice, salt and sherry. Pour over broccoli. Sprinkle cheese and almonds on top. Bake at 375° for 20 minutes until cheese browns.

Yield: 6-8 servings.

Sweet and Sour Red Cabbage

1 medium head red cabbage,
  shredded
2 cups water
½ teaspoon salt

1 cup sugar or 2 tablespoons
  sugar substitute
1 cup vinegar
¼ teaspoon ground cloves
Raisins (optional)

Cook cabbage in water on top of stove for 20 minutes over medium heat. Add salt, sugar, vinegar, cloves and raisins; simmer for 5-10 minutes. Ready to serve.

Note: Best if cooked the day before and reheated.

Yield: 6-8 servings.

Baked Dilled Carrots

1 pound carrots, cut into strips
1½ tablespoons margarine
¼ teaspoon dillweed

¼ teaspoon salt
Dash of pepper
2 tablespoons water

Place carrots on greased piece of heavy aluminum foil. Dot with margarine. Sprinkle with seasonings and water. Wrap in foil and bake at 350° for about 45 minutes or until tender. Also works well on outside grill.

Yield: 4-6 servings.

Braised Carrots and Turnips

1 pound carrots, peeled and
  sliced ½-inch thick
1 pound turnips, peeled, halved
  and sliced ¾-inch thick
2 cups chicken broth

2 teaspoons sugar
2 tablespoons butter
Salt and pepper to taste
Fresh chives, chopped

Place all ingredients, except the chives, in a large heavy saucepan; cook, partially covered, over medium heat, until tender, about 20 minutes. Check seasoning. Serve in warm dish garnished with chives.

Yield: 6-8 servings.

Honey and Brandy Glazed Carrots

3 pounds carrots, diagonally
  cut into 1-inch slices
3 cups water
2 tablespoons granulated sugar
1 teaspoon salt
¼ cup unsalted butter, divided

3 tablespoons honey
1 tablespoon brown sugar
¼ cup brandy
3 tablespoons chopped
  fresh parsley

Combine first 4 ingredients and ½ of the butter in large saucepan. Bring to a boil. Reduce heat; cover and simmer until carrots are tender, about 10 minutes. Drain well. Cook remaining butter, honey and brown sugar in large skillet over medium heat, stirring until butter melts and sugar dissolves. Add carrots and brandy; cook until carrots are coated with glaze, about 3 minutes. Before serving, sprinkle with parsley.

Note: Can be made in advance. Cover and let stand at room temperature. Reheat over medium to low heat.

Yield: 10-12 servings.

Latke-Crusted Cauliflower Pie

CRUST
2 cups (packed) grated raw
   potato
¼ cup grated onion
½ teaspoon salt
1 egg white, lightly beaten
Flour for your fingers
Oil

FILLING
1 tablespoon olive oil or butter
1 cup chopped onion
2 medium cloves garlic,
   minced

½ teaspoon salt
Black pepper to taste
½ teaspoon basil
¼ teaspoon thyme
1 medium cauliflower,
   broken into small pieces
1 cup sliced mushrooms
1 cup (packed) grated
   Cheddar cheese
2 eggs (or 1 whole egg
   + 1 egg white)
¼ cup milk
Paprika

CRUST: Preheat oven to 400°. Oil a 9-inch pie pan. Combine grated potato and onion, salt and egg white in a small bowl and mix well. Transfer to the pie pan and pat into place with lightly floured fingers building up the sides. Bake 30 minutes. Brush crust with a little oil and bake 10 more minutes. Remove from oven and reduce temperature to 375°.

FILLING: Heat olive oil in a large skillet. Add onion, garlic, salt, pepper and herbs; sauté over medium heat for about 5 minutes. Add cauliflower and mushrooms; stir and cover. Cook until tender, stirring occasionally, about 8-10 minutes. Spread half the cheese onto the baked crust. Place the sautéed vegetables on top; sprinkle on the remaining cheese. Beat the eggs and milk together and pour over the top. Dust lightly with paprika. Bake 35-40 minutes or until set. Serve hot or warm.

Note: If using a food processor with grating attachment, grate cheese, potato and onion in that order. No need to clean in between.

Yield: 4-6 servings.

Braised Celery and Apple Medley

1½ tablespoons olive oil
5¼ cups diced celery
1½ cups slivered onions,
  purple if possible
1 (8 ounce) can sliced water
  chestnuts, drained
3½ cups cubed red
  cooking apples

⅔ cup golden raisins
½ cup water
½ teaspoon dried tarragon
½ teaspoon salt
¼ teaspoon freshly
  ground pepper
¼-½ cup chopped
  walnuts, toasted

Toast walnuts in pie pan at 350° for 10-15 minutes. Warm olive oil in heavy saucepan or non-stick skillet over medium heat. Sauté celery and onion for 5 minutes. Add remaining ingredients, except nuts. Stir. Cover. Reduce heat and cook for 10 minutes or until firmly tender. Remove from heat. Stir in nuts.

Yield: 6-8 servings.

Corn Pudding

1 (16 ounce) can whole
  corn, drained
1 (16 ounce) can creamed corn
2 eggs, slightly beaten

8 ounces sour cream
½ cup margarine, melted
1 (8 ounce) box corn muffin mix

Mix all ingredients and place in a buttered 2-quart casserole. Bake at 350° for 55 minutes.

Yield: 8-10 servings.

Southwestern Corn Bake

2 (16 ounce) cans creamed corn
2 eggs, slightly beaten
¾ cup yellow cornmeal
1 teaspoon garlic salt

2 tablespoons vegetable oil
1 (4 ounce) can green chili
  peppers, diced
2 cups grated Cheddar cheese

Mix together all ingredients except chili peppers and cheese. Pour half the mixture into a 9x9x2-inch baking dish. Toss chili peppers and cheese together. Spread on top of corn mixture. Cover with remaining corn mixture. Bake in 350° oven for 35-40 minutes.

Yield: 8 servings.

Dandelions in Olive Oil
Mediterranean

2 pounds dandelion greens
½ cup olive oil (not salad oil)
4 medium onions,
   coarsely chopped

2 teaspoons salt
5 cloves garlic, minced
Juice of ½ lemon or
   lemon wedges

Rinse dandelion greens well; chop. Bring 2 quarts water to a boil; add dandelions. Boil 10 minutes; drain, squeeze out excess water. Heat oil in large skillet; add onions; sauté a few minutes. Add garlic; sauté 2 minutes, stirring frequently over low to medium heat. Add salt. Reserve a little of the onions for garnish; add the dandelions to skillet. Cook, stirring about 10 minutes. Pour onto serving plate; garnish with reserved onions. Squeeze lemon juice over dish or serve with lemon wedges on the side.

Yield: 4-6 servings.

Romanian Eggplant

2 large eggplants
Salt
½ cup olive oil
2 large onions, minced
2 large tomatoes, coarsely
   chopped or
2½ cups canned plum tomatoes,
   drained and chopped

2 tablespoons dillweed
Freshly ground pepper
1 tablespoon flour
½ cup finely chopped parsley
8-10 ripe olives, preferably
   oil-cured

Cut eggplant into ½-inch cubes. Place in a colander and sprinkle with salt. Drain for 30 minutes. Pat the cubes dry and set aside. In a large skillet heat a few tablespoons of the oil. Stir in the onions; sauté until transparent. Remove them from the skillet and reserve. Heat remaining oil in the skillet and sauté the eggplant over high heat, turning frequently until brown. Return the onions to the skillet. Add the tomatoes, dill and pepper to taste. Cover and simmer for 8-10 minutes. Sprinkle the flour over the mixture and stir in the parsley and olives. If the pan seems too dry, add a little water or dry white wine. Simmer gently, uncovered, 3-5 minutes.

Yield: 4-6 servings.

Berenjena Español
Spanish Eggplant

1 large eggplant	1 teaspoon salt
Salt	⅛ teaspoon pepper
4 slices bacon, diced	1 (6 ounce) can tomato purée
1 medium onion,	1 can water
finely chopped	½ cup grated cheese
1 green pepper, finely chopped	Buttered bread crumbs

Peel eggplant and cut into ½-inch cubes. Place in colander and sprinkle with salt. Drain for 30 minutes. Pat cubes dry and set aside. Fry bacon until crisp; add onion and green pepper. Cook about 5 minutes; pour off excess fat. Add eggplant, salt, pepper, tomato purée and water. Cook until eggplant is tender. Turn mixture into buttered 1½-quart casserole. Sprinkle with cheese and top with buttered bread crumbs. Bake at 350° for 35-45 minutes. Serve at once.

Yield: 6-8 servings.

Mushroom Casserole

½ cup chopped onion	2 tablespoons sherry
½ cup butter or margarine	1½ teaspoons dried parsley
1 cup beef consommé	½ cup seasoned Italian
⅛ teaspoon dried marjoram	bread crumbs
1 pound fresh mushrooms,	
sliced	

Sauté onions in butter in large deep frying pan until transparent and tender but not brown. Remove onions from pan and place in bowl. Add consommé and marjoram. In same frying pan, sauté mushrooms in butter. Add mushrooms to onion mixture. Mix in sherry and parsley. Pour into shallow 2-quart buttered casserole. (May be made ahead to this point. Refrigerate.) Top with seasoned bread crumbs. Bake uncovered at 350° for 20 minutes. If made ahead and refrigerated, bake for 30 minutes.

Yield: 6-8 servings.

Mushroom Strata

1 pound mushrooms,
   coarsely sliced
2 tablespoons margarine
½ cup each of chopped onions,
   celery and green pepper
½ cup mayonnaise
½ teaspoon salt
1 teaspoon pepper

7 slices buttered white bread,
   cut into 1-inch squares
   as used
2 eggs, beaten
1½ cups milk
1 (10¾ ounce) can
   mushroom soup
¼ cup grated cheese

Sauté mushrooms in margarine. In a bowl, combine vegetables and mayonnaise. Add salt, pepper and mushrooms. Place 3 slices of cut bread in bottom of 2-quart casserole; cover with mushroom/vegetable mixture. Add ½ of remaining bread. Mix eggs with milk; pour over mushroom mixture. Refrigerate several hours. An hour before baking, spoon mushroom soup over dish; top with remaining bread. Bake at 325° for 45 minutes. Sprinkle cheese on top. Continue baking 10 minutes longer.

Yield: 6 servings.

Onions Au Gratin

2 (14 ounce) jars small white
   whole onions, drained
¼ cup butter
3 tablespoons cornstarch
½ teaspoon salt

1½ cups milk
½ cup buttered bread crumbs
1 cup grated sharp
   Cheddar cheese

Place onions in buttered 9-inch square baking dish. Melt butter in saucepan; blend in cornstarch and salt. Add milk gradually and cook over low heat, stirring constantly until thick. Pour sauce over onions; sprinkle with buttered bread crumbs and top with grated cheese. Bake at 350° for 25 minutes.

Yield: 4-5 servings.

Shaker Onions

2 pounds small white onions,
   boiled and drained
½ cup butter
3 tablespoons brown sugar

1 tablespoon dry mustard
¼ teaspoon pepper
1½ teaspoons salt
⅓ cup chopped parsley

Place onions in a buttered, shallow 1-quart baking dish. Combine all remaining ingredients except parsley and pour over onions. Bake at 325° for 20 minutes or until heated through. Sprinkle with parsley before serving.

Yield: 8 servings.

Breaded Parsnips with Rosemary

6 parsnips, trimmed and pared
2 eggs, well-beaten
¼ cup bread crumbs

½ teaspoon dried rosemary
Salt and pepper to taste
¼ cup butter

Cook parsnips in boiling salted water for 10 minutes; drain. Cut into slices ½-inch thick. Dip into beaten eggs and roll in mixture of bread crumbs, rosemary, salt and pepper. Brown slices on both sides in butter over moderate heat.

Yield: 4 servings.

Maple Glazed Parsnips

8 small uniform parsnips,
   trimmed and pared
⅓ cup maple syrup

1½ tablespoons unsalted butter
2 teaspoons lemon juice
¼ teaspoon lemon zest

Cook parsnips in covered skillet in ½ inch boiling water over medium-high heat until tender but crisp (3-4 minutes). Remove parsnips and discard liquid. Combine remaining ingredients in same skillet; heat over medium heat until simmering. Return parsnips to skillet and cook, uncovered, turning frequently, until parsnips have absorbed the glaze, about 4 minutes.

Yield: 4 servings.

French-Style Peas

¼ cup butter
½ small head iceberg lettuce,
   coarsely chopped
2 (20 ounce) packages frozen
   peas, thawed
4-6 scallions, diced
1 teaspoon salt

1 teaspoon sugar
⅛ teaspoon pepper
1 bay leaf
2 tablespoons chopped
   fresh parsley
2 tablespoons chopped
   fresh chives

In large skillet, simmer lettuce in butter until soft. Add remaining ingredients. Cook until peas are done. Discard bay leaf. Serve with turkey, chicken or fish. Garlic and/or white wine to taste may be added.

Yield: 6-8 servings.

Herb-Rice Stuffed Peppers

4 large green peppers
1 large onion, chopped
2 stalks celery, thinly sliced
⅓ cup corn oil
1 (35 ounce) can whole
   tomatoes
1 teaspoon salt
½ teaspoon pepper

1½ cups uncooked rice
4 cloves garlic, chopped
¼ cup chopped fresh parsley
½ teaspoon dried mint
½ teaspoon dried basil
½ teaspoon dried oregano
1 (8 ounce) can tomato sauce
4 cups water

Wash peppers. Cut a slice from the top of each. Remove seeds. Sauté onion and celery in oil for 5 minutes. Set aside 4 whole tomatoes and the juice. Chop remaining tomatoes and add with salt and pepper to the sautéed mixture. Cook 3 minutes. Add rice, garlic and herbs; stir. Stuff peppers. Place whole tomato on top of each pepper. Place peppers in a 3-quart saucepan. Pour tomato sauce over peppers. Add tomato juice and water to pan. Liquid should reach top of peppers, not over top. Cover. Cook on medium heat on top of stove until rice is cooked and peppers are tender when pricked with a fork, 60-75 minutes.

Yield: 4 servings.

Baked Hash Browns

1 (2 pound) bag frozen hash
brown potatoes
1 medium onion, chopped
⅔ cup margarine or butter,
melted, divided

1 (12 ounce) carton sour cream
1 (10¾ ounce) can cream of
chicken soup
1½ cups grated mild cheese
½ cup crushed corn flakes

Thaw and crumble the potatoes. Sauté onion in 2 tablespoons margarine. Mix sour cream, soup and cheese. Add potatoes and onion. Pour into a 13x9x2-inch greased and floured baking dish. Top with corn flakes and remaining margarine. Bake at 350° for 1 hour.

Note: May use low-fat sour cream.

Yield: 4-6 servings.

Colcannon

½ cup finely chopped onion
¼ cup butter
¼ cup half-and-half

1 pound potatoes, boiled
and mashed
1½ cups coarsely chopped
cabbage, boiled

Sauté onion in butter until soft. Add cream and potatoes; stir until heated through. Beat cabbage into potatoes over a low heat until all is pale green and fluffy. Serve hot. Leftover colcannon is good fried in bacon fat, browned on both sides.

Note: This Irish potato dish is an excellent accompaniment for boiled ham. Traditionally served at Halloween, hiding in it a ring for a bride, a button for a bachelor, a coin for wealth and a thimble for a spinster.

Yield: 4 servings.

Golden Potato Soufflé

2 pounds potatoes	1 cup light cream
6 eggs	1 tablespoon sugar
1 orange, grated rind and juice	½ teaspoon salt
¼ cup butter	2 teaspoons baking powder

Peel the potatoes and cook until tender in boiling, salted water. Put potatoes through a ricer or mash. Cool. Beat the eggs and add the orange juice and rind. Melt the butter and blend with the cream and sugar; add salt and baking powder. Fold everything together with the cooled potatoes and mix thoroughly. Put in a 2-quart buttered casserole. Bake at 350° for 1 hour. Excellent with ham.

Yield: 8 servings.

Gourmet Potatoes

6 medium potatoes	1½ cups sour cream,
2 cups shredded sharp	room temperature
Cheddar cheese	⅓ cup finely chopped onion
¼ cup butter or margarine	1 teaspoon salt
	¼ teaspoon pepper

Boil potatoes in skins; cool, peel and shred coarsely. In saucepan, over low heat, combine cheese and butter, stirring occasionally until almost melted. Remove from heat and blend in sour cream, onions, salt and pepper. Fold in potatoes and turn into a greased 2-quart casserole. Bake at 350° for 20-25 minutes. May be assembled a day ahead and refrigerated until ready to heat.

Yield: 8 servings.

Potato Kugel

4-5 medium potatoes,
  peeled and grated
1 onion, finely grated
3 eggs
⅓ cup flour

1½ teaspoons salt
Pepper to taste
¼ cup oil or 2 tablespoons
  chicken fat

Combine potatoes and onion. Beat eggs until thick; add to potato mixture. Add remaining ingredients. Mix well with fork. Place in a greased 2-quart casserole. Bake at 350° for 1 hour or until kugel is light brown and crisp. Cut into sections; serve hot or cold.

Yield: 4 servings.

Rosemary Roasted Potatoes

3 medium shallots, peeled
1½ teaspoons minced fresh
  rosemary
1 teaspoon minced fresh thyme
¼ teaspoon black pepper
¾ teaspoon salt

⅛ teaspoon cayenne pepper
⅓ cup olive or vegetable oil
3 pounds small new potatoes,
  rinsed and scrubbed
Juice of ½ lemon
¼ cup minced fresh parsley

Adjust oven rack to lowest position and heat to 425°. Mince shallots and put in small bowl with rosemary, thyme, salt, black and cayenne peppers and olive oil. Stir well. Quarter potatoes and pat dry. Put on 10½x15½x1-inch jelly roll pan. Pour oil mixture over potatoes and turn to coat completely. Roast potatoes 35-40 minutes, turning several times with spatula until browned and soft when pierced. Cool to room temperature. Season to taste. Squeeze lemon juice over potatoes, sprinkle with parsley and toss to mix thoroughly. Serve at room temperature.

Yield: 6 servings.

Pommes de terre Dauphinoise
Scalloped Potatoes

6 cups peeled, thinly
   sliced potatoes
2-3 cloves garlic, peeled
   and crushed
2 cups milk

1½ cups heavy cream
¾ teaspoon salt
½ teaspoon white pepper
½ cup grated Swiss cheese

Combine potatoes with garlic, milk, cream, salt and pepper in large heavy saucepan. Bring to boil over medium heat, stirring constantly. When mixture has thickened, pour into a greased 11x7x2-inch baking pan. Sprinkle with grated cheese and bake at 400° for 1 hour or until potatoes are tender.

Note: Can be made ahead and reheated.

Yield: 10-12 servings.

Very Sherry Sweet Potato Soufflé

4 cups cooked mashed
   sweet potatoes
½ cup sherry
½ teaspoon salt
2 eggs, beaten

½ cup butter
¼ cup brown sugar
½ cup chopped walnuts
   (optional)

Whip all ingredients, except nuts, until light and fluffy. Place in 1½-quart casserole and bake at 350° until golden, about 30 minutes. Sprinkle walnuts over top.

Note: May be frozen before baking.

Yield: 6 servings.

Tantalizing Spinach

2 (10 ounce) packages
   chopped spinach,
   cooked and drained
3 ounces cream cheese,
   softened

½ cup sour cream
3 strips bacon, cooked
   and crumbled
¼ cup chopped green onion
1 tablespoon horseradish

Blend cream cheese and spinach together. Add remaining ingredients and spoon mixture into a 2-quart casserole. Bake at 350° for 30 minutes.

Note: May be made the day before and refrigerated. Low-fat cream cheese and sour cream may be used.

Yield: 4-6 servings.

Spinach Soufflé

SOUFFLÉ
2 tablespoons butter
2 tablespoons flour
½ cup milk
1 teaspoon onion juice
½ teaspoon salt
Pepper to taste
3 eggs, separated
2 (10 ounce) packages
   frozen chopped spinach,
   cooked and drained

CHEESE SAUCE
¼ cup butter
¼ cup flour
2 cups milk
½ teaspoon salt
¼ pound Cheddar
   cheese, diced

SOUFFLÉ: Using first 6 ingredients, make thick white sauce; cool slightly. Beat egg yolks slightly. While stirring, add sauce slowly. Add spinach and fold in stiffly beaten egg whites. Bake in buttered 1½-quart soufflé dish at 375° for 30 minutes. Serve with cheese sauce.

CHEESE SAUCE: Make white sauce; add salt and cheese, stirring until cheese is melted.

Yield: 6 servings.

Apple Squash Bake

1 (12 ounce) package frozen
  winter squash
1 cup applesauce
2 tablespoons sugar

½ teaspoon nutmeg
Dash salt
Buttered bread crumbs
¼ cup chopped pecans

Thaw squash and combine with applesauce, sugar, nutmeg and salt. Pour into buttered 1½-quart casserole. Sprinkle with crumbs and nuts. Bake at 350° for 30 minutes.

Yield: 4-6 servings.

Glazed Acorn Squash Rings

1 large acorn squash
⅓ cup orange juice
½ cup brown sugar
¼ cup light corn syrup

¼ cup butter
2 teaspoons grated lemon rind
⅛ teaspoon salt
Orange slices

Cut squash into ¾-inch slices. Remove seeds. Put in greased 13x9x2-inch baking dish. Bake at 350° for 30 minutes. Combine next six ingredients. Bring to boil and simmer 5 minutes. Pour mixture over squash. Bake uncovered for an additional 15-20 minutes. Baste as needed. Garnish with orange slices.

Yield: 4-6 servings.

Cheesy Summer Squash

1½ pounds summer squash,
 thinly sliced
¼ cup water
½ teaspoon salt
¼ teaspoon pepper

¼ teaspoon oregano
⅔ cup shredded Muenster cheese
¼ cup grated Parmesan cheese
¼ cup chopped pecans
1 tablespoon melted butter

Combine squash and water in saucepan; cover and simmer for 5 minutes. Drain well. Place half the squash in buttered shallow 1-quart baking pan. Sprinkle with half the salt, pepper, oregano and Muenster cheese. Repeat with remaining squash, seasonings and Muenster cheese. Top with Parmesan cheese. Mix nuts with butter and sprinkle over top. Bake uncovered at 350° for 15 minutes.

Note: Do not remove skin and seeds of squash if tender and young.

Yield: 4-6 servings.

Fried Red and Green Tomatoes

1 pound firm red tomatoes
1 pound green tomatoes
Salt and pepper to taste
2 large eggs
¼ cup milk
¼ cup water

Salt and pepper to taste
2 cups saltine cracker crumbs
1 cup flour
Vegetable oil
2 tablespoons bacon fat,
 if desired

Cut tomatoes into ⅓-inch slices. Pat dry and sprinkle both sides with salt and pepper. In a bowl, beat the eggs, milk, water and salt and pepper to taste. Put cracker crumbs into one shallow dish, the flour in a second. In a large skillet, heat ½-inch oil and bacon fat over moderate heat until deep-fat thermometer registers 375°. Dredge the tomato slices in flour, shaking off excess. Dip into egg mixture, dripping off excess. Coat with cracker crumbs. Fry a few at a time, turning carefully, for 30 seconds on each side, until golden. Using a slotted spatula, place on paper towels to drain. Keep warm. Serve hot with scrambled eggs or grilled meats at breakfast, lunch or dinner.

Yield: 4-6 servings.

Cheese-Tomato Pie

3 cups cubed slightly stale
  French bread
¾ teaspoon crushed
  dried basil
3 medium tomatoes
1½ cups grated Gruyère or
  Monterey Jack cheese

2 tablespoons chopped
  green onion
1¼ cups milk
3 eggs, beaten
½ teaspoon dry mustard
Dash of hot pepper sauce
Salt and pepper to taste

Place bread on bottom and sides of a greased 10-inch pie pan. Sprinkle with basil. Peel, core and slice tomatoes ¼-inch thick. Arrange over bread, overlapping slightly. Sprinkle with cheese and green onions. Mix milk, eggs, mustard, pepper sauce, and salt and pepper together. Carefully pour over layers in pan. Bake at 375° for 30-40 minutes or until puffed and brown. Let stand for 10 minutes before serving.

Note: Delicious using ¾ tablespoon minced fresh basil leaves layered over tomatoes.

Yield: 6 servings.

Turnips in Orange Juice

2 pounds turnips, peeled and
  cut into 1-inch cubes
½ teaspoon salt
½ cup orange juice
2 tablespoons brown sugar

¼ teaspoon ground ginger
3 tablespoons melted butter
  or margarine
1 cup fresh orange sections

Boil turnips; drain and mash. Beat in the salt, orange juice, sugar, ginger and shortening. Put into a buttered 1½-quart baking dish; garnish with orange sections. Bake at 350° for 7-10 minutes.

Note: May also be heated in a saucepan without orange sections, put into a serving dish and garnished with orange sections.

Yield: 4-6 servings.

Creole Praline Yam Casserole

YAMS
6 cups mashed cooked yams
¼ cup butter, softened
1 tablespoon brown sugar
1 teaspoon salt
Dash of white pepper
Hot milk
¼ cup dark seedless raisins

TOPPING
⅓ cup brown sugar,
   firmly packed
2 tablespoons flour
½ teaspoon salt
3 tablespoons butter
⅓ cup chopped pecans

YAMS: Put yams in a large bowl; add butter, brown sugar, salt, pepper and enough hot milk to moisten. Beat with electric beater until fluffy. Stir in raisins and turn into shallow, lightly greased 2-quart casserole.

TOPPING: Mix together the brown sugar, flour and salt. Cut in butter until mixture is crumbly. Stir in nuts and sprinkle over yams. Bake uncovered at 350° for 30 minutes.

Yield: 6-8 servings.

Zucchini-Tomato Skillet

¼ cup corn oil or olive oil
4 medium-size zucchini
   (7-8 inches), cut into
   ½-inch slices
1 medium onion, chopped
4 large cloves garlic, crushed
½ teaspoon dried basil
4 medium-size tomatoes,
   peeled, cut in wedges
Salt and pepper to taste

Heat oil in large skillet. Add zucchini and stir until slightly browned. Push to one side of pan. Add onion and garlic on other side of pan. Sauté until slightly golden. Sprinkle with basil and fry over low heat until zucchini is crisp-tender. Gently stir in tomatoes just to heat. Sprinkle with salt and pepper.

Yield: 8 servings.

Tomato-Zucchini Pot Pie

2 medium size zucchini, sliced
2 tablespoons margarine
1 onion, chopped
2 garlic cloves, minced
2 tomatoes, peeled and diced
1 cup grated Cheddar cheese

3 eggs, beaten
¾ cup biscuit baking mix
1¼ cups milk
¼ cup sour cream
Pinch of thyme
Pinch of dill

Sauté zucchini in margarine. Add onion and garlic. Cook 5 minutes. Gently add tomatoes. Put mixture in 9-inch pie plate. Cover with cheese. Mix remaining ingredients. Pour over zucchini. Bake at 400° for about 35 minutes.

Yield: 4-6 servings.

Tour-R-Lou
Greek Vegetable Casserole

2 medium potatoes,
  peeled and sliced
2 onions, sliced
4 medium zucchini squash,
  scraped and thickly sliced
2 ribs celery, sliced
2 cloves garlic, minced
2 tablespoons fresh mint or 1
  tablespoon dried (optional)

¼ cup fresh Italian parsley
1 can tomato sauce diluted
  with 1 can water
¼ cup olive oil
½ pound green beans,
  cooked tender-crisp
Salt and pepper to taste
Flavored bread crumbs

Combine all ingredients except crumbs in 2-quart baking dish. Sprinkle the top with bread crumbs. Bake at 325° for about one hour. May also be simmered for 1½ hours on top of stove.

Note: Good served with feta cheese and crunchy bread or rolls.

Yield: 6-8 servings.

Roasted Vegetables

1 red pepper, seeded
1 green pepper, seeded
1 yellow pepper, seeded
1 zucchini
1 yellow squash

1 medium onion
Olive oil
Salt
Herbs

Cut vegetables into large pieces. Spread over a shallow baking pan. Drizzle with olive oil. Add salt and herbs. Sage is nice, as is rosemary or basil. Bake at 450° for 45 minutes. Check several times. Stir with fork during baking. Vegetables should be thoroughly cooked and slightly brown.

Note: Roasted vegetables are great on their own. May be used with penne pasta with garlic and olive oil. Use with salad also, but let cool completely, then toss with greens. Use a sherry vinegar to make the salad dressing.

Yield: 4 servings.

DESSERT TIME
Ida Pulis Lathrop (1859-1937)
Oil on canvas, c. 1910
AIHA purchase 1987.6

This painting is executed with almost photographic
realism, so that one easily responds to the bloom of the
grapes and the fuzziness of the peaches. Ida Pulis Lathrop,
a self-taught artist, was born in Albany and married
Cyrus Clark Lathrop. They raised two daughters;
Gertrude, a successful sculptor, and Dorothy, a painter,
writer and illustrator of children's books.

Brandy Alexander Pie

1 envelope unflavored gelatin	¼ cup brown crème de cacao
½ cup cold water	1 cup heavy cream, whipped
⅔ cup sugar, divided	1 9-inch graham cracker crust
Pinch of salt	Chocolate curls for garnish
3 eggs, separated	(optional)
¼ cup cognac	

In a medium saucepan, sprinkle gelatin over cold water. Add ⅓ cup sugar, salt and 3 egg yolks. Stir by hand until well-blended. Place over low heat and stir constantly until mixture has thickened and gelatin has dissolved. Do not allow to boil. Remove from heat. Stir in cognac and crème de cacao. Place in refrigerator until mixture mounds when dropped from a spoon. In a medium bowl, beat 3 egg whites until stiff peaks form. Gradually beat in remaining ⅓ cup sugar. Fold into chilled gelatin mixture. Fold in whipped cream. Pour mixture into pie crust and refrigerate overnight. Garnish.

Yield: 8 servings.

Chocolate Chip Nut Pie

1 9-inch pie crust, unbaked	½ cup dark corn syrup
1 cup semi-sweet chocolate chips	3 eggs
1½ cups chopped nuts	1 teaspoon vanilla
(walnuts, pecans or cashews)	Sweetened whipped cream
½ cup firmly packed brown	¼ cup chocolate chips, melted,
sugar	or chocolate syrup

Sprinkle chips over bottom of pie crust. Sprinkle chopped nuts evenly over chips. In small bowl, combine sugar, corn syrup, eggs and vanilla. Beat well. Pour over nuts. Bake at 375° for 25-35 minutes until top is deep golden brown. When cool, garnish with whipped cream spread around outer 2 or 3 inches of pie and drizzle with melted chips or chocolate syrup.

Yield: 8-10 servings.

Japanese Fruit Pie

7 tablespoons margarine,
    melted
1 cup sugar
2 eggs, slightly beaten
½ cup finely chopped nuts
½ cup raisins

½ cup coconut
1 tablespoon vinegar
1 teaspoon vanilla
1 9-inch pie crust, unbaked
Whipped cream

Mix first 8 ingredients. Pour into pie crust and bake at 350° for 40 minutes. Cool. Garnish with whipped cream.

Yield: 8 servings.

Green Tomato Pie

3 cups peeled, thinly sliced
    green tomatoes
1½ cups sugar
¼ teaspoon cinnamon
¼ teaspoon salt

¼ cup flour
5 tablespoons lemon juice
5 teaspoons grated lemon rind
2 tablespoons softened butter
Pastry for 9-inch (2-crust) pie

To peel tomatoes easily, immerse in boiling water until skins will slip off, about 3 minutes. Mix together sugar, cinnamon, salt, flour, lemon juice, lemon rind, and butter. Arrange tomatoes in layers in crust, sprinkling each layer with sugar mixture. Adjust top crust, flute edges and cut vents. Bake in 425° oven until tomatoes are soft and crust is lightly browned, about 35-40 minutes.

Yield: 6-8 pieces.

Lemon Cream Pie with Apricot Sauce

PIE

1 envelope unflavored gelatin
⅔ cup sugar, divided
¼ teaspoon salt
2 eggs, separated
6 tablespoons cold water
6 tablespoons lemon juice

2 teaspoons grated lemon peel
1 cup heavy cream, whipped
1 9-inch graham cracker crust
   or baked pastry crust

SAUCE
1 (16 ounce) can apricot halves

PIE: Combine gelatin, ⅓ cup sugar and salt in saucepan. Beat egg yolks; beat in water and lemon juice; add to gelatin mixture. Mix well. Cook over low heat, stirring constantly until gelatin dissolves and mixture thickens slightly. Remove from heat; add lemon peel. Chill, stirring occasionally, until mixture mounds slightly when dropped from a spoon. Beat egg whites until stiff. Add remaining ⅓ cup sugar gradually and beat until very stiff. Fold into gelatin mixture. Fold in cream. Pour into 9-inch crust. Chill until firm.

SAUCE: Drain apricots, reserving ¼ cup syrup. Purée apricots and reserved syrup.

Chill. Serve over pie. Garnish with mint leaves. May also be served without the crust as a pudding.

Yield: 6-8 servings.

Quick Pineapple Cheese Pie

1 (8 ounce) package cream
   cheese, softened
¼ cup sugar
1 cup heavy cream, whipped,
   or 1 cup whipped topping

1½ cups crushed pineapple,
   drained well
1 9-inch graham cracker pie
   crust, baked

Whip softened cream cheese and sugar together well. Fold in cream, then pineapple. Spoon into the pie crust. Chill 2 hours or until filling is set.

Yield: 6-8 servings.

Shaker Double Crust Lemon Pie

Pastry for 9-inch (2-crust) pie
2 cups sugar
⅓ cup flour
¼ teaspoon salt
⅔ cup water

2 tablespoons butter or
  margarine, softened
3 eggs
2½ teaspoons grated orange peel
1 large or 2 small lemons, peeled
  and sliced ⅛-inch thick

In large bowl, combine sugar, flour and salt. Add water, butter, eggs and orange peel; beat until well-blended. Stir in lemon slices. Pour mixture into bottom crust. Top with second crust and flute; cut slits in several places in top crust. Bake in preheated oven at 400° for 35-45 minutes or until golden brown. Cool completely on wire rack before serving. Refrigerate leftovers.

Yield: 8 servings.

Pumpkin-Apple Pie

⅓ cup packed brown sugar
1 tablespoon cornstarch
½ teaspoon cinnamon
¼ teaspoon salt
⅓ cup water
2 tablespoons butter
  or margarine
3 cups pared and sliced apples
1 egg

⅓ cup sugar
¾ cup cooked or canned
  mashed pumpkin
½ teaspoon cinnamon
¼ teaspoon ginger
⅛ teaspoon cloves
¼ teaspoon salt
¾ cup evaporated milk
1 unbaked 9-inch pie crust

Combine brown sugar, cornstarch, ½ teaspoon cinnamon and ¼ teaspoon salt in 2-quart saucepan. Stir in water and butter. Cook over medium heat, stirring constantly, until mixture comes to a boil. Add apples; cook 4 minutes more. Remove from heat.

Combine next 8 ingredients in bowl. Beat until blended. Pour apple mixture into pie crust. Carefully spoon an even layer of pumpkin mixture over apple mixture. Bake in 425° oven 10 minutes. Reduce temperature to 375° and bake 40 minutes more, or until filling is set around the edge. Cool on rack.

Yield: 6-8 servings.

Pumpkin-Pecan Pie

3 eggs, divided
1 cup canned pumpkin
1 cup sugar, divided
½ teaspoon cinnamon
¼ teaspoon ginger
⅛ teaspoon cloves

⅔ cup corn syrup
2 tablespoons margarine, melted
½ teaspoon vanilla
1 cup pecans
1 9-inch pie crust, unbaked

Blend 1 egg, pumpkin, ⅓ cup sugar and the 3 spices. Spread evenly in bottom of pie crust. Mix together 2 eggs and the remaining ingredients; carefully spoon over pumpkin layer. Bake in 350° oven for one hour until filling is set around edges. Cool.

Yield: 6-8 servings.

Sweet Potato Pie

4 large sweet potatoes or yams, 3 to 4 cups
2 eggs
1 cup evaporated milk
½ cup butter
½ teaspoon allspice

¼ teaspoon nutmeg
1 teaspoon cinnamon
¾-1¼ cups sugar, depending on sweetness of potatoes
1 9-inch pie crust, unbaked

Wash and peel sweet potatoes; dice and boil until tender; drain and mash. Add the remaining ingredients and beat until smooth. Pour filling into pie crust. Bake in 350° oven for 1 hour or until firm.

Note: May use canned sweet potatoes or yams.

Yield: 8 servings.

Turtle Pie

12 caramels
1 (14 ounce) can sweetened
   condensed milk, divided
1 9-inch pastry crust, baked
2 (1 ounce) squares
   unsweetened chocolate

¼ cup butter or margarine
2 eggs
2 tablespoons water
1 teaspoon vanilla
Dash of salt
½ cup chopped pecans

In small heavy saucepan, over low heat, melt the caramels and ⅓ cup condensed milk. Spread evenly on bottom of baked pie crust. In medium saucepan, over low heat, melt chocolate and shortening. In large mixing bowl, beat eggs, remaining condensed milk, water, vanilla and salt. Add chocolate mixture; mix well. Pour into crust. Top with pecans. Bake in 325° oven for 35 minutes or until center is set. Cool. Chill. Refrigerate leftovers, if any.

Yield: 8 servings.

Creamy Rice Pudding

½ cup rice
1 quart whole milk
½ cup sugar
½ teaspoon salt

¼ teaspoon nutmeg
⅛ teaspoon cinnamon
Raisins (optional)

In top of double boiler mix all ingredients. Cover and cook over boiling water until rice absorbs milk and is soft, about two hours. If necessary, replenish boiling water in lower part of double boiler during cooking. Add raisins when an hour has passed, if desired. Serve warm or chilled.

Note: Do not use skim or low-fat milk.

Yield: 6 servings.

Upside-Down Date Pudding

PUDDING

1 cup pitted chopped dates
1 cup boiling water
½ cup granulated sugar
½ cup brown sugar
1 egg
2 tablespoons melted butter
   or margarine
1½ cups sifted flour
1 teaspoon baking soda

½ teaspoon baking powder
½ teaspoon salt
1 cup chopped walnuts
Whipped cream

BROWN SUGAR SAUCE

1½ cups brown sugar
1 tablespoon butter
1½ cups boiling water

PUDDING: Combine dates and water; set aside to cool. Blend sugars, egg and butter. Sift together dry ingredients. Combine with egg mixture. Stir in nuts and dates. Pour into 11x7x1½-inch lightly greased baking dish. Combine ingredients for Brown Sugar Sauce and pour over pudding. Bake in 350° oven for 40 minutes. Cut into squares. Invert on serving plates. Serve warm with whipped cream.

Yield: 15 servings.

Hot Fudge Pudding Cake

1 cup sifted flour
2 teaspoons baking powder
1 teaspoon salt
⅔ cup granulated sugar
6 tablespoons cocoa, divided
½ cup milk

2 tablespoons butter, melted
1 teaspoon vanilla
½ cup chopped walnuts
   or pecans
1 cup brown sugar, packed
1½ cups boiling water

Mix flour, baking powder, salt, sugar and 2 tablespoons cocoa. Add milk, butter and vanilla. Mix only until smooth. Fold in nuts. Put into greased 8x1¼-inch round baking dish. Mix brown sugar and 4 tablespoons cocoa. Sprinkle over mixture in baking dish. Pour boiling water over top. Bake in 350° oven for 40 minutes. Serve warm or cold with cream, if desired.

Note: Weird and wonderful – cake with sauce on the bottom.

Yield: 8 servings.

Bread Pudding with Whiskey Sauce

PUDDING
1 loaf French bread
1 quart milk
3 eggs, beaten
2 cups sugar
2 tablespoons vanilla
1 cup raisins
3 tablespoons margarine,
    melted

WHISKEY SAUCE
1 cup sugar
1 egg
½ cup of butter or
    margarine, melted
Whiskey to taste

PUDDING: Break bread into pieces; soak in milk. Crush with hands until well mixed. Add eggs, sugar, vanilla, and raisins. Stir well. Pour margarine into bottom of a shallow heat-proof baking dish. Add pudding mixture. Bake in 350° oven 45 minutes or until very firm. Cool. Cube pudding; put into individual heat-proof dessert dishes. To serve, add whiskey sauce and heat under broiler.

SAUCE: Cream sugar and egg until well mixed. Add butter. Mix well to dissolve sugar. Add whiskey. Sauce should be creamy smooth.

Yield: 6-8 servings.

Chocolate Bread Pudding

1 quart milk, scalded
2 (1 ounce) squares
    unsweetened chocolate
2 cups dry bread cubes
1 tablespoon butter

¼ teaspoon salt
¾ cup sugar
4 eggs, slightly beaten
1 teaspoon vanilla

Melt chocolate in hot milk; soak bread in milk 5 minutes. Add butter, salt, and sugar. Pour slowly over eggs; add vanilla and mix well. Pour into greased 2-quart casserole. Bake in pan of hot water in 350° oven until firm, about 50 minutes. Serve warm with whipped cream.

Yield: 8 servings.

Brother James' Rhubarb Bread Pudding

8 slices bread, firm texture	½ teaspoon cinnamon
1½ cups milk, scalded	¼ teaspoon salt
¼ cup butter	2 cups diced rhubarb
5 eggs, lightly beaten	¾ cup wheat germ
1 cup honey or 1½ cups sugar	

Toast bread; remove crusts. Cut toast into ½-inch cubes and place in buttered 11x7x2-inch pan. Combine milk and butter; stir to melt butter. Pour over toast cubes and let stand for 15 minutes. Mix together eggs, honey, cinnamon, salt and rhubarb. Stir into bread mixture. Sprinkle with wheat germ. Bake in 325° oven for 45 minutes. Serve warm with topping. Suggested are half-and-half, softened vanilla ice cream, whipped cream, or best of all, Hot Lemon Sauce.

Yield: 8-10 servings.

Jiffy Low-Cal Pot de Crème

¾ cup skim milk	6 individual packages
1 cup semi-sweet chocolate bits	granulated sugar substitute
1 egg	1 teaspoon vanilla
	Low-cal frozen whipped topping

Heat milk to boiling point. Place the chocolate, egg, sugar substitute and vanilla in the electric blender container. Add hot milk and blend at low speed for 1 minute. Stir with spatula to remove bubbles and pour into pot de crème cups or small dessert dishes. Chill several hours before serving. Garnish with a dab of "light" whipped topping.

Yield: 5-6 servings.

Chocolate Soufflés

Butter
Sugar
6 ounces semi-sweet chocolate
6 jumbo eggs (if extra large,
    add 1)

2 tablespoons liqueur,
    raspberry (Chambord) or
    orange (Grand Marnier)
Whipped cream

Lavishly butter and lightly sugar 6 1-cup ramekins and refrigerate until ready to bake. Preheat oven at 350° (oven must be hot when soufflés are ready to bake). Melt chocolate slowly over hot but not boiling water. Separate eggs, placing whites in a stainless steel or copper bowl suitable for beating them and placing the yolks in a large bowl for combining all ingredients. While chocolate is melting slowly, beat the egg whites until firm but not dry. Whisk egg yolks together with liqueur. Add melted chocolate slowly into yolks; blend well. Fold whites into chocolate mixture until well incorporated. Spoon mixture, in even amounts, into prepared ramekins. Place in oven on a baking sheet to facilitate handling. Cook for 12 minutes (for slightly runny center) to 15 minutes (for a firm soufflé). Serve while hot with a dollop of whipped cream.

Note: Soufflés have been perceived as difficult, cranky items. "It ain't necessarily so." This recipe may be prepared in a few minutes and contains fewer calories than most. To change the yield, the formula for each serving is 1 ounce chocolate to 1 jumbo egg, and flavor accordingly.

Yield: 6 soufflés.

Chocolate Mousse

1 pound semi-sweet chocolate
3 eggs, separated
1-2 tablespoons cognac or
  brandy (optional)

1 pint heavy cream, whipped
Shaved pieces of chocolate
  for decoration

Melt chocolate in microwave or in double boiler. Remove from heat. Slowly add beaten egg yolks, stirring constantly. Add cognac or brandy if desired. Set aside. Beat egg whites until stiff. Add cream to chocolate mixture, gently folding together. Fold in egg whites. Pour into bowl or individual serving dishes and decorate if desired. Refrigerate, covered, 2-3 hours or overnight.

Yield: 8-10 servings.

Frozen Chocolate Mousse Cake

1 teaspoon butter
1 tablespoon sifted
  confectioners' sugar
1 (3 ounce) package
  ladyfingers

1 (6 ounce) package semi-
  sweet chocolate morsels
3 tablespoons water
4 eggs, separated
¼ cup sugar
1 cup heavy cream, whipped

Butter sides and bottom of 8-inch springform pan. Sprinkle with confectioners' sugar; swirl pan to coat evenly. Separate ladyfingers. Line sides of pan with ladyfingers, rounded side against pan. Combine semi-sweet morsels and water over hot (not boiling) water in double boiler. Stir until morsels are melted and mixture is smooth. Transfer to large bowl. Add egg yolks, one at a time, beating well after each addition. Set aside. In 1½-quart bowl, beat egg whites until soft peaks form. Fold beaten egg whites and whipped cream into chocolate mixture. Pour into ladyfinger-lined pan. Freeze until firm (about 4 hours).

Yield: 10-12 servings.

Biscuit Tortoni

½ cup coarsely crushed
   Italian macaroons
½ cup finely chopped
   toasted almonds
2 large eggs, separated

3 tablespoons super-fine
   granulated sugar, divided
1 cup heavy cream
¼ cup confectioners' sugar
Pinch of salt
Pinch of cream of tartar

Combine macaroons and almonds. Beat egg yolks with 1 table-spoon granulated sugar until light and lemon colored. In chilled bowl beat cream with confectioners' sugar until stiff. In another bowl beat egg whites with cream of tartar and salt, gradually adding 2 tablespoons granulated sugar, until the meringue holds stiff glossy peaks. Stir all but 1 tablespoon of the almond maca-roon mixture into the yolk mixture; fold in the egg whites and cream. Pour into a greased 9½x2½-inch springform pan and freeze at least 3 hours. Loosen the tortoni from the sides of the pan with a hot knife. Sprinkle remaining macaroon mixture on top and return to freezer until ready to serve.

Yield: 6-8 servings.

Lemon Charlotte

4 lemons, rind and juice
1½ cups sugar
5 eggs
1 pint heavy cream, whipped

2 dozen lady fingers
4 egg whites
½ cup sugar

Dissolve sugar in lemon juice in top of double boiler. Beat 5 eggs; gradually add to lemon mixture, stirring until thickened. Cool. Add cream. Line springform pan with lady fingers; pour in half of mixture; add a layer of lady fingers and rest of mixture. Refriger-ate overnight. Before serving spread top with meringue of 4 egg whites and ½ cup sugar. Brown lightly under broiler.

Yield: 6-8 servings.

Fresh Fruit Romanoff

3 cups raspberries, strawberries
   or sliced peaches
1 pint vanilla ice cream,
   slightly softened

½ pint heavy cream, whipped
1 tablespoon lemon juice
¼ cup Cointreau or brandy
Very fine sugar, to taste

Beat ice cream slightly with a fork and fold gently with whipped cream, lemon juice, Cointreau and sugar. Fold in fruit. Serve immediately.

Note: Ingredients can be prepared ahead and assembled just before serving.

Yield: 8 servings.

Pavlova

4 egg whites, at room
   temperature
¼ teaspoon salt
¼ teaspoon cream of tartar
1 cup fine granulated sugar
4 teaspoons cornstarch

2 teaspoons white wine vinegar
1 teaspoon vanilla
1 cup heavy cream, whipped
3 cups strawberries, sliced
   and sprinkled with sugar
   and Grand Marnier

Beat egg whites with salt and cream of tartar until whites hold a stiff peak. Gradually add sugar, a few tablespoons at a time, beating until whites are stiff and glossy. Beat in cornstarch, then vinegar and vanilla. Butter and lightly flour an 8-inch springform pan. Fill gently with meringue mixture, spreading it higher around the edges than in the center. Bake undisturbed in 275° oven for 1-1¼ hours or until firm and lightly browned. It will remain moist inside. Cool slightly; unmold onto serving plate and cool completely. Just before serving, spread with whipped cream and then the berries.

Note: First made in Melbourne for ballerina Dame Nellie Pavlova.

Yield: 4-6 servings.

Snowball

1 envelope unflavored gelatin	Juice of 2 lemons
¼ cup cold water	Dash of salt
1 cup boiling water	1 pint heavy cream, divided
1 cup sugar	1 small angel food cake
1 cup orange juice	1 cup moist coconut

Dissolve gelatin in cold water. Add boiling water, sugar, orange juice, lemon juice and salt. Mix. Set in refrigerator until half jelled. Whip ½ pint heavy cream until stiff. Add to jelled mixture; result will be runny. Line round 2-quart bowl with waxed paper. Break cake into bite-sized pieces. In the bowl, alternate layers of syrupy mixture and cake bits, beginning and ending with syrupy mixture. Fold over excess of paper. Store in refrigerator, preferably overnight, until firm. To serve, invert bowl on serving dish. Peel paper from mold. Cover with ½ pint stiffly whipped cream and coconut.

Yield: 8 servings.

Strawberry Angel Delight

2 (3 ounce) packages strawberry jello	1 cup heavy cream, whipped, or whipped topping
1 cup boiling water	1 large angel food cake, cubed
1 (16 ounce) package frozen sliced strawberries, slightly thawed	Whipped cream Whole strawberries

Dissolve jello in boiling water. Add berries and allow to partially thicken. Fold in cream or topping. Toss with cake cubes and place in greased springform pan or large mixing bowl. Chill until firm. Turn out on serving dish; frost with whipped cream and garnish with whole berries.

Yield: 10-12 servings.

Hot Gingered Fruit
A Festival of Trees Café Favorite

1 (20 ounce) can sliced
pineapple, drained,
reserve juice
1 (29 ounce) can peach
slices, drained
2 (16 ounce) cans apricot
halves, drained

1 (29 ounce) can pear
slices, drained
10 maraschino cherries,
halved
¾ cup firmly packed light
brown sugar
¼ cup melted margarine
½ teaspoon ground ginger

Reserve 2 tablespoons pineapple juice. Pat fruit dry; arrange all except cherries in 2-quart casserole. Top with cherries. Combine remaining ingredients and reserved pineapple juice in a saucepan. Cook over low heat until sugar melts; pour over fruits. Bake at 325° for 40 minutes. A great winter brunch accompaniment.

Yield: 12 servings.

Chocolate Sauce

10 squares unsweetened
chocolate
2½ cups granulated sugar
2½ teaspoons salt
¼ cup cornstarch

2 cups light corn syrup
1 can evaporated milk
½ cup butter or margarine
¼ cup vanilla

Melt chocolate in top of double boiler. Add dry ingredients, corn syrup and milk. Stir to blend. Heat until smooth. Do not boil. Add butter. When cool, stir in vanilla. Store in a covered glass jar in refrigerator. To heat, place uncovered cold jar in pan of cold water; bring water to a slow boil. Serve over ice cream and/or coconut cake or with fresh fruit.

Yield: 4 cups.

Hawaiian Baklava

1 (16 ounce) package frozen
   phyllo dough
1 cup finely chopped pecans
1 cup finely chopped
   macadamia nuts
1 cup flaked coconut
¼ cup packed brown sugar
1 teaspoon cinnamon

½ teaspoon nutmeg
1 cup butter or
   margarine, melted
¾ cup sugar
¾ cup water
2 tablespoons honey
Juice of one lemon

Thaw phyllo dough at room temperature. Cut sheets in half cross-wise; cover with damp towel. Butter the bottom of a 13x9x2-inch baking pan. Combine the nuts, coconut, brown sugar, cinnamon and nutmeg; set aside. Layer 15 half-sheets of phyllo in the pan, brushing with melted butter between each sheet. Sprinkle half of the nut mixture atop phyllo. Repeat with another 15 phyllo sheets, the remaining nut mixture and butter. Top with remaining phyllo sheets, brushing with butter as above. Score the top into 1½-inch diamonds. Bake in 350° oven 40-45 minutes. Prepare syrup by combining the sugar, water, honey and lemon juice. Boil gently, uncovered, 10 minutes. Remove from heat. Stir in juice. Pour syrup over pastry. Cut into diamonds. Cool.

Yield: 36 pieces.

Hot Lemon Sauce

¼-½ cup sugar
1 tablespoon cornstarch
1 cup water
2-3 tablespoons butter

½ teaspoon grated lemon rind
1½ tablespoons lemon juice
⅛ teaspoon salt

Combine sugar, cornstarch and water; stir until thickened in double boiler over hot, not boiling, water. Remove from heat and stir in remaining ingredients. Serve warm.

Note: Serve over gingerbread or over plain cake and call it Cottage Pudding.

Yield: 1 cup sauce.

Apricot-Banana Shortcake

FILLING
2 tablespoons sugar
1 tablespoon cornstarch
¾ cup unsweetened
   pineapple juice
1 tablespoon lemon juice
½ teaspoon vanilla
2 cups sliced fresh apricots
   (8 medium)
2 medium bananas, sliced

CAKE
2 cups all-purpose flour
2 tablespoons sugar
1 tablespoon baking powder
½ teaspoon salt
½ cup butter or margarine
1 egg, slightly beaten
⅔ cup milk
1 cup whipping cream
2 tablespoons sugar
Toasted coconut (optional)

FILLING: Combine sugar and cornstarch. Stir in pineapple juice. Cook, stirring until thickened and bubbly. Cook and stir 2 minutes more. Remove from heat; stir in lemon juice and vanilla. Fold in apricots and bananas. Cool.

CAKE: Stir together flour, sugar, baking powder and salt. Cut in butter until mixture resembles coarse crumbs. Combine egg and milk; add all at once to flour mixture; stir just to moisten. Spread in greased 8x1½-inch round baking pan; build up edges slightly. Bake at 450° for 15-18 minutes. Cool in pan for 10 minutes. Remove from pan. Split into 2 layers; carefully lift off top layer. Whip cream and sugar just to soft peaks. Spoon filling and whipped cream between layers and over top. Sprinkle with coconut. Serve immediately.

Yield: 8 servings.

Pear Strudel

2 (16 ounce) cans sliced
    pears, drained
½ cup diced pitted dates
⅓ cup sugar
½ teaspoon cinnamon
¼ teaspoon ginger
⅛ teaspoon salt

¾ cup dried bread
    crumbs, divided
½ (16 ounce) package
    phyllo dough
½ cup melted butter
1 egg, beaten
Confectioners' sugar

In a large bowl, mix pears, dates, sugar, cinnamon, ginger, salt, and ¼ cup bread crumbs. On an 18x12-inch sheet of wax paper, place 1 sheet of phyllo; brush with melted butter. (Remember to keep phyllo covered with a damp cloth so that it does not dry.) Repeat the process with each sheet. The sheets are layered as they are buttered. Sprinkle with remaining ½ cup of bread crumbs. Spoon the pear mixture to cover ½ of the dough, starting at one edge. Roll the dough; tuck the ends towards the center. Make 16 slashes with a knife on the top. Place on cookie sheet greased with vegetable shortening. Brush with beaten egg. Bake in 375° oven for 20 minutes; cover lightly with foil and bake an additional 20 minutes. Before serving, sprinkle with confectioners' sugar.

Yield: 8-10 servings.

Caramel Corn

6 quarts popped corn
2 cups brown sugar
1 cup margarine
1 teaspoon salt

1 cup light corn syrup
1 teaspoon vanilla
½ teaspoon baking soda

Bring sugar, margarine, salt, and corn syrup to a boil. Remove from heat; stir in vanilla and baking soda. Slowly pour over popped corn. Mix thoroughly. Bake on greased jelly roll pans in 250° oven for 40-45 minutes. When popcorn is cool enough to handle, break into pieces.

Yield: 6 quarts.

Glazed Pecans

½ cup half-and-half	1 teaspoon vanilla
¼ cup water	4 cups pecan halves
1 cup sugar	

Combine all ingredients except pecans in a medium saucepan; stir well. Place over medium heat, stirring constantly, until sugar dissolves. Continue cooking until mixture registers 220° on candy thermometer. Remove from heat. Add pecans, stirring until well coated. Spread pecans on waxed paper and separate with a fork. Cool.

Yield: 4 cups.

2-Minute Microwave Fudge

1 pound confectioners' sugar	1 teaspoon vanilla
½ cup cocoa	½ cup butter
¼ teaspoon salt	1 cup chopped nuts (optional)
¼ cup milk	

In 1½-cup casserole stir sugar, cocoa, salt, milk and vanilla until partially blended. Put butter on top in center of dish. Microwave on high until mixture feels warm on the bottom. Stir vigorously until smooth. Blend in nuts, pour into wax-paper lined 8-inch square pan. Chill 1 hour in refrigerator or 20-30 minutes in freezer. Cut into squares.

Yield: 48 pieces.

Super-Easy Fudge

½ cup butter or margarine	1 can prepared chocolate
1 (12 ounce) package	fudge frosting
semi-sweet chocolate bits	1 cup chopped nuts

Heat first 3 ingredients in top of double boiler 20-30 minutes to melt bits. Stir occasionally. Beat with electric mixer at low speed over hot water for 2-3 minutes. Add nuts. Pour into a greased 8-inch square pan. Refrigerate until set.

Yield: 64 pieces.

Peanut Butter Balls

1 (18 ounce) jar peanut butter,
  crunchy or plain
2 (16 ounce) boxes
  confectioners' sugar
¾ pound butter

3 teaspoons vanilla
Chopped nuts (optional)
1 (12 ounce) package
  chocolate bits
¼ paraffin cake

Combine peanut butter, sugar, butter, vanilla and nuts. Mix thoroughly until creamy and chill. Make into balls and chill. Melt chocolate bits and paraffin in double boiler over warm water. Dip peanut butter balls into chocolate mixture and place on waxed paper to harden.

Yield: Many.

Danish Carrot Hazelnut Torte

CAKE
7 ounces ground hazelnuts
15 ounces finely
  shredded carrots
½ cup sugar
6 egg whites

FILLING
1 cup apricot marmalade or
  jam, divided
3 ounces marzipan
1 cup heavy cream
3 tablespoons grated
  semi-sweet chocolate

CAKE: Mix first 3 ingredients. Beat egg whites until stiff; fold gently into first mixture and place in two 9½-inch springform pans lined with parchment baking paper. Bake at 375° for 30-40 minutes. Use tester to be sure cakes are done. Cool.

FILLING: Warm jam. Spread 1 layer with ½ the jam. Roll out marzipan and place a layer on top of jam. Cover with remaining jam. Place other layer of cake on top and press to stick. Allow to stand for 2-6 hours. Cover with whipped cream and decorate with chocolate shavings.

Yield: 12-16 servings.

Apple Cheese Torte
A Luncheon Gallery Favorite

14 Pecan Sandy cookies,
  finely rolled
3 tablespoons margarine,
  melted
1 (8 ounce) package cream
  cheese, softened
½ cup sugar, divided

1 egg
1 tablespoon vanilla
4 medium baking apples,
  peeled, cored and thinly
  sliced
2 teaspoons lemon juice
1 teaspoon cinnamon

Combine cookie crumbs and margarine. Press into bottom of 9½x2½-inch springform pan. In small bowl, beat cream cheese, ¼ cup sugar, egg and vanilla at medium speed until smooth. Pour onto prepared crust. Combine apple slices, remaining ¼ cup sugar, lemon juice and cinnamon. Arrange apples in circular pattern on top of cheese mixture. Bake in 450° oven for 10 minutes; reduce heat to 400° and continue baking 25 minutes. Serve warm or chilled. Refrigerate leftovers.

Yield: 8-12 servings.

Chiffon Cake

2¼ cups cake flour, sifted
1½ cups sugar
3 teaspoons baking powder
1 teaspoon salt
¾ cup water
¼ teaspoon almond extract

1 teaspoon vanilla
½ cup oil
5 egg yolks
7 egg whites
½ teaspoon cream of tartar

Sift flour, sugar, baking powder and salt. Mix water, flavorings and oil; add to sifted ingredients; add egg yolks. Beat one minute. In separate bowl, beat egg whites and cream of tartar until very stiff; fold into batter gradually. Bake in ungreased 10-inch tube pan for 65 minutes in 325° oven.

Note: 1 cup cake flour equals 1 cup all-purpose flour minus 2 tablespoons.

Yield: 20 servings.

White Chocolate Cheesecake

CRUST

2 cups graham cracker crumbs
⅓ cup ground blanched
   almonds
¼ cup melted butter

FILLING
8 ounces white chocolate

4 (8 ounce) packages cream
   cheese, softened
½ cup plus 2 tablespoons sugar
4 large eggs
2 large egg yolks
2 tablespoons flour
1 teaspoon vanilla

CRUST: Combine ingredients and pat gently into a 10-inch springform pan. Refrigerate while preparing filling.

FILLING: Melt chocolate in metal bowl over barely simmering water. Stir until smooth. Remove from heat. Beat cream cheese until fluffy; add sugar and beat in eggs and egg yolks 1 at a time. Beat in flour and vanilla. Add chocolate in slow steady stream. Pour filling into crust. Place pan on cookie sheet. Bake in 250° oven for 1 hour or until done.

Optional: Place fresh raspberries on crust before adding the filling, or serve with a raspberry sauce. Cake may be frozen.

Yield: 12 servings.

Imperial Pound Cake

1 pound margarine
   (not low fat)
1 pound confectioners' sugar

6 eggs
3 cups sifted cake flour
2 teaspoons vanilla

Grease angel cake pan all over very thoroughly. Cream margarine and sugar. Add eggs one at a time beating about 1 minute after each addition. Beat in flour and vanilla. Bake at 325° for 1 hour or until cake tester comes out clean. Let set 10 minutes; invert until cake drops. Remove pan to let cake cool.

Note: 1 cup cake flour equals 1 cup all-purpose flour minus 2 tablespoons.

Yield: 30 servings.

Praline Pecan Cheesecake
A Luncheon Gallery Favorite

CRUST
1 package butter-recipe cake mix
½ cup butter or margarine, softened

4 (1.2 ounce) toffee candy bars, coarsely crushed, or 1 (6 ounce) bag brickle-bits

FILLING
3 (8 ounce) packages cream cheese, softened
⅓ cup sugar
3 tablespoons flour
1-1½ teaspoons rum extract
3 eggs

TOPPING
Reserved crumb mixture
½ cup brown sugar, firmly packed
1 cup chopped pecans
⅓ cup caramel ice cream topping

CRUST: Combine cake mix and shortening at low speed until crumbly. Set aside 1 cup of mixture for topping. Press remaining mixture in bottom and 1½ inches up sides of 9 or 10-inch spring-form pan.

FILLING: Combine cream cheese, sugar, flour and rum extract. Add eggs; mix well. Stir in candy. Pour into crust.

TOPPING: Combine reserved crumb mixture, brown sugar and nuts. Sprinkle over filling. Bake in 325° oven for 1¼ hours or until center is firm and top is brown. Remove from oven. Drizzle caramel topping over cake. Bake additional 8 minutes. Cool 30 minutes. Run knife around sides of pan to loosen cake. Cool completely. Remove sides of pan. Store in refrigerator 4-5 hours or overnight.

Note: Cut with wet knife.

Yield: 16 servings.

Coconut Pound Cake
with Christmas Variations

1 pound butter or margarine,
  softened
2 cups sugar
6 large eggs
2 cups flour
7 ounces finely grated coconut
  (double coconut is
  even better)

ADDITIONS FOR
CHRISTMAS CAKE
2 cups golden raisins
1 cup currants
1 cup finely chopped
  almonds or pecans
1 (8 ounce) can crushed
  pineapple, fully drained,
  and soaked with 2
  tablespoons Grand Marnier
8 ounces well-chopped
  candied cherries

Cream butter with sugar. Add eggs, flour and coconut. Make optional additions now. Mix. Bake in well-greased and floured 9-inch Bundt pan for 90 minutes in 350° oven or in two 8x4x2½-inch loaf pans, greased and floured, for 60 minutes. Cool. When just warm, invert to remove. Serve plain or with ice cream and chocolate sauce or with fresh strawberries or raspberries.

Note: Cake keeps indefinitely if well-wrapped and frozen. Cuts well when frozen.

Yield: 10-12 servings, 20-24 Christmas revelers.

Matzo Sponge Cake

9 eggs, separated
1¼ cups sugar

¾ cup matzo cake meal
1 teaspoon vanilla

Beat whites until stiff. Beat yolks and sugar until lemon-colored; fold in beaten whites, then the cake meal and vanilla. Bake in 350° oven, in ungreased 10-inch tube pan, until top springs back when touched lightly, about 40 minutes. Invert pan on funnel; let hang until cake is cold.

Yield: 10-12 servings.

Easy Chocolate Cake

1½ cups sifted flour	¼ teaspoon salt
1 cup sugar	1 cup water
1 teaspoon baking soda	½ cup salad oil
⅓ cup cocoa	1 teaspoon vanilla

Sift together dry ingredients; add water, oil and vanilla. Stir until smooth. Put in greased 9-inch square pan or in single layer cake pan. Bake 25-30 minutes in 350° oven.

Note: Dry ingredients can be mixed and placed in plastic bags for future use at home or away. Add wet ingredients before baking.

Yield: 9 servings.

Low-Fat Chocolate Bundt Cake

2 cups flour	3 (4 ounce) jars puréed
1 cup unsweetened	prune baby food
cocoa powder	2 teaspoons vanilla
2 cups sugar	3 egg whites, beaten
2 teaspoons baking soda	1 cup skim milk
1 teaspoon baking powder	2 tablespoons instant
¼ teaspoon salt	coffee granules
	1 cup boiling water

Sift together first 6 ingredients into mixing bowl. Add baby food, vanilla, egg whites and milk; stir just until blended. Combine coffee and boiling water; stir until dissolved. Stir into batter until blended. Pour into 9-inch Bundt pan sprayed with non-stick spray. Bake at 350° for 40-50 minutes until center tests done with toothpick. Cool cake in pan 10 minutes. Invert onto wire rack.

Note: Baby food replaced 1 cup butter. Only 4 grams of fat in whole cake. Calories per slice, 100-125.

Yield: 12 servings.

Chocolate Carrot Cake

CAKE
2 cups sugar
1 cup vegetable oil
4 eggs
2 teaspoons vanilla
2 cups flour
½ teaspoon salt
1 teaspoon baking soda
1 teaspoon baking powder
1 teaspoon cinnamon
2 cups grated carrots

3 (1 ounce) squares semi-
  sweet chocolate, grated
1 cup finely chopped walnuts

ICING
1 (8 ounce) package cream
  cheese, softened
2 cups sifted confectioners'
  sugar
2-3 tablespoons milk
½ teaspoon vanilla

CAKE: Blend sugar, oil, eggs, and vanilla. Sift together flour, salt, baking soda, baking powder, and cinnamon; add to egg mixture. Add carrots, chocolate and walnuts. Mix well. Pour into a greased and floured 9-inch tube pan. Bake in 350° oven for 1 hour or until cake tester comes out clean.

ICING: Mix ingredients together and frost cake.

Note: Cake keeps well in refrigerator, wrapped in foil, for 2-3 days. Cake, not frosted, may be frozen.

Yield: 10-12 servings.

Chocolate Butter Crumbles

Waverly saltine crackers
1 cup sugar
1 cup butter

1 (12 ounce) package
  semi-sweet chocolate chips
Chopped nuts (optional)

Line cookie sheet with foil and coat with non-stick vegetable spray. Spread a layer of saltines to cover. Bring sugar and butter to a rolling boil; cool slightly and spread on saltines. Bake at 400° for 5 minutes. Remove from oven; sprinkle with chocolate chips. Let stand for 3-5 minutes, then spread like frosting. Top with chopped nuts if desired. Cool in refrigerator and break into pieces.

Yield: 12-15 generous pieces.

Carrot Pineapple Cake

CAKE
2 cups sugar
4 eggs
1½ cups oil
2 cups flour
1½ teaspoons baking soda
2 teaspoons baking powder
2 teaspoons cinnamon
1 teaspoon salt
2 cups shredded carrots

½ cup chopped walnuts
1 (8 ounce) can crushed
 pineapple, drained

ORANGE GLAZE FROSTING
2 cups confectioners'
 sugar, sifted
1 teaspoon vanilla
3 tablespoons orange juice

CAKE: In large bowl combine sugar, eggs and oil. Combine and stir in flour, sifted with baking soda, baking powder, cinnamon and salt. Stir in carrots, walnuts and crushed pineapple. Pour into a greased 9x13x2-inch pan. Bake 45 minutes at 350°. Cool for 10 minutes before frosting.

FROSTING: Mix sifted confectioners' sugar, vanilla and orange juice.

Yield: 12 servings.

Fresh Apple Cake

2 eggs, well beaten
1¼ cups oil
2 cups sugar
2 teaspoons vanilla
2 tablespoons lemon juice
1 tablespoon grated lemon rind
3 cups sifted flour

1 teaspoon salt
1½ teaspoons cinnamon
1½ teaspoons baking soda
3 cups chopped or thinly
 sliced apples
1 cup chopped walnuts
1 cup raisins

Beat eggs; add oil, sugar, vanilla, lemon juice and rind; mix well. Gradually add flour, salt, soda and cinnamon. Stir in apples, nuts and raisins. Pour into greased and floured 10-inch tube pan. Bake in a 350° oven for 1 hour. No frosting is necessary.

Yield: 12-16 servings.

Queen Elizabeth's Date Nut Cake

CAKE

1 cup boiling water
1 cup chopped dates
1 teaspoon baking soda
1 cup sugar
¼ cup butter, softened
1 egg, beaten
1 teaspoon vanilla
1½ cups flour, sifted
1 teaspoon baking powder

1 teaspoon salt
½ cup chopped nuts

FROSTING

5 tablespoons brown sugar
5 tablespoons half-and-half
2 tablespoons butter
¼ cup chopped nuts or
    ¼ cup shredded coconut

CAKE: Combine boiling water, dates and baking soda; let stand. Cream together sugar, butter, egg and vanilla. Combine flour, baking powder, salt and nuts; add to creamed mixture. Add water and date mixture. Mix well. Pour into greased 9x13x2-inch pan. Bake at 350°, testing after 40 minutes.

FROSTING: Boil sugar, cream and butter for 2 minutes. Pour over cake. Sprinkle with nuts or coconut.

Yield: 12-16 servings.

Molasses Spice Cake

½ cup shortening
1 cup sugar
2 tablespoons molasses
1 teaspoon baking soda
1 cup sour milk

2 cups flour
½ teaspoon cinnamon
¼ teaspoon cloves
⅛ teaspoon nutmeg
1 teaspoon salt

Cream shortening. Add sugar and molasses gradually. Dissolve baking soda in milk. Sift together dry ingredients; add to creamed mixture alternating with milk. Beat well. Bake in a greased 8x8x2-inch pan in a 350° oven for 45 minutes.

Note: Sour milk may be made by adding 1 tablespoon vinegar or 1 tablespoon lemon juice to 1 cup milk. Let stand 5 minutes.

Yield: 8-10 servings.

Orange Poppy Seed Loaf Cake

CAKE

3 cups flour
2½ cups sugar
1½ teaspoons salt
1½ teaspoons baking powder
3 eggs
1½ cups milk
1 cup plus 2 tablespoons oil
2 tablespoons poppy seeds

1½ teaspoons vanilla
1½ teaspoons almond extract

GLAZE

¼ cup orange juice
¾ cup sugar
½ teaspoon vanilla
½ teaspoon almond extract
½ teaspoon oil

CAKE: Mix ingredients until smooth. Pour into two 9x5x3-inch greased and floured loaf pans. Bake in 325° oven for 70 minutes. Check at 50 minutes. If browning, cover with foil tent for remaining 20 minutes. Remove from oven. Let cool 10 minutes. Spoon glaze over cake. Allow to set 30 minutes before removing from pan.

GLAZE: While cake is baking, heat ingredients until sugar is dissolved.

Yield: 2 loaves.

Low-Fat Lemon Poppy Seed Cake

CAKE

1 (18½ ounce) package
  yellow cake mix
½ cup sugar
⅓ cup vegetable oil
¼ cup water
1 cup plain non-fat yogurt
1 cup egg substitute

3 tablespoons lemon juice
2 tablespoons poppy seeds

GLAZE

½ cup confectioners'
  sugar, sifted
2 tablespoons lemon juice

CAKE: Combine cake mix and sugar in large bowl. Add oil, water, yogurt, egg substitute, and lemon juice; beat well. Stir in poppy seeds. Pour batter into a 9-cup greased Bundt pan. Bake at 350° for 40-45 minutes until done. Cool for 10 minutes and remove from pan. Drizzle with lemon glaze.

GLAZE: Mix ingredients well.

Yield: 12 servings.

Sour Cream Raisin Spice Cake

1½ cups seedless raisins
2 cups flour, sifted
1½ cups sugar
½ cup cocoa
1 teaspoon salt
1 teaspoon baking soda
1 teaspoon cinnamon
1 teaspoon nutmeg

1 teaspoon cloves
1 cup chopped nuts
1 cup sour cream
2 eggs
3 tablespoons melted
   shortening or oil
1 teaspoon vanilla

Rinse raisins, drain and snip with scissors. (This takes time but is necessary and well worth the effort.) Sift dry ingredients and spices together in a large bowl. Mix in raisins and nuts. Add sour cream, eggs, shortening and vanilla all at once. Beat well and pour into an 8-inch greased tube pan. Bake in a 350° oven for 75 minutes until done. Invert on wire rack 5 minutes before removing from pan. No frosting is necessary.

Yield: 12-16 servings.

Holiday "Strudel"

½ cup butter
¾ cup vanilla ice cream
⅓ cup egg nog
2 cups flour

1 cup slivered almonds
Apricot jam
White raisins (optional)

Mix butter, ice cream, egg nog and flour in food processor. Place dough between two sheets of plastic wrap, the size of a jelly roll pan 10½x15½x1-inch. Gently roll dough out to size of plastic wrap. Roll lengthwise and refrigerate until ready to use. Unroll; remove top layer of plastic wrap. Spread with jam, almonds and raisins. Reroll removing lower layer of plastic wrap. Bake curved slightly to fit pan at 350° for 50 minutes.

Yield: 8 servings.

Banana-Pineapple Cake

CAKE

3 cups flour, sifted
2 cups sugar
1 teaspoon salt
1 teaspoon cinnamon
1 teaspoon baking soda
1 cup chopped almonds
3 eggs
1½ cups vegetable oil
1 teaspoon almond flavoring

2 cups chopped ripe bananas
1 (8 ounce) can crushed
 pineapple

FROSTING

1 (8 ounce) package cream
 cheese
½ cup butter or margarine
1 pound confectioners' sugar
1 tablespoon instant chocolate

CAKE: Mix and sift together the first 5 ingredients. Stir in almonds. Beat eggs slightly; combine with oil, flavoring, bananas and undrained pineapple. Add to dry ingredients; mix thoroughly but do not beat. Spoon into well-oiled 10-inch tube pan. Bake at 325° for 1 hour and 20-25 minutes. Invert on cake rack. Remove pan. Cool thoroughly before frosting. Place cake on plate and frost top and sides. Refrigerate until ready to serve.

FROSTING: Soften cream cheese and butter to room temperature. Cream together with sugar and chocolate.

Options: Substitute other nuts for almonds and use vanilla instead of almond flavoring.

Yield: 12-16 servings.

Chocolate Chip Coconut Bars

1 stick margarine
1 cup graham cracker crumbs
1 cup coconut
1 cup chocolate chips

1 cup chopped walnuts
1 (14 ounce) can sweetened
 condensed milk

Melt margarine in 8-inch square pan. Layer graham cracker crumbs, coconut, chocolate chips and walnuts. Pour condensed milk over top. Bake in a 350° oven for 30 minutes. Let cool; cut into bars.

Yield: 12-16 bars.

Peach Upside-Down Cake

1 cup flour
1 teaspoon baking powder
½ cup plus 3 tablespoons
   unsalted butter, softened
   and divided
½ cup granulated sugar
2 eggs, at room temperature

2 tablespoons peach schnapps
   or brandy
⅔ cup lightly packed dark
   brown sugar
1½ pounds small peaches,
   peeled, pitted and
   quartered

In a small bowl, thoroughly mix the flour and baking powder. In a medium bowl, beat ½ cup butter until pale and creamy, about 2 minutes. Add the granulated sugar and beat until light and fluffy, about 3 minutes. Add the eggs one at a time, beating well after each addition. Fold flour into the batter until no white streaks remain. Stir in the schnapps. In a heavy 9-inch cast iron skillet, melt the 3 tablespoons butter. Add the brown sugar and cook over moderate heat, stirring occasionally, until melted and bubbly, 3-5 minutes. Remove from heat. Arrange the peach quarters in the skillet in 2 tight circles, starting with the outer ring. Cook over moderately high heat until peach juices bubble, about 3 minutes. Remove from heat and quickly turn over each piece of peach. Return to heat and cook 3 minutes longer. Remove from heat. Using a large spoon, evenly distribute the cake batter smoothly over the hot peaches. The batter will swell as it cooks to cover fruit completely. Bake in middle of 375° oven for 20 minutes or until cake tester inserted in the center comes out clean. Let the cake cool for 5 minutes before inverting it onto a large platter. Serve warm or at room temperature with vanilla ice cream or lightly sweetened whipped cream.

Yield: 8 servings.

No-Bake Corn Flake Drops

1 cup semi-sweet morsels
¼ cup light corn syrup

1 tablespoon water
2 cups corn flakes

Melt morsels in top of double boiler. Add corn syrup and water; mix well. Remove from heat. Add corn flakes. Stir until corn flakes are coated. Drop by teaspoon on waxed paper and let set.

Yield: 1½ -2 dozen.

Peanut Butter Blossoms

1¾ cups flour
1 teaspoon baking soda
½ teaspoon salt
½ cup sugar
½ cup firmly packed
  brown sugar

½ cup shortening, softened
½ cup peanut butter
1 egg
2 tablespoons milk
1 teaspoon vanilla
48 milk chocolate candy kisses

Combine all ingredients except candy in large mixing bowl. Mix on lowest speed of mixer until dough forms. Shape dough into balls, using a rounded teaspoonful for each. Roll balls in sugar; place on ungreased cookie sheets. Bake at 375° for 10 minutes. Top each cookie immediately with a candy kiss; press down firmly so cookie cracks around edge.

Yield: 48 cookies.

Peanut Butter Swirl Bars

½ cup crunchy peanut butter
⅓ cup butter or margarine,
  softened
¾ cup granulated sugar
¾ cup brown sugar
2 eggs

2 teaspoons vanilla
1 cup flour
1 teaspoon baking powder
¼ teaspoon salt
1 (12 ounce) package
  chocolate chips

In a large bowl beat peanut butter, butter and the 2 sugars until creamy. Add eggs and vanilla; mix well. Combine flour, baking powder and salt. Add gradually to creamed mixture. Stir well. Spread in a greased 13x9x2-inch pan. Sprinkle chocolate chips evenly over dough. Bake 5 minutes at 350°; remove from oven and run a knife through chips to marbleize. Return to oven; bake 20 minutes more. Cut into 1x2-inch bars before they cool.

Yield: 4 dozen bars.

Black and White Cookies

½ cup shortening, softened
2 squares unsweetened
   chocolate, melted
1 egg
1 cup brown sugar
1 teaspoon vanilla

1⅔ cups flour
½ teaspoon baking soda
½ teaspoon salt
½ cup milk
½ cup chopped walnuts

Cream shortening and chocolate together. In another bowl mix egg, sugar and vanilla. Add egg mixture to shortening mixture. Gradually add flour, salt, baking soda and milk. Mix well. Add nuts. Drop by heaping teaspoonful on greased cookie sheet. Bake at 350° for 10-12 minutes. Frost half of each cookie with a vanilla frosting and the other half with a chocolate frosting.

Yield: 36 cookies.

Chocolate Chocolate Chip Cookies

2 cups butter, softened
2 cups granulated sugar
2 cups brown sugar
4 eggs
2 teaspoons vanilla
4 cups flour
5 cups oatmeal, finely
   chopped in blender

1 teaspoon salt
2 teaspoons baking powder
2 teaspoons baking soda
1 (8 ounce) chocolate bar,
   grated or finely chopped
2 (12 ounce) packages
   chocolate chips
3 cups chopped nuts

Cream sugars into butter. Beat eggs into the mixture and add vanilla. Mix dry ingredients into creamed mixture. Stir in grated chocolate bar, chocolate chips and nuts. Shape into 1-inch balls and place on ungreased cookie sheet 2-inches apart. Flatten slightly. Bake in 375° oven 8-10 minutes.

Yield: 100 cookies.

Chocolate Macaroons

2 egg whites
¼ teaspoon salt
½ cup sugar
½ teaspoon vanilla

1 (6 ounce) package semi-sweet
  chocolate pieces, melted
1½ cups shredded coconut

Beat egg whites until foamy; add salt. Sift sugar, gradually add to egg whites, beating well after each addition, until mixture stands in peaks. Fold in vanilla, cooled melted chocolate and coconut. Drop from teaspoon onto ungreased cookie sheets covered with brown paper. Bake in 325° oven for 20 minutes. Cool before removing from paper.

Yield: 24 cookies.

Viennese Brownies

CAKE
2 ounces unsweetened
  chocolate
½ cup butter or margarine
1 cup sugar
¾ cup flour
½ teaspoon baking powder
½ teaspoon salt
2 eggs

FILLING
1 (8 ounce) package cream
  cheese, softened
⅓ cup sugar
1 egg, beaten
¼ teaspoon vanilla

CAKE: Melt chocolate and butter together. Combine sugar, flour, baking powder and salt; add to chocolate mixture. Add eggs and mix well. Pour half chocolate mixture into a greased 8-inch pan. Spread with cream cheese mixture. Add remaining chocolate mixture. Bake in a 350° oven for 45 minutes. Let cool; cut into bars.

FILLING: Combine all ingredients and mix well.

Yield: 12-16 bars.

Chocolate Layered Squares

FIRST LAYER
2 ounces unsweetened
   baking chocolate
½ cup butter
2 eggs, beaten
1 cup sugar
½ cup flour
1 cup chopped nuts
1 teaspoon vanilla

SECOND LAYER
1½ cups confectioners' sugar
½ cup butter, softened
½ cup heavy cream

THIRD LAYER
2 ounces unsweetened
   baking chocolate
1 tablespoon butter

FIRST LAYER: Over very low heat, melt the chocolate and butter. Set aside to cool slightly. Add the eggs, sugar, flour, nuts and vanilla. Spread evenly in a 9x13x2-inch pan. Bake for 10 minutes at 350°.

SECOND LAYER: Combine the confectioners' sugar, butter and cream; cook over low heat to the soft ball stage, about 20-25 minutes. Spread over baked layer.

THIRD LAYER: Melt the chocolate and butter over very low heat. Drizzle over the top of the second layer. Cool until set; cut into squares.

Yield: 2½ dozen.

Molasses Oatmeal Cookies

1¾ cups flour
1 teaspoon baking powder
½ teaspoon salt
1 teaspoon baking soda
1 teaspoon cinnamon
1¼ cups sugar
⅓ cup molasses

2 eggs, beaten
½ cup melted shortening
   or vegetable oil
2 cups rolled oats
½ cup chopped walnuts or
   other nuts (optional)
1 cup raisins or chopped dates

Sift together flour, baking powder, salt, baking soda and cinnamon. Mix sugar, molasses, eggs and shortening. Add to dry ingredients. Add oats, nuts and raisins. Mix well. Chill dough for 15 minutes. Drop by teaspoon on greased baking sheet. Bake in a 350° oven for 12-15 minutes.

Note: May bake as needed rather than all at once.

Yield: 3-4 dozen.

Cherry Flakes

2¼ cups sifted flour
1 teaspoon baking powder
½ teaspoon baking soda
½ teaspoon salt
1 cup sugar
¾ cup butter or margarine
2 eggs
2 tablespoons milk

1 teaspoon vanilla
1 cup chopped pecans
   or walnuts
1 cup cut dates
½ cup chopped maraschino
   cherries, drained
2½ cups crushed corn flakes
30 maraschino cherries

Sift together and set aside flour, baking powder, baking soda and salt. Add sugar to softened shortening; cream well. Blend in eggs, milk and vanilla. Add the dry ingredients; mix thoroughly. Stir in nuts, dates and chopped cherries. If desired, chill dough for easier handling. Drop rounded teaspoons of dough onto crushed corn flakes; coat thoroughly forming into balls. Place on greased baking sheet; top each with half a maraschino cherry. Bake at 350° for 12-15 minutes.

Yield: 5 dozen.

World's Best Cookies

1 cup butter
1 cup sugar
1 cup brown sugar,
   firmly packed
1 egg
1 cup oil
1 teaspoon vanilla
1 cup rolled oats

1 cup crushed corn flakes
½ cup shredded coconut
½ cup chopped walnuts
   or pecans
3½ cups flour, sifted
1 teaspoon baking soda
1 teaspoon salt

Cream butter and sugars until light and fluffy. Add egg, oil and vanilla; mix well. Add oats, corn flakes, coconut and nuts; mix well. Add flour, salt and baking soda; mix well. Form into walnut-size balls and place on an ungreased cookie sheet. Flatten with a fork dipped in cold water. Bake for 12 minutes at 325°. Allow to cool a few minutes before removing from pan.

Yield: 8 dozen cookies.

Nutmeg Cookie Logs

3 cups flour
1 teaspoon nutmeg
1 cup butter or margarine,
    softened
2 teaspoons vanilla

3 teaspoons rum extract
¾ cup sugar
1 egg
Nutmeg

Sift together flour and nutmeg. Cream butter, vanilla, rum extract and sugar. Blend in egg and the dry ingredients gradually; mix thoroughly. Shape pieces of dough on lightly floured surface into long roll, ½-inch in diameter. Cut into 3-inch lengths; place on ungreased baking sheets. Bake at 350° for 12-15 minutes. Cool. Frost with creamy frosting. Sprinkle with nutmeg.

Yield: Approximately 6 dozen.

Sesame Seed Twist Cookies

1½ cups sugar
1 cup shortening, softened
6 eggs, reserve 1
1 teaspoon anise extract
2 teaspoons vanilla
Grated peel of 1 lemon
5 cups flour

1 teaspoon salt
1 teaspoon baking powder
½ teaspoon baking soda
1 teaspoon nutmeg
¾ cup milk or eggnog,
    divided
Sesame seeds

Cream together sugar and shortening. Add 5 eggs, anise extract, vanilla and lemon peel. Sift together flour, salt, baking powder, baking soda and nutmeg. Add dry ingredients to creamed mixture and add ½ cup milk or eggnog. Mix dough well. If too soft, refrigerate for an hour. Using a rounded tablespoon of dough, roll between hands until about 8 inches long. Put ends together and twist. Place on a greased cookie sheet. Brush cookies with beaten mixture of 1 egg and ¼ cup milk or eggnog. Sprinkle with sesame seeds. Bake at 350°, until light brown on bottom, 20-25 minutes.

Yield: Approximately 5 dozen.

Kourabiedes
Greek Wedding Cookies

1 pound sweet butter	3 tablespoons brandy
½ cup confectioners' sugar	⅓ cup orange juice
2 egg yolks, beaten	1 teaspoon baking powder
⅔ cup blanched almonds,	4½-5 cups flour
finely chopped	Confectioners' sugar

Cream softened butter until very light; beat in sugar, egg yolks, almonds, brandy and orange juice. Sift baking powder with flour and blend into butter mixture. Shape into small balls or crescents and bake on ungreased baking sheet at 350° for 15-20 minutes until lightly golden. Sift confectioners' sugar on waxed paper; place cookies on sugar and sift additional sugar on tops and sides. Cool before storing.

Yield: 36 cookies.

Lebkuchen
German Christmas Cookie

COOKIE

1 pound dark brown sugar	¼ teaspoon cloves
3 tablespoons butter, softened	Pecan halves
3 eggs	
2 cups flour	**ICING**
2 teaspoons baking powder	1½ cups confectioners'
1 teaspoon cinnamon	sugar, sifted
1 teaspoon nutmeg	3 drops almond extract
	Milk

COOKIE: Beat sugar, butter and eggs well. Sift flour, baking powder and spices together; slowly add to sugar mixture. Spread evenly in a greased 10½x15½x1-inch pan. Bake 20-25 minutes at 375° or until toothpick comes out clean. Cut into bars; frost immediately and top with pecan halves. May need to be cut again as they are removed from pan.

ICING: Mix sugar with almond extract. Add enough milk to moisten and make a smooth consistency.

Yield: Approximately 30 bars.

Pfeffernüsse
German Christmas Cookie

1 quart dark corn syrup	1 teaspoon cinnamon
½ pound butter	½ teaspoon cloves
2 teaspoons baking soda	½ teaspoon allspice
1 cup sugar	11 cups flour
1 teaspoon pepper	¼ cup brandy, generous
½ teaspoon ginger	

Put syrup and butter into a large pot; bring to boil. Remove from heat. Add baking soda. Pour over dry ingredients that have been sifted together. Add brandy; mix well. Shape dough into sausage-like rolls. Refrigerate overnight. Cut into desired size. Bake on greased cookie sheet in 350° oven for 10-15 minutes. Dust with confectioners' sugar if desired. Cookies will keep indefinitely stored in tightly covered container.

Yield: Approximately 6 dozen.

Rugalach

COOKIE DOUGH

1 (8 ounce) package cream cheese, softened

1 cup butter or margarine, softened

2 cups flour

FILLING

½ cup sugar

1½ teaspoons cinnamon

½ cup brown sugar

1 cup finely chopped nuts

1 tablespoon butter, melted

Cream butter, flour and cream cheese together. Refrigerate for 2-3 hours. Mix filling ingredients together. Roll dough into 3 or 4 nine-inch circles. Cut each circle into 16 triangles. Sprinkle filling over all the triangles. Roll from wide end of triangle to point. Place point side down on cookie sheet. Bake in a 350° oven for 20 minutes. Store in refrigerator. May be frozen.

Note: Optional fillings: commercial poppy seed filling, fruit conserve or marmalade.

Yield: 48-64 cookies.

Angel Whispers

COOKIE
1 cup butter or margarine, softened
½ cup confectioners' sugar
1 teaspoon lemon extract
2 cups flour, sifted
¼ teaspoon salt

FILLING
1 egg, slightly beaten
⅔ cup sugar
3 tablespoons lemon juice
1½ tablespoons butter, softened
Grated lemon peel

COOKIE: Cream butter to consistency of mayonnaise. Add confectioners' sugar, and while continuing to beat, add lemon extract, flour and salt. Blend well and chill. Form into balls using level teaspoon of dough. Flatten slightly. Place on ungreased cookie sheet 1 inch apart. Bake 8-10 minutes at 400° or until edges are slightly brown. Cool. Put lemon filling between two cookies.

FILLING: Blend ingredients together in double boiler and cook, stirring constantly, until thickened. Chill until firm.

Yield: 5 dozen double cookies.

Apricot Balls

2 pounds dried apricots, finely chopped
1 can sweetened condensed milk

3 cups coconut
1 cup chopped walnuts
Confectioners' sugar

Combine first 4 ingredients. Stir and make into walnut-size balls. Roll in confectioners' sugar.

Yield: 3-4 dozen balls, depending on size.

Rum Balls

3 cups crushed vanilla wafers
1 cup finely chopped nuts
2 cups confectioners' sugar
4 tablespoons cocoa
½ cup rum

¼ cup light corn syrup
Granulated sugar (optional)
Chopped nuts (optional)
Sprinkles (optional)

Mix dry ingredients; add corn syrup and rum. Mix well. Shape into balls. Roll in granulated sugar, nuts or sprinkles.

Yield: Depends on size of balls.

Honey Walnut Balls

1 cup butter (not margarine),
  softened
½ cup confectioners'
  sugar, sifted
2 tablespoons honey

2 cups flour
¾ cup chopped walnuts
1 teaspoon vanilla
¼ teaspoon salt
Confectioners' sugar, sifted

In a large mixing bowl beat together butter, the ½ cup confectioners' sugar, and honey. Add flour, walnuts, vanilla and salt; mix thoroughly, using hands if necessary. Shape into 1-inch balls. Place 1½ inches apart on a greased cookie sheet. Bake in a 325° oven, 14-16 minutes or until the cookies are barely tinged with brown. While cookies are still warm, roll in confectioners' sugar. Cool. Roll cookies in confectioners' sugar again.

Yield: 48 cookies.

Caramel Apple Bars

CRUST
½ cup butter or margarine
¼ cup vegetable shortening
1 cup brown sugar, packed
1¾ cups flour
1 cup oatmeal, dry
1 teaspoon salt
½ teaspoon baking soda
½ cup chopped pecans
  (optional)

FILLING
4½ cups peeled and coarsely
  chopped apples
3 tablespoons flour
1 (14 ounce) package caramels
3 tablespoons butter
  or margarine

CRUST: Cream butter, shortening and brown sugar until fluffy. Add flour, oatmeal, salt and baking soda; mix well. Stir in pecans. Reserve 2 cups. Press remaining mixture into 13x9x2-inch baking pan.

FILLING: Toss apples with flour and spoon over crust. In a saucepan melt the caramels and butter over low heat. Drizzle over apples. Top with reserved oatmeal mixture. Bake in 400° oven for 25-30 minutes, until lightly browned. Cool before cutting into bars. Serve plain or with ice cream or whipped cream.

Yield: Approximately 42 bars.

Glazed Walnut Bars

BARS
1 cup flour
¼ cup butter
2 eggs
1½ cups brown sugar, packed
1 teaspoon vanilla
2 tablespoons flour
¼ teaspoon baking soda

½ teaspoon salt
1 cup chopped walnuts
½ cup coconut

GLAZE
⅔ cup confectioners'
    sugar, sifted
1-2 tablespoons orange juice

Cut shortening into 1 cup flour and press in bottom of greased 11x7x2-inch pan. Bake in a 350° oven for 10 minutes until brown. Mix eggs, brown sugar and vanilla; add 2 tablespoons flour, soda and salt. Add nuts and coconut. Mix well and spread over baked layer. Return to oven and bake for 20 minutes. Cool. Mix confectioners' sugar and orange juice; spread over baked mixture. Cut into bars.

Yield: 12-16 bars.

Lemon Squares

2 cups flour
1 cup butter (or half butter,
    half margarine), softened
½ cup confectioners' sugar
4 eggs, beaten
2 cups granulated sugar

½ teaspoon salt
6 tablespoons lemon juice
¼ cup flour
2 teaspoons confectioners'
    sugar
Grated rind of 2 lemons

Cream together the 2 cups flour, butter and ½ cup confectioners' sugar. Spread evenly in a 13x9x2-inch pan. Bake at 350° for 15 minutes. Crust should be a pale gold at edge. In a bowl, mix eggs, granulated sugar and salt; blend in lemon juice. Sift ¼ cup flour and 2 teaspoons confectioners' sugar into egg mixture; fold in. Stir in lemon rind by hand. Pour mixture over crust and return to oven for 30 minutes. Sift confectioners' sugar over top after taking from the oven, if desired.

Yield: 12-15 squares.

INDEX

A

Angel Hair Pasta with Broccoli 107
Angel Whispers 238
APPETIZERS
  Aram Sandwiches 21
  Asparagus Roll-Ups 22
  Baked Carrot Spread 18
  Banana Rumaki 22
  Borekas 23
  Cheese Crisps 27
  Cheese Petit Fours 28
  Chicken Liver Pâté 33
  Chicken Wings 23
  Chili con Queso 19
  Chipped Beef Dip 18
  Crabmeat Spread 31
  Crustless Zucchini Quiche 26
  Danish Cheese Mold 28
  Deviled Ham Mousse 34
  Devilish Pâté 30
  Fruited Cheese Log 29
  Gouda Cup 29
  Great Guacamole 20
  Green Pepper Jelly 34
  Hot Chili Dip 18
  Hot Crab Puffs 30
  "Hot" Cream Cheese Topping 29
  Hot Mushroom Cocktail Spread 19
  Hot Mushroom Turnovers 25
  Hummus 20
  Lobster (or Seafood) Spread 31
  Nut-Filled Brie 27
  Raw Vegetable Pizza 26
  Roasted Garlic Canapés 22
  Rosemary Cheese Wafers 30
  Rye Cheese Delights 28
  Salmon Ball 32
  Sausage Biscuit Bites 24
  Seafood Cream Cheese Spread 32
  Shrimp Dip 20
  Shrimp Mousse 33
  Spinach Balls 25
  Swedish Meatballs 149
  Taco Dip 21
  Tiny Broccoli Quiches 24
  Turkey Ball 33
APPLES
  Apple Cheese Torte 218
  Apple Danish 51
  Apple Squash Bake 191
  Apple-Brandy Pork Chops 158
  Apples Under Glaze 166
  Baked Sausage with Apples 162
  Braised Celery and Apple Medley 180
  Caramel Apple Bars 239
  Chicken Waldorf Salad 92
  Cottage Cole Slaw 82

Fresh Apple Cake 224
Hot Apple Oatmeal 60
Lemon Cream Cheese Salad 79
Pumpkin-Apple Pie 201
Variegated Salad 88
APRICOTS
  Apricot Balls 238
  Apricot Refresher 36
  Apricot Sauce for Ham 164
  Apricot-Banana Shortcake 214
  Lemon Cream Pie with
    Apricot Sauce 200
Aram Sandwiches 21
ASPARAGUS
  Asparagus Roll-Ups 22
  Danish Fish Bake 123
  Fresh Asparagus and Ham Pie 160
Autumn Soup 72
Avgolemono Soup 71

B

Baked Carrot Spread 18
Baked Crabmeat Salad 115
Baked Dilled Carrots 177
Baked Hash Browns 186
Baked Orange-Pineapple Chicken 133
Baked Pineapple 166
Baked Rice 109
Baked Sausage with Apples 162
Baked Tomato Macaroni 111
Balsamic Vinaigrette Salad Dressing 98
BANANAS
  Apricot-Banana Shortcake 214
  Banana Rumaki 22
  Banana-Pineapple Cake 228
Barley Bake 112
Barm Brack Bread 53
Basque Potato Soup 69
BEANS
  24-Hour Bean Salad 81
  Busy People's Beans 175
  Celebrity Chili 152
  Chuck Wagon Calico Beans 163
  Country Herb Soup 78
  Green Bean Salad 80
  Green Beans in Olive Oil 174
  Herbed White Bean Salad 81
  Lemon-Walnut Green Beans 174
  Minestrone 77
  Pasta e Fagioli 74
  Peasant Bean Soup 65
  San Diego Relish 96
  Sweet and Sour Bean Casserole 175
  Tour-R-Lou 195
  Union Street Lunch's
    Bacon-Bean Soup 66
  Vegetarian Cholent 176

INDEX

BEEF
Beef and Sausage Stew 147
Beef Stroganoff Dèja Vu 145
Beef Wellington with
    Mushroom Pâté 142
Bobotie 156
Celebrity Chili 152
Cheesy Beef and Pasta in a Pot 108
Chuck Wagon Calico Beans 163
Cold Corned Beef Loaf 152
Elegant Calves' Liver 170
Erster Sauerbraten 146
Five Hour Stew 147
Grilled Salisbury Steaks 150
Jewish Pot Roast 145
Liver Baked with Onion and Herbs ... 167
Meatball Soup 76
Mexican Lasagna 107
Moussaka 155
No-Boil Lasagna 109
Red Flannel Hash 151
Reuben Sandwich Casserole 102
Shaker Braised Flank Steak 144
Sirloin Tip Casserole 143
Sour Cream Steak 143
Status Stew 148
Stir-Fry Steak Slices
    with Winter Radishes 144
Surprise Beef Patties 149
Swedish Meatballs 149
Taco Salad 90
Tailgaters' Loaf 151
Tourtière 158
Twin Meat Loaves 148
Zweiter Sauerbraten 146
Beer Bread 42
Berenjena Español 182
Berry Patch Muffins 48
Best 'Wurst Sandwich 100
Better Than Eggnog 35
BEVERAGES
Apricot Refresher 36
Better Than Eggnog 35
Champagne Punch 38
Cranberry Holiday Drink 39
Geppel's Gloggs 40
Holiday Wassail 39
Irish Cream Whiskey 40
Kahlua 39
Madison Avenue Punch 38
Mulled Cider 37
Popular Party Punch 35
Shaker Cold Rhubarb Tea 35
Shaker Mocha "Punch" 36
Spicy Tea Punch 36
Sunshine Punch 37
Biscuit Tortoni 209
Black and White Cookies 231
Blend of the Bayou 121

Blueberry Coffee Cake 42
Bobotie 156
Borekas 23
Braised Carrots and Turnips 178
Braised Celery and Apple Medley 180
Bran Muffins – For Your Heart's Sake ... 49
Bran Muffins for Busy Bakers 48
Brandy Alexander Pie 198
Bread Pudding with Whiskey Sauce 205
Breaded Parsnips with Rosemary 184
BREADS
Apple Danish 51
Barm Brack Bread 53
Beer Bread 42
Blueberry Coffee Cake 42
Cherry Coffee Cake 43
Corn Bread 44
Cranberry Nut Bread 45
English Tea Scones 50
Healthy Heart Scones 50
Irish Soda Bread 47
Italian Herb Bread 53
Lemon Bread 46
Oatmeal Molasses Bread 54
Olibollen 56
Orange Nut Coffee Cake 44
Pear Nut Bread 46
Praline Biscuits 52
Pretzels 57
Rhubarb Coffee Cake 43
Sour Cream Cheese Coffee Cake 45
Spoon Bread 60
Zucchini Bread 47
BROCCOLI
Angel Hair Pasta with Broccoli 107
Broccoli Puff 175
Broccoli Salad 91
Broccoli Salad with Basil Dressing 82
Broccoli-Cheese Casserole 177
Cream of Broccoli Soup 66
Parmesan Vegetable Tossed Salad 88
Tiny Broccoli Quiches 24
Brother James' Cabbage Soup 67
Brother James' Rhubarb
    Bread Pudding 206
Busy People's Beans 175

C

CABBAGE
Brother James' Cabbage Soup 67
Colcannon 186
Cottage Cole Slaw 82
Crunchy Noodle Salad 95
Farmers' Soup/Stew 73
Spicy Cole Slaw 83
Sweet and Sour Red Cabbage 177
Caesar Salad with Grilled Chicken 90
CAKES
Apricot-Banana Shortcake 214

Banana-Pineapple Cake 228
Carrot Pineapple Cake 224
Chiffon Cake 218
Chocolate Carrot Cake 223
Coconut Pound Cake 221
Easy Chocolate Cake 222
Fresh Apple Cake 224
Frozen Chocolate Mousse Cake 208
Hot Fudge Pudding Cake 204
Imperial Pound Cake 219
Low-Fat Chocolate Bundt Cake 222
Low-Fat Lemon Poppy Seed Cake ... 226
Matzo Sponge Cake 221
Molasses Spice Cake 225
Orange Poppy Seed Loaf Cake 226
Peach Upside-Down Cake 229
Queen Elizabeth's Date Nut Cake 225
Sour Cream Raisin Spice Cake 227

CANDY
2-Minute Microwave Fudge 216
Apricot Balls 238
Caramel Corn 215
Glazed Pecans 216
Peanut Butter Balls 217
Super Easy Fudge 216

Caramel Apple Bars 239
Caramel Corn 215
Carolina Crabmeat Quiche 114

CARROTS
Baked Carrot Spread 18
Baked Dilled Carrots 177
Braised Carrots and Turnips 178
Carrot Leek Soup 64
Carrot Pineapple Cake 224
Carrot Soup 64
Chocolate Carrot Cake 223
Danish Carrot Hazelnut Torte 217
Honey and Brandy Glazed Carrots .. 178
Marinated Carrots 95

CASSEROLES
Apple Squash Bake 191
Baked Rice 109
Barley Bake 112
Berenjena Español 182
Blend of the Bayou 121
Bobotie 156
Broccoli-Cheese Casserole 177
Celebrity Chili 152
Cheddary Ham 'n Eggs Casserole 104
Cheesy Beef and Pasta in a Pot 108
Chicken and Sausage with Rice 132
Chicken Casserole with
    Avocado Garnish 137
Chicken 'n Stuffing Casserole 131
Corn Pudding 180
Creole Praline Yam Casserole 194
Danish Fish Bake 123
Gourmet Potatoes 187
Hot Chicken Salad 131

Hot Seafood Salad Supreme 119
Macaroni and Cheese, Welsh Style 110
Mushroom Casserole 182
Mushroom Strata 183
Mushroom-Rice-Nut Casserole 108
Poulet Blanchard 128
Red Flannel Hash 151
Seafood Casserole 115
Shrimp and Artichoke Casserole 118
Sirloin Tip Casserole 143
Southwestern Corn Bake 180
Sweet and Sour Bean Casserole 175
Tour-R-Lou 195
Turkey Noodle Casserole 140

CAULIFLOWER
Cold Cauliflower Salad 83
Latke-Crusted Cauliflower Pie 179
Parmesan Vegetable Tossed Salad 88
Celebrity Chili 152

CEREALS
Granola 60
Hot Apple Oatmeal 60
Champagne Punch 38

CHEESE
Broccoli-Cheese Casserole 177
Cheddar-Potato Soup 70
Cheddary Ham 'n Eggs Casserole 104
Cheese Crisps 27
Cheese Petit Fours 28
Cheese Soufflé 104
Cheese Soup 71
Cheese-Tomato Pie 193
Cheesy Beef and Pasta in a Pot 108
Cheesy Summer Squash 192
Danish Cheese Mold 28
Fruited Cheese Log 29
Gouda Cup 29
Gourmet Potatoes 187
Ham and Cheese Ring 161
"Hot" Cream Cheese Topping 29
Macaroni and Cheese, Welsh Style 110
Nut-Filled Brie 27
Old-fashioned Baked Eggs 105
Quesadillas with Three Cheeses 165
Rosemary Cheese Wafers 30
Rye Cheese Delights 28
Seafood Cream Cheese Spread 32
Spanakopeta 164
Turkey-Cheese-Mushroom Timbale ... 138

CHERRIES
Cherry Coffee Cake 43
Cherry Flakes 234
Duckling with Black Cherry Sauce ... 141
Spicy Cherry Glaze for Ham 165

CHICKEN
Baked Orange-Pineapple Chicken 133
Caesar Salad with Grilled Chicken 90
Chicken and Pasta in
    Hot and Sour Peanut Sauce 127

INDEX

Chicken and Pasta Salad 91
Chicken and Sausage with Rice 132
Chicken Breast Veronique 136
Chicken Breasts Provençal 133
Chicken Casserole with
   Avocado Garnish 137
Chicken Fricassee with Dumplings ... 130
Chicken Imperial 134
Chicken in Phyllo 135
Chicken Liver Pâté 33
Chicken Livers in Foil 137
Chicken 'n Stuffing Casserole 131
Chicken Stew 129
Chicken Waldorf Salad 92
Chicken Wings 23
Chinese Chicken Salad 89
Ham-Chicken Bake 160
Hot Chicken Salad 131
Mediterranean Chicken 129
Pineapple Chicken Stir-Fry 127
Poulet Blanchard 128
Stuffed Chicken Breasts
   with Proscuitto, Mozzarella 134
Stuffed Ham Rolls with
   Creamed Chicken Sauce 162
Thai Curry Chicken
   with Vegetables 128
Vintage Chicken 136
Wine-Baked Chicken
   and Artichoke Hearts 135
Chiffon Cake 218
Chili con Queso 19
Chinese Chicken Salad 89
Chipped Beef Dip 18

CHOCOLATE
2-Minute Microwave Fudge 216
Black and White Cookies 231
Chocolate Bread Pudding 205
Chocolate Butter Crumbles 223
Chocolate Carrot Cake 223
Chocolate Chip Coconut Bars 228
Chocolate Chip Nut Pie..................... 198
Chocolate Chocolate Chip Cookies ... 231
Chocolate Layered Squares 233
Chocolate Macaroons 232
Chocolate Mousse 208
Chocolate Sauce 212
Chocolate Soufflés 207
Easy Chocolate Cake 222
Frozen Chocolate Mousse Cake 208
Hot Fudge Pudding Cake 204
Jiffy Low-Cal Pot de Crème 206
Low-Fat Chocolate Bundt Cake 222
No-Bake Corn Flake Drops 229
Peanut Butter Balls 217
Peanut Butter Blossoms..................... 230
Peanut Butter Swirl Bars 230
Rum Balls 238
Super-Easy Fudge 216

Turtle Pie.. 203
Viennese Brownies 232
White Chocolate Cheesecake 219
Chuck Wagon Calico Beans.................... 163
Coconut Pound Cake 221
Colcannon 186
Cold Cauliflower Salad 83
Cold Corned Beef Loaf 152
Cold Cucumber-Dill Sauce 125
Cold Peach Soup 62

COOKIES
Angel Whispers 238
Black and White Cookies 231
Cherry Flakes 234
Chocolate Butter Crumbles 223
Chocolate Chocolate Chip Cookies 231
Chocolate Macaroons 232
Glazed Walnut Bars 240
Honey Walnut Balls 239
Kourabiedes 236
Lebkuchen 236
Molasses Oatmeal Cookies 233
No-Bake Corn Flake Drops 229
Nutmeg Cookie Logs 235
Peanut Butter Blossoms..................... 230
Peanut Butter Swirl Bars 230
Pfeffernüsse 237
Rugalach 237
Rum Balls 238
Sesame Seed Twist Cookies 235
World's Best Cookies 234
Corn Bread 44
Corn Pudding.. 180
Cottage Cole Slaw 82
Country Griddlecakes 59
Country Herb Soup 78
Crabmeat Delight 114
Crabmeat Rice Salad 93
Crabmeat Spread 31

CRANBERRIES
Cranberry Butter 55
Cranberry Holiday Drink 39
Cranberry Muffins 49
Cranberry Nut Bread 45
Cranberry Relish 167
Cranberry Soufflé Salad 79
Double Fruit Pancakes....................... 58
Fresh Cranberry Waffles 58
Cream of Broccoli Soup 66
Cream of Celery Soup 67
Cream of Mushroom Soup 68
Creamy Anchovy-Dill Salad Dressing 97
Creamy Citrus Salad Dressing 97
Creamy Rice Pudding 203
Creole Praline Yam Casserole 194
Crunchy Noodle Salad............................ 95
Crunchy Red Potato Salad 85
Crustless Zucchini Quiche 26
Cucumber With Cumin and Yogurt 83

Cucumber-Yogurt Soup 63

D

Dandelions in Olive Oil 181
Danish Carrot Hazelnut Torte 217
Danish Cheese Mold 28
Danish Fish Bake 123
DATES
    Queen Elizabeth's Date Nut Cake 225
    Upside-Down Date Pudding 204
DESSERTS *(See Cakes, Cookies,*
    Pies, and Sauces also)
    Apple Cheese Torte 218
    Biscuit Tortoni 209
    Caramel Apple Bars 239
    Chocolate Chip Coconut Bars 228
    Chocolate Layered Squares 233
    Chocolate Mousse 208
    Chocolate Soufflés 207
    Danish Carrot Hazelnut Torte 217
    Fresh Fruit Romanoff 210
    Hawaiian Baklava 213
    Holiday "Strudel" 227
    Hot Gingered Fruit 212
    Jiffy Low-Cal Pot de Crème 206
    Lemon Charlotte 209
    Lemon Squares 240
    Pavlova 210
    Pear Strudel 215
    Praline Pecan Cheesecake 220
    Snowball 211
    Strawberry Angel Delight 211
    Viennese Brownies 232
    White Chocolate Cheesecake 219
Deviled Eggs with Mushrooms 105
Deviled Ham Mousse 34
Devilish Pâté 30
DIPS/SPREADS
    Baked Carrot Spread 18
    Chicken Liver Pâté 33
    Chili con Queso 19
    Chipped Beef Dip 18
    Crabmeat Spread 31
    Cranberry Butter 55
    Deviled Ham Mousse 34
    Devilish Pâté 30
    Gouda Cup 29
    Gourmet Tuna Spread 99
    Great Guacamole 20
    Green Pepper Jelly 34
    Hot Chili Dip 18
    "Hot" Cream Cheese Topping 29
    Hot Mushroom Cocktail Spread 19
    Hummus 20
    Lobster (or Seafood) Spread 31
    Roasted Garlic Canapés 22
    Salmon Ball 32
    Seafood Cream Cheese Spread 32
    Shrimp Dip 20

Shrimp Mousse 33
Taco Dip 21
Turkey Ball 33
Double Fruit Pancakes 58
DUCK
    Duckling with Black Cherry Sauce ... 141
    Roast Duckling 139

E

Easy Chocolate Cake 222
Easy Marinated Spareribs 159
Easy Rhubarb Jam 51
Egg Sauce 126
EGGPLANT
    Berenjena Español 182
    Hudson Valley Vegetarian
        Sandwich 99
    Moussaka 155
    Romanian Eggplant 181
EGGS
    Carolina Crabmeat Quiche 114
    Cheddary Ham 'n Eggs Casserole 104
    Cheese Soufflé 104
    Deviled Eggs with Mushrooms 105
    Egg Sauce 126
    Old-fashioned Baked Eggs 105
    Pecan French Toast 106
    Scrambled Eggs-Fines Herbes 106
Elegant Calves' Liver 170
English Tea Scones 50
Erster Sauerbraten 146

F

Farmers' Soup/Stew 73
Feather Light Pancakes 56
Fettuccine with Shrimp
    and Snow Peas 120
Fillet of Sole Marguery 123
FISH
    Danish Fish Bake 123
    Fillet of Sole Marguery 123
    Fish Fillets – Quick and Easy! 114
    Gourmet Tuna Spread 99
    Grilled Salmon Sandwich 102
    Herb-Roasted Orange Salmon 121
    Psari Plaki 122
    Salmon Ball 32
    Salmon Loaf with Celery Sauce 124
    Salmon Mousse 124
    Smoked Salmon Fettuccine 122
    Tuna Cakes 125
    Tuna Sandwiches
        with Lemon Butter 100
Fish Sauce 126
Five Hour Stew 147
Fluffy Today/Thin Tomorrow
    Flapjacks 57
French Onion Soup Gratiné 68

INDEX

French-Style Peas 185
Fresh Apple Cake 224
Fresh Asparagus and Ham Pie 160
Fresh Cranberry Waffles 58
Fresh Seafood Salad 93
Fried Red and Green Tomatoes 192
Frozen Chocolate Mousse Cake 208
FRUIT
    Apricot-Banana Shortcake 214
    Coconut Pound Cake 221
    Cold Peach Soup 62
    Creamy Citrus Salad Dressing 97
    Double Fruit Pancakes 58
    Fresh Fruit Romanoff 210
    Fruit Cream Cheese Pancake 59
    Fruit Salad Dressing 97
    Hot Gingered Fruit 212
    Melon Soup 62
    Strawberry Soup 62
Fruited Cheese Log 29

G

Garden Vegetable Soup 75
Garlic Pickles 96
Garlic Shrimp with Linguine 116
Gazpacho 63
Geppel's Gloggs 40
Glazed Acorn Squash Rings 191
Glazed Pecans 216
Glazed Walnut Bars 240
Golden Potato Soufflé 187
Gouda Cup 29
Gourmet Potatoes 187
Gourmet Tuna Spread 99
Granola 60
GRAPES
    Chicken Breast Veronique 136
    Fresh Seafood Salad 93
Great Guacamole 20
Green Bean Salad 80
Green Beans in Olive Oil 174
Green Pea/Red Radish Salad 84
Green Pepper Jelly 34
Green Tomato Pie 199
Grilled Salisbury Steaks 150
Grilled Salmon Sandwich 102
Grilled Turkey Breast 138
Guzek's Osso Buco 168

H

Ham and Cheese Ring 161
Ham Loaf with Pineapple Sauce 161
Ham-Chicken Bake 160
Hawaiian Baklava 213
Healthy Heart Scones 50
Herb-Rice Stuffed Peppers 185
Herb-Roasted Orange Salmon 121
Herbed White Bean Salad 81
Holiday "Strudel" 227

Holiday Wassail 39
Honey and Brandy Glazed Carrots 178
Honey Walnut Balls 239
Hot Apple Oatmeal 60
Hot Chicken Salad 131
Hot Chili Dip 18
Hot Crab Puffs 30
"Hot" Cream Cheese Topping 29
Hot Fudge Pudding Cake 204
Hot German Potato Salad 84
Hot Gingered Fruit 212
Hot Lemon Sauce 213
Hot Mushroom Cocktail Spread 19
Hot Mushroom Turnovers 25
Hot Seafood Salad Supreme 119
"Hot" Vinaigrette Salad Dressing 98
Hudson Valley Vegetarian Sandwich 99
Hummus 20

I

Imperial Pound Cake 219
Irish Cream Whiskey 40
Irish Soda Bread 47
Italian Barley Soup 74
Italian Herb Bread 53
Italian Shrimp Pasta Toss 120

J

Japanese Fruit Pie 199
Jewish Pot Roast 145
Jiffy Low-Cal Pot de Crème 206

K

Kahlua 39
Kourabiedes 236

L

LAMB
    Bobotie 156
    Lamb Meatballs en Brochette 154
    Lamb Shanks 153
    Moussaka 155
    Mrs. Lynch's Irish Stew 153
    New England Lamb Stew 156
Latke-Crusted Cauliflower Pie 179
Layered Spinach Salad 87
Lebkuchen 236
LEMONS
    Hot Lemon Sauce 213
    Lemon Bread 46
    Lemon Charlotte 209
    Lemon Cream Cheese Salad 79
    Lemon Cream Pie
        with Apricot Sauce 200
    Lemon Squares 240
    Lemon-Cucumber Tea Sandwiches .. 101
    Lemon-Walnut Green Beans 174
    Low-Fat Lemon Poppy Seed Cake ... 226

Variegated Salad 88
Liver Baked with Onion and Herbs 167
Lobster (or Seafood) Spread 31
Low-Cal Salad Dressing 98
Low-Fat Chocolate Bundt Cake 222
Low-Fat Lemon Poppy Seed Cake 226

M

Macaroni and Cheese, Welsh Style 110
Madison Avenue Punch 38
Mandarin Orange Salad 89
Maple Glazed Parsnips 184
Marinade for Salmon Steaks 126
Marinated Carrots 95
Matzo Sponge Cake 221
Meatball Soup 76
Mediterranean Chicken 129
Melon Soup 62
Mexican Lasagna 107
Minestrone 77
Molasses Oatmeal Cookies 233
Molasses Spice Cake 225
Moussaka 155
Mrs. Lynch's Irish Stew 153
MUFFINS
Berry Patch Muffins 48
Bran Muffins – For Your
    Heart's Sake 49
Bran Muffins for Busy Bakers 48
Cranberry Muffins 49
Pumpkin Pecan Muffins 52
Mulled Cider 37
MUSHROOMS
Cream of Mushroom Soup 68
Deviled Eggs with Mushrooms 105
Hot Mushroom Cocktail Spread 19
Hot Mushroom Turnovers 25
Mushroom Casserole 182
Mushroom Strata 183
Mushroom-Rice-Nut Casserole 108
Turkey-Cheese-Mushroom Timbale ... 138

N

Nantucket Bay Scallops
    and Saffron Risotto 117
Nectarine Pork Chops 159
New Age Fried Rice 110
New England Lamb Stew 156
No-Bake Corn Flake Drops 229
No-Boil Lasagna 109
Nutmeg Cookie Logs 235
NUTS
2-Minute Microwave Fudge 216
Apricot Balls 238
Banana-Pineapple Cake 228
Braised Celery and Apple Medley 180
Cherry Coffee Cake 43
Cherry Flakes 234

Chinese Chicken Salad 89
Chocolate Carrot Cake 223
Chocolate Chip Coconut Bars 228
Chocolate Chocolate Chip Cookies 231
Chocolate Layered Squares 233
Cranberry Nut Bread 45
Danish Carrot Hazelnut Torte 217
Fresh Apple Cake 224
Glazed Pecans 216
Glazed Walnut Bars 240
Hawaiian Baklava 213
Holiday "Strudel" 227
Honey Walnut Balls 239
Hot Chicken Salad 131
Molasses Oatmeal Cookies 233
Mushroom-Rice-Nut Casserole 108
Nut-Filled Brie 27
Orange Nut Coffee Cake 44
Peanut Butter Balls 217
Peanut Butter Blossoms 230
Peanut Butter Swirl Bars 230
Pear Nut Bread 46
Pecan French Toast 106
Praline Biscuits 52
Praline Pecan Cheesecake 220
Pumpkin Pecan Muffins 52
Pumpkin-Pecan Pie 202
Queen Elizabeth's Date Nut Cake 225
Rugalach 237
Rum Balls 238
Sour Cream Raisin Spice Cake 227
Super-Easy Fudge 216
Upside-Down Date Pudding 204
Walnut Rolls 54
Zucchini Bread 47

O

Oatmeal Molasses Bread 54
Old-fashioned Baked Eggs 105
Olibollen 56
ONIONS
French Onion Soup Gratiné 68
Green Beans in Olive Oil 174
Liver Baked with Onion and Herbs . 167
Onions Au Gratin 183
Shaker Onions 184
ORANGES
Baked Orange-Pineapple Chicken 133
Chinese Chicken Salad 89
Cranberry Relish 167
Herb-Roasted Orange Salmon 121
Mandarin Orange Salad 89
Orange Nut Coffee Cake 44
Orange Poppy Seed Loaf Cake 226
Orange Rolls 55
Turnips in Orange Juice 193
Oyster Bisque 78

INDEX

Shaker Onions 184

ORANGES
Baked Orange-Pineapple Chicken 133
Chinese Chicken Salad 89
Cranberry Relish 167
Herb-Roasted Orange Salmon 121
Mandarin Orange Salad 89
Orange Nut Coffee Cake 44
Orange Poppy Seed Loaf Cake 226
Orange Rolls 55
Turnips in Orange Juice 193
Oyster Bisque 78

P

PANCAKES/WAFFLES
Country Griddlecakes 59
Double Fruit Pancakes 58
Feather Light Pancakes 56
Fluffy Today/Thin Tomorrow
  Flapjacks 57
Fresh Cranberry Waffles 58
Fruit Cream Cheese Pancake 59
Parmesan Vegetable Tossed Salad 88

PARSNIPS
Breaded Parsnips with Rosemary 184
Maple Glazed Parsnips 184

PASTA
Angel Hair Pasta with Broccoli 107
Baked Tomato Macaroni 111
Cheesy Beef and Pasta in a Pot 108
Chicken and Pasta Salad 91
Chicken and Pasta in
  Hot and Sour Peanut Sauce 127
Fettuccine with Shrimp
  and Snow Peas 120
Garlic Shrimp with Linguine 116
Italian Shrimp Pasta Toss 120
Macaroni and Cheese, Welsh Style 110
Mexican Lasagna 107
Minestrone 77
No-Boil Lasagna 109
Pasta e Fagioli 74
Pasta Picnic Salad 94
Pasta with Bay Scallops 116
Smoked Salmon Fettuccine 122
Tortellini Salad 94
Turkey Noodle Casserole 140

PÂTÉ
Chicken Liver Pâté 33
Devilish Pâté 30
Pavlova 210
Pea Soup 69

PEACHES
Cold Peach Soup 62
Peach Upside-Down Cake 229
Peanut Butter Balls 217
Peanut Butter Blossoms 230
Peanut Butter Swirl Bars 230

PEARS
Pear Nut Bread 46
Pear Strudel 215
Seafoam Delight 80
Spinach-Pear Salad 87

PEAS
Fettuccine with Shrimp
  and Snow Peas 120
French-Style Peas 185
Green Pea/Red Radish Salad 84
Layered Spinach Salad 87
Lenticchie in Umido 176
Lentil Soup 65
Pea Soup 69
San Diego Relish 96
Peasant Bean Soup 65
Pecan French Toast 106
Pennsylvania Potato Dressing
  for Poultry 132
Peruvian Shrimp and Corn Chowder 76
Pfeffernüsse 237

PICKLES
Garlic Pickles 96
Rags (Quick Pickles) 96

PIES
Brandy Alexander Pie 198
Chocolate Chip Nut Pie 198
Green Tomato Pie 199
Japanese Fruit Pie 199
Lemon Cream Pie
  with Apricot Sauce 200
Pumpkin-Apple Pie 201
Pumpkin-Pecan Pie 202
Quick Pineapple Cheese Pie 200
Shaker Double Crust Lemon Pie 201
Sweet Potato Pie 202
Turtle Pie 203

PINEAPPLE
Baked Orange-Pineapple Chicken 133
Baked Pineapple 166
Banana-Pineapple Cake 228
Carrot Pineapple Cake 224
Easy Rhubarb Jam 51
Ham Loaf with Pineapple Sauce 161
Lemon Cream Cheese Salad 79
Pineapple Chicken Stir-Fry 127
Quick Pineapple Cheese Pie 200
Pommes de terre Dauphinoise 189
Popular Party Punch 35

PORK/HAM
Apple-Brandy Pork Chops 158
Baked Sausage with Apples 162
Beef and Sausage Stew 147
Cheddary Ham 'n Eggs Casserole 104
Chicken and Sausage with Rice 132
Easy Marinated Spare Ribs 159
Fresh Asparagus and Ham Pie 160
Ham and Cheese Ring 161
Ham Loaf with Pineapple Sauce 161

Basque Potato Soup 69
Cheddar-Potato Soup 70
Colcannon 186
Crunchy Red Potato Salad 85
Golden Potato Soufflé 187
Gourmet Potatoes 187
Hot German Potato Salad 84
Pennsylvania Potato Dressing
    for Poultry 132
Pommes de terre Dauphinoise 189
Potato and Leek Soup 70
Potato Kugel 188
Potato Salad Mold 85
Red Flannel Hash 151
Rosemary Roasted Potatoes 188
Poulet Blanchard 128
POULTRY *(See Chicken, Duck and Turkey)*
Praline Biscuits 52
Praline Pecan Cheesecake 220
Pretzels 57
Psari Plaki 122
PUDDINGS
Bread Pudding
    with Whiskey Sauce 205
Brother James' Rhubarb
    Bread Pudding 206
Chocolate Bread Pudding 205
Creamy Rice Pudding 203
Lemon Cream Pie with
    Apricot Sauce 200
Upside-Down Date Pudding 204
PUMPKIN
Autumn Soup 72
Pumpkin Pecan Muffins 52
Pumpkin-Apple Pie 201
Pumpkin-Pecan Pie 202

Q
Queen Elizabeth's Date Nut Cake 225
Queen Victoria Soup 72
Quesadillas with Three Cheeses 165
QUICHES
Carolina Crabmeat Quiche 114
Crustless Zucchini Quiche 26
Tiny Broccoli Quiches 24
Turkey-Cheese-Mushroom Timbale ... 138
Quick Pineapple Cheese Pie 200

R
Rags (Quick Pickles) 96
RAISINS
Bran Muffins – For Your
    Heart's Sake 49
Bran Muffins for Busy Bakers 48
English Tea Scones 50
Sour Cream Raisin Spice Cake 227
Raspberry Vinaigrette Salad Dressing 99
Raw Vegetable Pizza 26

Red Crest Tomato Aspic 80
Red Flannel Hash 151
RELISHES
Cranberry Relish 167
Green Pepper Jelly 34
Marinated Carrots 95
San Diego Relish 96
Reuben Sandwich Casserole 102
RHUBARB
Brother James' Rhubarb
    Bread Pudding 206
Easy Rhubarb Jam 51
Rhubarb Coffee Cake 43
Roast Loin of Pork with Rhubarb 157
Shaker Cold Rhubarb Tea 35
RICE
Baked Rice 109
Chicken and Sausage with Rice 132
Crabmeat Rice Salad 93
Creamy Rice Pudding 203
Herb-Rice Stuffed Peppers 185
Mushroom-Rice-Nut Casserole 108
Nantucket Bay Scallops
    and Saffron Risotto 117
New Age Fried Rice 110
Stuffed Ham Rolls
    with Creamed Chicken Sauce 162
Roast Duckling 139
Roast Loin of Pork with Rhubarb 157
Roasted Garlic Canapés 22
Roasted Vegetables 196
ROLLS
Orange Rolls 55
Walnut Rolls 54
Romaine-Spinach Salad 86
Romanian Eggplant 181
Rosemary Cheese Wafers 30
Rosemary Roasted Potatoes 188
Rugalach 237
Rum Balls 238
Rye Cheese Delights 28

S
SALAD DRESSINGS
Balsamic Vinaigrette Salad Dressing 98
Creamy Anchovy-Dill
    Salad Dressing 97
Creamy Citrus Salad Dressing 97
Fruit Salad Dressing 97
"Hot" Vinaigrette Salad Dressing 98
Low-Cal Salad Dressing 98
Raspberry Vinaigrette
    Salad Dressing 99
SALADS
24-Hour Bean Salad 81
Baked Crabmeat Salad 115
Broccoli Salad 91
Broccoli Salad with Basil Dressing 82
Caesar Salad with Grilled Chicken 90

INDEX

Chicken and Pasta Salad 91
Chicken Waldorf Salad 92
Chinese Chicken Salad 89
Cold Cauliflower Salad 83
Crabmeat Rice Salad 93
Cranberry Soufflé Salad 79
Crunchy Noodle Salad 95
Crunchy Red Potato Salad 85
Cucumber With Cumin and Yogurt ... 83
Fresh Seafood Salad 93
Green Bean Salad 80
Green Pea/Red Radish Salad 84
Herbed White Bean Salad 81
Hot German Potato Salad 84
Layered Spinach Salad 87
Lemon Cream Cheese Salad 79
Mandarin Orange Salad 89
Marinated Carrots 95
Parmesan Vegetable Tossed Salad 88
Pasta Picnic Salad 94
Potato Salad Mold 85
Red Crest Tomato Aspic 80
Romaine-Spinach Salad 86
Seafoam Delight 80
Spinach-Pear Salad 87
Sweet Potato Salad 86
Tabbouleh Salad 92
Taco Salad 90
Tortellini Salad 94
Variegated Salad 88
Salmon Ball 32
Salmon Loaf with Celery Sauce 124
Salmon Mousse 124
San Diego Relish 96
SANDWICHES
Aram Sandwiches 21
Best 'Wurst Sandwich 100
Gourmet Tuna Spread 99
Grilled Salmon Sandwich 102
Hudson Valley Vegetarian Sandwich ... 99
Lemon-Cucumber Tea Sandwiches 101
Reuben Sandwich Casserole 102
Stuffed Franks 101
Tuna Sandwiches
with Lemon Butter 100
SAUCES
Apricot Sauce for Ham 164
Chocolate Sauce 212
Cold Cucumber-Dill Sauce 125
Egg Sauce 126
Fish Sauce 126
Hot Lemon Sauce 213
Marinade for Salmon Steaks 126
Spicy Cherry Glaze for Ham 165
Sausage Biscuit Bites 24
Scrambled Eggs-Fines Herbes 106
Seafoam Delight 80
SEAFOOD
Baked Crabmeat Salad 115

Blend of the Bayou 121
Carolina Crabmeat Quiche 114
Crabmeat Delight 114
Crabmeat Rice Salad 93
Crabmeat Spread 31
Fettuccine with Shrimp
and Snow Peas 120
Fresh Seafood Salad 93
Hot Crab Puffs 30
Hot Seafood Salad Supreme 119
Lobster (or Seafood) Spread 31
Nantucket Bay Scallops
and Saffron Risotto 117
Oyster Bisque 78
Pasta with Bay Scallops 116
Seafood Casserole 115
Seafood Cream Cheese Spread 32
Shrimp and Scallops Gruyère 119
Sesame Seed Twist Cookies 235
Shaker Braised Flank Steak 144
Shaker Cold Rhubarb Tea 35
Shaker Double Crust Lemon Pie 201
Shaker Mocha "Punch" 36
Shaker Onions 184
SHRIMP
Blend of the Bayou 121
Danish Fish Bake 123
Fettuccine with Shrimp
and Snow Peas 120
Fillet of Sole Marguery 123
Fresh Seafood Salad 93
Garlic Shrimp with Linguine 116
Hot Seafood Salad Supreme 119
Italian Shrimp Pasta Toss 120
Peruvian Shrimp
and Corn Chowder 76
Seafood Casserole 115
Seafood Cream Cheese Spread 32
Shrimp à la Creole 118
Shrimp and Artichoke Casserole 118
Shrimp and Scallops Gruyère 119
Shrimp Dip 20
Shrimp Mousse 33
Sirloin Tip Casserole 143
SLAWS
Cottage Cole Slaw 82
Spicy Cole Slaw 83
Smoked Salmon Fettuccine 122
Snowball 211
SOUFFLÉS
Cheese Soufflé 104
Chocolate Soufflés 207
Golden Potato Soufflé 187
Spinach Soufflé 190
Very Sherry Sweet Potato Soufflé 189
SOUPS/STEWS
Autumn Soup 72
Avgolemono Soup 71
Basque Potato Soup 69

Beef and Sausage Stew 147
Brother James' Cabbage Soup 67
Carrot Leek Soup 64
Carrot Soup 64
Cheddar-Potato Soup 70
Cheese Soup 71
Chicken Stew 129
Cold Peach Soup 62
Country Herb Soup 78
Cream of Broccoli Soup 66
Cream of Celery Soup 67
Cream of Mushroom Soup 68
Cucumber-Yogurt Soup 63
Farmers' Soup/Stew 73
Five Hour Stew 147
French Onion Soup Gratiné 68
Garden Vegetable Soup 75
Gazpacho 63
Italian Barley Soup 74
Lentil Soup 65
Meatball Soup 76
Melon Soup 62
Minestrone 77
Mrs. Lynch's Irish Stew 153
New England Lamb Stew 156
Oyster Bisque 78
Pasta e Fagioli 74
Pea Soup 69
Peasant Bean Soup 65
Peruvian Shrimp
  and Corn Chowder 76
Potato and Leek Soup 70
Queen Victoria Soup 72
Status Stew 148
Strawberry Soup 62
Sweet Potato Soup 75
Union Street Lunch's
  Bacon-Bean Soup 66
Veal Stew – A Taste of Italy 171
Sour Cream Cheese Coffee Cake 45
Sour Cream Raisin Spice Cake 227
Sour Cream Steak 143
Southwestern Corn Bake 180
Späetzle 112
Spanakopeta 164
Spicy Cherry Glaze for Ham 165
Spicy Cole Slaw 83
Spicy Tea Punch 36

SPINACH
Borekas 23
Layered Spinach Salad 87
Romaine-Spinach Salad 86
Spanakopeta 164
Spinach Balls 25
Spinach Soufflé 190
Spinach-Pear Salad 87
Tantalizing Spinach 190
Variegated Salad 88
Spoon Bread 60

SQUASH
Apple Squash Bake 191
Cheesy Summer Squash 192
Crustless Zucchini Quiche 26
Glazed Acorn Squash Rings 191
Tomato-Zucchini Pot Pie 195
Zucchini Bread 47
Zucchini Sausage Bake 163
Zucchini-Tomato Skillet 194
Status Stew 148
Stir-Fry Steak Slices
  with Winter Radishes 144
STRAWBERRIES
Pavlova 210
Strawberry Angel Delight 211
Strawberry Soup 62
Stuffed Chicken Breasts
  with Proscuitto, Mozzarella 134
Stuffed Franks 101
Stuffed Ham Rolls with
  Creamed Chicken Sauce 162
Stuffed Turkey Rolls Florentine 139
Sunshine Punch 37
Super-Easy Fudge 216
Surprise Beef Patties 149
Swedish Meatballs 149
Sweet and Sour Bean Casserole 175
Sweet and Sour Red Cabbage 177
SWEET POTATOES
Creole Praline Yam Casserole 194
Sweet Potato Pie 202
Sweet Potato Salad 86
Sweet Potato Soup 75
Very Sherry Sweet Potato Soufflé 189

T
24-Hour Bean Salad 81
2-Minute Microwave Fudge 216
Tabbouleh Salad 92
Taco Dip 21
Taco Salad 90
Tailgaters' Loaf 151
Tantalizing Spinach 190
Thai Curry Chicken with Vegetables 128
Tiny Broccoli Quiches 24
TOMATOES
Baked Tomato Macaroni 111
Cheese-Tomato Pie 193
Fried Red and Green Tomatoes 192
Gazpacho 63
Green Tomato Pie 199
Red Crest Tomato Aspic 80
Tomato-Zucchini Pot Pie 195
Zucchini-Tomato Skillet 194
Tortellini Salad 94
Tour-R-Lou 195
Tourtière 158
Tuna Cakes 125
Tuna Sandwiches with Lemon Butter ... 100

INDEX

TURKEY
Aram Sandwiches 21
Grilled Turkey Breast 138
Stuffed Turkey Rolls Florentine 139
Turkey Ball 33
Turkey Noodle Casserole 140
Turkey Picadillo 140
Turkey-Cheese-Mushroom Timbale ... 138
TURNIPS
Braised Carrots and Turnips 178
Turnips in Orange Juice 193
Turtle Pie 203
Twin Meat Loaves 148

U
Union Street Lunch's
Bacon-Bean Soup 66
Upside-Down Date Pudding 204

V
Variegated Salad 88
VEAL
Guzek's Osso Buco 168
Veal Julienne 170
Veal Loaf 168
Veal Parmigiana 169
Veal Scallopini with Peas 172
Veal Stew – A Taste of Italy 171

VEGETABLES
Garden Vegetable Soup 75
Roasted Vegetables 196
Tour-R-Lou 195
Vegetarian Cholent 176
VENISON
Venison Pot Roast 172
Zweiter Sauerbraten 146
Very Sherry Sweet Potato Soufflé 189
Viennese Brownies 232
Vintage Chicken 136

W
Walnut Rolls 54
White Chocolate Cheesecake 219
Wine-Baked Chicken
and Artichoke Hearts 135
World's Best Cookies 234

Z
ZUCCHINI
Crustless Zucchini Quiche 26
Tomato-Zucchini Pot Pie 195
Zucchini Bread 47
Zucchini Sausage Bake 163
Zucchini-Tomato Skillet 194
Zweiter Sauerbraten 146

The Albany Collection:
Treasures and Treasured Recipes

Women's Council Cookbook
Albany Institute of History & Art
125 Washington Avenue, Albany, New York 12210

Please send me _____ copies of The Albany Collection at $21.95 each $_____
add postage and handling $ 3.00 each $_____
New York residents add 8% sales tax $ 3.76 each $_____

Name _____

Address_____

City_____State_____Zip_____
Please make checks payable to *Women's Council Cookbook*

- -

The Albany Collection:
Treasures and Treasured Recipes

Women's Council Cookbook
Albany Institute of History & Art
125 Washington Avenue, Albany, New York 12210

Please send me _____ copies of The Albany Collection at $21.95 each $_____
add postage and handling $ 3.00 each $_____
New York residents add 8% sales tax $ 3.76 each $_____

Name _____

Address_____

City_____State_____Zip_____
Please make checks payable to *Women's Council Cookbook*

Albany Institute of History & Art

125 Washington Avenue
Albany, NY 12210 • 518-463-4478

1 free admission

For use Thursday through Sunday, Noon to 5 pm.

Albany Institute of History & Art

125 Washington Avenue
Albany, NY 12210 • 518-463-4478

1 free admission

For use Thursday through Sunday, Noon to 5 pm.